Supermarket Own Brand Guide

Choosing the best value food and drink

Martin Isark

MITCHELL BEAZLEY

Supermarket Own Brand Guide
by Martin Isark

First published in Great Britain in 2006 by Mitchell Beazley, an imprint of
Octopus Publishing Group Ltd, 2–4 Heron Quays, London E14 4JP

ISBN 1 84533 189 3

A CIP record for this book is available from the British Library

Set in Cosmo, Dax and Bliss
Printed and bound in Italy by Rotolito

Commissioning Editor: Hilary Lumsden
Executive Art Editor: Yasia Williams-Leedham
Managing Editor: Julie Sheppard
Editor: Naomi Waters
Dietetic Advisor: Jane Thompson
Design: Lizzie Ballantyne
Index: Nigel D'Auvergne
Production: Faizah Malik

The publishers will be grateful for any information that will assist them in keeping
future editions up to date. Although all reasonable care has been taken during the
preparation of this book, neither the publishers nor the author can accept any
liability for any consequence arising from the use thereof, or the information
contained therein.

Contents

Introduction

Is it worth buying an "own label" or is the leader in the market always superior? Over the last decade, as the big brands have become ever more powerful, the supermarkets have realised that, in order to compete, they too must pull out all the stops. And how they have! You'll be surprised, I think, with what you find in these pages.

This book is about quality, value for money and nutritional health. Using these criteria, I have tasted over 2,000 supermarket "own labels" or "exclusives", together with the leading brand and packed in as much information as possible about the food and drink products (all from the 10 leading supermarkets) that you load into your shopping trolley every week. Of the 16 chapters, the first 10 concern groceries, chapters 11 to 13 cover non-alcoholic drinks and 14 to 16 alcoholic drinks. In the latter, I have also included products from Oddbins, Majestic and Threshers.

I have been involved in the food and drink industry as a professional taster and writer since the early 1990s, chewing, slurping and spitting more than 100,000 food and drink products. It was as drinks' writer for *Scotland on Sunday* that, in the autumn of 2003 I compiled a *Winter Wine Guide*; a list of the best (and worst!) quality and value wine to be found on the shelves of the supermarkets and large retailers. Astounded store managers and shoppers reported that wines I had rated highly had been stripped from the shelves within 24 hours. It seemed, then, that consumers were as passionate about quality and value for money as I was. And so the idea for this book was born.

For 12 months, almost daily, I have talked to supermarket shoppers and staff and listened to their views. Of course, the staff members know exactly which of their "own labels" are excellent value and quality, but it's harder for the shopper. We have to try for ourselves, and that can be expensive and frustrating. So here you are: from cheese to Chardonnay, Weetabix to whisky, soup to sherry and bread to beer, I've checked them all – Aldi, Asda, Co-op, Kwik Save, Marks & Spencer, Morrisons, Sainsbury's, Somerfield, Tesco and Waitrose – and, where relevant, the big drinks retailers. Throughout, my only purpose is to search out the good and the fairly priced. There are some excellent "own labels". At best, they mirror, or even better, the brand, and can be as little as half its price. At worst, you'll end up throwing them away!

"How can 'own labels' be of a similar quality and yet cheaper than brands?" I hear you ask. Easy. A large chunk of the selling price of a big brand is devoted to advertising and needlessly lavish packaging, whereas there is no need to advertise the "own label" and costs can certainly be cut on the packaging. Even if you save only a few pence by buying good "own Labels", in a big shopping trip this will add up to more than the price of this book!

Healthy eating is a hot topic at the moment, from government anxieties about pressures on the National Health Service to media exploitation of our insecurities about self-image. Many of you will already be aware of how little help most front labels are to the shopper with food intolerances and special dietary requirements. Things are improving, however. The Food Standards Agency is in the process of introducing new rules stating that allergenic ingredients should be labelled on all pre-packed food and drink. To save you time, in this book there are letters displayed against the tasting notes throughout to indicate whether a product is suitable for different dietary groups. This should be of assistance to vegan shoppers (V); to those with coeliac disease who require products that are gluten free (GF); to those with lactose intolerance (L); or to those with nut and seed allergies (N/S). For more information about these dietary requirements, and for sources of further information please see pages 11 to 13. Although every care has been taken to produce accurate information, recipes do change – one hopes for the better – so, to be absolutely sure, always check the nutrition and ingredient labels. Easier said than done, this. For example, how many of us have squinted in frustration over that tiny print, which could actually communicate some very vital information?

It's a sad fact that retailers are very quick to jump on health bandwagons, provided, of course, that those bandwagons guarantee they will sell more products. Such retailers are very skillful at hiding bad nutritional information. If their product has high salt, sugar and saturated fat, they do their best to disguise these levels under less obvious umbrella terms. Thus, salt is often displayed as the lower level "sodium" (multiply it by 2.5 to get the salt content), sugar under the more palatable "carbohydrate" and saturated fat unspecified under the vague term "fat". Not the best way to keep the nation fit and healthy! Details of how much of these nutrients we should be eating are given on pages 9 to 10, but it's important to realise that they are only a guide, as your weight, age and sex are also factors to bear in mind. In this book, key words at the top of a sub-section indicate products with high levels of certain ingredients that you may want to check.

These days, food additives are impossible to avoid, so prevalent are they in a culture where the appearance of the products we buy is of paramount importance. We shop less frequently too, and, since we expect our food to have a long "sell by" date, these expectations must be fulfiled artificially by the manufacturers; so in go the preservatives. Not that food is the only source of possibly harmful additives: they are also plentifully present in both hard and soft drinks. While most of the ingredients are listed on the back label of food and soft drink products, very few alcoholic drink labels list the full ingredients. Overall, clear, consumer-friendly labelling is rare: many additives will be listed under their E number rather than their name. Since a growing number of people are increasingly intolerant of such additives, on pages 14 to 16 I have included lists of E numbers, with their names, the products where they are most likely to be found and the problems they could cause.

All alcoholic drinks have their units of alcohol displayed per bottle or can, so counting there is easy. It is advised that women should keep to a maximum of three units a day and men four units. More recently it has also been suggested that two alcohol-free days a week are advisable. Consider on top of this the varying alcoholic strengths of wine and beer and you realise the sums are very difficult to calculate.

There are lots of problems then, to be faced in our weekly trawl through the supermarket. Here's hoping that the facts and information in this book will help you solve your problems – whether you're shopping on a tight budget or catering for a special diet – and help you to find food that tastes good. Load that trolley with confidence and happy eating and drinking!

How to Use this Book

1. In writing this book I have obtained information from 10 leading supermarkets. I have not included products that were in the process of being reformulated or where the retailer was changing supplier. This book is not a PR exercise, though. You'll find both the excellent and the abysmal here.

2. The book has 16 chapters and lists more than 1,800 products. The first 10 chapters cover groceries; chapters 11 to13 non-alcoholic drinks; and 14 to 16 alcoholic drinks (Oddbins, Majestic and Threshers are also included here).

3. Each chapter is divided into 10 or more sub-sections. For example, chapter 1, "Cereals", contains 12 sub-sections including Cornflakes, Frosties, Bran Flakes, Fruit and Fibre, Swiss Style Muesli, Muesli, Fruit and Nut Muesli and so forth.

4. Each sub-section has the market leading brand (or one of them, if there should be two), as a benchmark to taste against. In the case of "Cornflakes", for example, it is Kellogg's Cornflakes. Each of the supermarkets' "own labels" was compared only against the brand. The only criterion is – is it worth buying the "own label" or should you stick to the brand?

5. I cannot tell you which is the best supermarket. That becomes irrelevant if the Co-op is round the corner and Waitrose is 20 miles away. This book is about avoiding expensive "own label" mistakes at your regular, local or occasional supermarket. There are still plenty of buyer's mistakes on the shelves!

6. At the top of each sub-section certain key ingredients found in the products below are listed, warning of high levels of ingredients like sugar, salt and fat, or ingredients such as yeast, wheat and egg, which are known allergens.

7. Where labelling is concerned, while vegetarians are increasingly well catered for, unfortunately vegans are often ignored. Therefore, I asked every retailer which products are suitable for vegans and these are individually marked (V).

8. The increase in food intolerance amongst shoppers has meant that an ever larger number of people must avoid certain ingredients. Coeliacs with their gluten intolerance (G), those who are lactose intolerant (L) and people allergic to nuts and seeds (N/S) will see letters against the relevant product. Although every care has been taken, remember that recipes do change with time and size, so always check the ingredient label yourself when you buy the product.

9. In the Scoring Chart, the brand (the benchmark) is not scored. All the food or drink "own labels" are tasted against the brand in the appropriate section.

   a. If the product tastes as good as the brand and is also cheaper, it is placed above the brand, and will be scored a 7, 8, 9 or 10, depending on the price.

b. However, if the taste is not as good as the brand, it is placed below the brand, *whatever* the price. But choose carefully: the score 5, at only slightly inferior quality and perhaps much cheaper than the brand, might be the best alternative for you.

c. There are two scores, 6 and on certain occasions 10, that represent products that taste, in my opinion, much better than the brand. A score of 6 is given when the product is more expensive than the brand, but well worth it on all taste fronts. The perfect 10 can also mean that the "own label" is of very much better quality than the brand and is also cheaper.

d. In some sections the "own labels" don't get even close to the brand taste-wise and therefore they all sit below the brand. Other sections reveal that all the "own labels" are of similar quality and also cheaper and so they are all positioned above the brand. In many sections the brand sits at half way.

This scoring system, I hope, leaves you in no doubt whether to buy the "own label" or the brand. Below is a summary.

Scoring Chart

(10) Half the price (or less) of the brand and of equal quality; or cheaper than the brand and of very much better quality.

(9) Not quite half price, and of equal quality to the brand.

(8) Less expensive than the brand, but still of similar quality.

(7) Slightly less expensive than the brand, and still of equal quality.

(6) More expensive than the brand, but very much better quality.

The brand is not scored.

(5) Cheaper, but a step down in quality compared to the brand. Or it could be more expensive than the brand, but no better in quality; or the same quality as the brand at the same price.

(4) Cheaper, but of noticeably inferior quality when compared to the brand.

(3) Cheaper, but the flavour/taste does not compete with the brand and therefore is not an alternative.

(2) Don't waste your cash.

(1) Disgusting!

Healthy Eating

The recommended daily allowances (often abbreviated to RDA on labels) of a particular nutrient were first devised in the 1970s. Today nutritionists talk about dietary reference values. These are only a guideline, since not one of us, thankfully, is a standardised unit: sex, age, height, weight, fitness and medical conditions will all influence the calculation for the optimum amount of any nutrient. Even a rough guide, however, is helpful when you are trying to eat and drink healthily. Many manufacturers don't give the help they should, with high levels of sugars, salt and saturated fat disguised under vaguer umbrella terms. If you want to live healthily, it's up to you to take control, and see past those deceptive marketing techniques.

The government website **www.eatwell.gov.uk** is excellent. It is easy to use and has all the latest nutritional information. Also useful is **www.eufic.org**, the website of the European Food Information Council. Based in Brussels, its aim is to improve public understanding of nutrition and food safety.

Guidelines for alcohol consumption were first introduced in the 1980s and related to drinks that were served in a pub (one unit equalled half a pint beer, lager or cider, one single measure of spirits, one small glass of wine, one small measure of fortified wine, *e.g.* port or sherry). However, today many drinks have increased in alcohol content, especially wine, cider and bottled beer. Therefore the only sure way to check your units of alcohol is to use the formula on page 10.

Current guidelines for a healthy diet:

- **Eat 5 portions of fruit and vegetables a day.**
- **Reduce salt intake to 6g a day.**

When the salt content is high it will often be labelled as "sodium" per tiny portion rather than for the whole packet. You have to multiply the sodium level by 2.5 to find the salt level (1g salt = 0.4g sodium; 6g salt = 2.4g sodium)).

- **Women consume a total of 70g of fat per day and men 95g.**

Unsaturated (poly-unsaturated and mono-unsaturated) fats: these are the good fats that help to lower rather than raise cholesterol, and help to improve your body's well being. Food examples are: olive oil, vegetable oil, nuts and seeds, oily fish and avocados.

Saturated fats: the upper limit for a man is 30g; for a woman 20g. These are the ones to consume with care. They raise the level of your cholesterol and therefore increase the risk of a heart attack. As with salt (*see* above), when the saturated fat content is high, too often it is labelled under the umbrella term of "fat".

You may well have to call the customer service number on the packet or even surf the manufacturer's website for a more detailed breakdown. Food examples are: dairy products, pastries and meats.

Trans fats: These are just as bad for you as saturated fats and should be added together with saturated fat content if the product contains both. Food examples are: chips, fast foods, pastry, biscuits and cakes.

• Reduce added sugar to 60g a day.

The sugar content of a food will often be found by looking for the "Carbohydrate (of which sugars)" figure in the nutrition information panel on the label, or, when only the total carbohydrate figure is given, by looking in the ingredients list. This is where any added sugars are listed, starting with the biggest. A manufacturer may use several types in a product – *e.g.* sucrose, glucose or glucose syrup – so that the word "sugar" doesn't appear first on the list.

• Women need on average 2,000 kcals and men 2,500 kcals per day.

Energy is measured in units called calories. Most foods are labelled with their calorie count, but check it against the weight or portion you actually eat rather than a suggested "normal" serving.

Alcohol units – men should consume no more than 4 units per day and women 3.

The formula for working this out for all drinks is:
The total millilitres multiplied by percentage of alcohol, divided by 1,000.

Therefore:

- 500ml bottle of beer at 5% ABV (alcohol by volume), can be worked out as:
  500 x 5 = 2,500 ÷ 1,000 = 2.5 units.
- 175ml glass of wine at 13% ABV, can be worked out as:
  175 x 13 = 2,275 ÷1,000 = 2.28 units
- 25ml glass of whisky at 40% ABV, can be worked out as:
  25 x 40 = 1,000 ÷ 1,000 = 1 unit
- 25ml glass of vodka at 37.5% ABV,can be worked out as:
  25 x 37.5 = 9,375 ÷ 1,000 = .938 units

Weekly guideline:

- Men 3–4 units per day, 21–28 units per week, no significant risk
- Men 4–5 units per day, 28–35 units per week, moderate risk
- Men 5+ units per day, 35+ units per week, high risk
- Women 2–3 units per day, 14–21 units per week, no significant risk
- Women 3–5 units per day, 21–35 units per week, moderate risk
- Women 5 + per day, 35+ units per week, high risk

Food Intolerance Advice

The letters G, L, V and N/S in this book are intended to be taken as guide only, and whilst the utmost care has been taken in their research, products are often tweaked and therefore ingredients do change. Moreover, it's important to check the ingredient list of every packet as they can alter with size and special offers.

Anyone excluding a food group from their diet for health reasons must take care to ensure their nutritional intake is not compromised *e.g.* those following a dairy-free diet must ensure an adequate calcium intake from other sources.

Lactose
Lactose intolerance is the most common food intolerance in the UK.
The best information can be found on the website: www.eatwell.gov.uk.
Products/ingredients to avoid for those with a lactose intolerance

- Biscuits
- Breakfast cereals (processed)
- Butter
- Cake
- Cheese
- Chocolate
- Cream
- Ice cream
- Instant potato
- Margarine
- Milk
- Salad dressings
- Yogurt
- Creamed soups

Gluten
Products/ingredients to avoid for those with Coeliac disease (Gluten Free)

- Barley
- Beer and lager (unless labelled gluten free)
- Biscuits
- Bran
- Bread
- Bulgar wheat
- Cake
- Cereal filler
- Cereal protein
- Cous cous
- Liquorice
- Malt
- Modified wheat starch
- Oats
- Pasta
- Pastry
- Rusk
- Rye
- Semolina
- Spelt wheat
- Triticale wheat
- Wheat breakfast cereals
- Wheat flour
- Wheat germ
- Wheat starch

NUTS & SEEDS

Products/ingredients to avoid for people with nut (including peanuts; which are legumes not nuts, although people with peanut allergies may also be allergic to tree nuts) and seed allergies or intolerance. Note that some people may be fine with sesame seeds, but may react to one or more of the other seeds.

- Almonds (also avoid almond essence)
- Brazils
- Bread and buns using nuts and seeds
- Cashews
- Chestnuts
- Frangipane
- Hazelnuts (also called cob nuts and filberts)
- Linseeds (often used in breads)
- Macadamia nuts
- Marzipan
- Oils made from nuts
- Oils made from seeds
- Peanuts (also called ground nuts, earth nuts and monkey nuts)
- Pecans
- Pistachio nuts
- Poppy seeds (often used in breads)
- Praline
- Queensland nuts
- Sesames Seeds (sometimes found in Aqua Libra)
- Spreads made using nuts and seeds
- Walnuts

Unfortunately, such is the sensitivity of some people's intolerance that a mere trace of a nut or seed can trigger a reaction. Therefore, products without nuts or seeds that have been prepared or produced in a factory that uses them, have the possibility of containing a nut and/or seed trace. Indeed, many of the products sold from a delicatessen counter fall into this category and warnings are now being displayed at many supermarket deli counters.

For further information contact:

Allergy UK

3 White Oak Square, Swanley, Kent BR8 7AG
Helpline Tel: 01322 619 898 (9.00am–9.00pm Monday– Friday);
www.allergyuk.org

Coeliac UK

P O Box 220, High Wycombe, Buckinghamshire HP11 2HY
Tel: 01494 437 278; www.coeliac.co.uk

The Anaphylaxis Campaign

P O Box 275, Farnborough, Hampshire GU14 6XS
Tel: 01252 542 029; www.anaphylaxis.org.uk

Vegan Advice

The most common form of vegetarian diet is one that excludes meat and fish but includes milk, milk products and eggs as well as all foods of plant origin. A vegan diet is based on cereals vegetables, fruits, nuts and seeds. Someone following a vegan diet excludes all foods of animal origin.

Products/ingredients to avoid for Vegans

- Animal fats including lard, suet and dripping (as an ingredient, for frying or for greasing pans)
- Aspic
- Butter
- Butter Ghee
- Cheese
- Chitin, blood albumen caseinates, egg albumen or shellac
- Cream
- E120 Cochineal, Carmine
- E153 Carbon Black (normally of vegetable origin but can be animal derived)
- E542 (edible bone phosphate)
- Eggs
- Fish
- Gelatine
- Glycerol
- Honey
- Lactose
- Meat
- Milk
- Poultry
- Proteins, amino acids (normally of vegetable origin but can be animal derived), bone charcoal, animal-derived rennet, pepsin
- Shellfish
- Stearates and Stearic acid (if not of vegetable origin)
- Stock made from animal flesh or bones in soup and sauces
- Vitamin D3
- Whey
- Wines, wine vinegar, beers and ciders clarified using isinglass
- Yogurt

For further information contact:

Vegan Society

St Leonards-on-Sea, East Sussex TN37 7AA
Tel: 0845 458 8244; www.vegansociety.com

E Numbers

All food additives (listed as E Numbers) permitted and used in the UK are passed as safe for human consumption. However, some are known to be harmful and should be avoided by people with food intolerance or where they contravene the consumer's ethical, religious or special dietary requirements. The side effects listed below, such as hyperactivity in children, only occur in a small number of cases. Many of the colours below are banned in Norway and the USA.

COLOURS

E Number – 102
Name: Tartrazine
Found in: confectionery, cordials, pickles, soft drinks.
Problems: Hyperactivity in children.

E Number – 104
Name: Quinoline Yellow
Found in: jam, processed meat, soft drinks.
Problems: Hyperactivity in children.

E Number – 107
Name: Yellow 2G
Found in: jam, soft drinks.
Problems: Hyperactivity in children. Known to cause allergic reactions to asthmatics and people with an aspirin intolerance.

E Number – 110
Names: Sunset Yellow FCF; Orange Yellow S
Found in: cordial, confectionery, packet soup.
Problems: Hyperactivity in children. Allergic reactions (rashes, swelling, vomiting).

E Number – 120
Names: Cochineal, Carminic acid; Carmines
Found in: confectionery, liqueurs.
Problems: Hyperactivity in children.

E Number – 122
Names: Azorubine; Carmoisine
Found in: brown sauce, confectionery, marzipan, jelly, flavoured yogurt.
Problems: Hyperactivity in children. Asthmatics and people with aspirin sensitivity may have a reaction to it.

E Number – 123
Name: Amaranth
Found in: ice cream, gravy granules, jam, jelly, fruit-pie fillings, soup.
Problems: Hyperactivity in children. People with aspirin sensitivity may react to it.

E Number – 124
Names: Brilliant scarlet 4R; Ponceau 4R; Cochineal Red A
Found in: salami, seafood dressing, jelly, fruit pie fillings, soup.
Problems: Hyperactivity in children. Asthmatics and people with aspirin sensitivity may have a reaction to it.

E Number – 127
Name: Erythrosine
Found in: custard powder, biscuits, glacé cherries, canned cherries and strawberries.
Problems: Hyperactivity in children. Can cause sensitivity to light.

E Number – 128
Name: Red 2G
Found in: cooked meats, sausages, jam.
Problems: Hyperactivity in children.

E Number – 129
Name: Allura red AC
Found in: biscuits, cake mixes.
Problems: May be an allergen to people with sensitive skin and asthmatics.

E Number – 131
Name: Patent blue V
Found in: Scotch eggs.
Problems: Hyperactivity in children. May be an allergen to people with sensitive skin. Low blood-pressure, breathing problems.

E Number – 132
Names: Indigotine, Indigo carmine
Found in: biscuits, confectionery.
Problems: Hyperactivity in children. May be an allergen to people with sensitive skin and high blood-pressure.

E Number – 133
Names: Brilliant Blue FCF, FD&C Blue 1
Found in: tinned processed peas.
Problems: Hyperactivity in children.

E Number – 142
Name: Green S
Found in: gravy granules, ice cream, mint sauce, sweets, tinned peas.
Problems: Should be avoided if you suffer from food-colour intolerance.

E Numbers – 150a, 150b, 150c, 150d
Names: Plain caramel, Caustic sulphite caramel, Ammonia caramel.
Found in: soy sauce, beer, whisky, dark rum, colas, sauces, gravy powder, chocolate.
Problems: Hyperactivity in children.

E Number – 151
Names: Brilliant Black BN, Black PN
Found in: soft drinks, sauces, red-fruit jam, ice creams, flavoured milk.
Problems: Hyperactivity in children.

E Number – 154
Name: Brown FK
Found in: smoked kippers, smoked mackerel, ham, crisps.
Problems: Hyperactivity in children.

E Number – 155
Name: Brown HT
Found in: chocolate cake.
Problems: Hyperactivity in children.

E Number – 160B
Names: Annatto, Bixin, Norbixin
Found in: cheese, custard, fish fingers.
Problems: Hyperactivity in children. Annatto may cause allergic reactions.

PRESERVATIVES

E Number – 210
Name: Benzoic acid
Found in: fruit juice, cordial, salad cream, pickles, jam.
Problems: Hyperactivity in children. May cause allergic skin reactions or gastric irritation.

E Numbers – 211, 212, 213, 214
Names: Sodium benzoate, Potassium benzoate, Calcium benzoate, Ethyl4-hydroxybenzoate
Found in: fruit juice, cordial, salad cream, pickles, jam.
Problems: Hyperactivity in children. May be an allergen to people with sensitive skin and asthmatics.

E Numbers – 220, 221 222, 223, 224, 225, 226, 227, 228
Names: Sulphur dioxide and its salts, Sodium sulphite, Sodium bisulsulphite, Sodium metabisulphite, Potassium Metabisulphite, Potassium sulphite, Calcium sulphite, Calcium hydrogen Sulphite, Potassium bisulphite.
Found in: fruit juice, cordials, beer, wine, vinegar, dried fruit.
Problems: Hyperactivity in children. May be an allergen to asthmatics.

E Number – 235
Name: Natamycin
Found in: meat, cheese.
Problems: nausea, vomiting, anorexia, diarrhoea and skin irritation.

E Numbers – 249, 252
Names: Potassium nitrite/nitrate
Found in: meat.
Problems: dizzynesss, headaches, difficult breathing.

E Numbers – 250, 251
Name: Sodium nitrite/nitrate
Found in: meat.
Problems: Hyperactive Children's Support Group recommends to avoid them.

E Numbers – 281, 282, 283
Names: Sodium propionate, Calcium propionate, Potassium propionate
Found in: flour products.
Problems: Can trigger migraines.

E Numbers – 310, 311, 312,
Names: Propyl gallate, Octyl gallate, Dodecyl gallate
Found in: margarine, fats, oils.
Problems: gastric or skin irritation.

E Numbers – 320, 321
Names – Butulated hydroxyanisole, Butylated hydroxytoluene
Found in: fat, oil, margarine, nuts, instant potato products.
Problems: Hyperactive Children's Support Group recommends to avoid them.

VEGETABLE GUMS, EMULSIFIERS, STABILISERS

E Number – 420
Name: Sorbitol
Found in: low-calorie foods, dried fruit, confectionery, pastries.
Problems: Can cause gastric disturbance.

E Number – 421
Name: Mannitol
Found in: low-calorie foods.
Problems: nausea, vomiting, diarrhoea.

E Number – 422
Name: Glycerin
Found in: liqueurs, low-calorie foods, dried fruits, confectionery.
Problems: Large quantities can cause thirst, headaches, nausea, high blood sugar.

E Number – 440 (a)
Name: Pectin
Found in: fruits, olives.
Problems: Large quantities cause flatulence.

E Number – 441
Name: Gelatine
Found in: chilled dairy products, jelly, confectionery, meat products.
Problems: People that are allergic to Sulphites should avoid it.

E Number – 518
Name: Magnesium Sulphate
Used as: an acidity regulator and firming agent.

Problems: It is also a laxative.

E Number – 542
Name: Bone phosphate
Used as: an anti-caking agent.
Problems: Not suitable for vegans.

E Numbers – 620, 621, 622, 623, 624, 625
Names: L-Glutamic acid, Monosodium glutamate (MSG), Monopotassium glutamate, Calcium diglutamate, Monoammonium glutamate
Found in: pork pies, cooked and cured meat, sausages, soup, Chinese and Japanese food.
Problems: raging thirst, dizziness, nausea, cold sweats.

E Number – 901
Name: Beeswax – white and yellow
Used as: a glazing agent.
Problems: allergic reactions.

E Number – 904
Name: Shellac
Used as: a glazing agent.
Problems: skin irritation.

E Number – 924
Name: Potassium bromate
Found in: flour products.
Problems: nausea, vomiting, diarrhoea.

E Number – 928
Name: Benzol Peroxide
Used as: a bleaching agent in flour.
Problems: for asthmatics and people with allergies.

E Number – 951
Name: Aspartame
Used as: artificial sweetener in over 5,000 products.
Problems: Memory loss, increases appetite, and may be addictive.

E Number – 966
Name: Lactitol
Found in: breakfast cereals, chewing gum, mustard, sauces, ice cream, jam, jelly, "no added sugar" products.
Problems: Large amounts can cause diarrhoea.

Alcohol Duty

Alcoholic drinks are taxed more heavily than petrol, and bring in billions of pounds of revenue for the government.

Note the duty paid below, and you'll understand why the price of our alcoholic drinks are so high! Indeed, this dreaded duty is the reason why up to 20% of all drink sold in the UK is smuggled in by the booze runners.

Duty (not including VAT):

Cider – is 9p for 330ml bottle.

Beer & Lager – is 18p* for a 330ml bottle at 4% ABV and will increase as the alcohol increases.

Wine (Red, Rosé White) – is £1.26 for a 750ml bottle – that's provided the wine does not have an ABV above 15%.

Champagne & Sparkling Wine – is £1.65 – for a 750ml bottle.

Fortified Wine (Sherry & Port) – is £1.68 for a 750 ml bottle.

Brown & White Spirits – is £5.48 for a 700ml bottle at 40% ABV – that's around 14p per degree of alcohol. Reduce the spirit to 37.5% and producer/retailers save about 35p in duty.

* Duty is half this for beer or lager from boutique brewers, but it only applies to the first 59 barrels produced per week (5,000 hectolitres).

1
Cereals

Don't always assume that cereals are the healthy breakfast option. Over the years ingredient tweaking has resulted in many over-salted and over-sugared products. Even cereals advertising "no added salt and sugar" may naturally contain some. So, check the nutrition information on the packet side carefully – and often – as recipes can change.

Branded cereals like Kellogg's Cornflakes are big business, and once upon a time they were the only ones to buy if you wanted the best quality. Then, while supermarket "own labels" were cheaper, their quality was poor. How things have changed! "Own label" breakfast cereals at their best are identical to the big brand – except for the price. Check these out.

Kellogg's Cornflakes

Iron, Salt, Vitamins

(8) **ASDA** Corn Flakes, 500g, 84p   **(GF) (N/S)**
A great purchase for the beat-the-brand shopper. These match the flavour of Kellogg's, flake for flake.

(8) **TESCO** Corn Flakes, 500g, 84p
Another brand beater. The same shape, colour and crunch, with or without milk!

(8) **SAINSBURY'S** Corn Flakes, 500g, 87p   **(GF) (L) (N/S)**
Make room in the trolley. Equal to Kellogg's on all fronts, except for the price.

(8) **MORRISONS** Corn Flakes, 500g, 89p
A beat-the-brand buy. Much cheaper and there's little or no difference in taste and crunch.

(8) **WAITROSE** Corn Flakes, 500g, 89p   **(GF) (L) (N/S)**
A slightly more golden colour, but the crunch and flavour equal the brand.

(7) **ALDI** Harvest Morn Corn Flakes, 500g, 99p   **(L)**
Side by side, it was difficult to taste any difference between Kellogg's and Harvest Morn.

(7) **MARKS & SPENCER** Corn Flakes, 500g, £1.09
With or without milk, there is little difference in colour, crunch, crispness and flavour.

KELLOGG'S CORNFLAKES, 500g, £1.29
Crunchy and tasty, and with milk they certainly have what it takes to relish the bowlful. Indeed, like most cornflakes, 30g will deliver 25% of your RDA of vitamins and iron.

(5) **SOMERFIELD** Corn Flakes, 500g, 89p   **(V)**
Cheaper alternative to the brand; however, taste-wise they are just a small step below.

(5) **CO-OP** Corn Flakes, 500g, 92p   **(L)**
Just a notch below the brand, but they are still worth a punt at this price.

(1) **SAINSBURY'S** Low Price Corn Flakes, 500g, 44p
The overpoweringly sweet "corn on the cob" flavour makes them difficult to swallow – even at 44p.

(1) **TESCO** Value Corn Flakes, 500g, 44p   **(V)**
Don't! I've tasted better cow cereal. Tesco's cereal buyer should be made to eat these.

(1) **ASDA** Smartprice, 500g, 66p
Taste-wise, this Smartprice is a non-starter. Almost identical in flavour to Tesco Value Corn Flakes, but 22p more!

Kellogg's Frosties

Iron, Salt, Sugar, Vitamins

---

(10)   **ALDI** New Day Frosted Flakes, 625g, 99p (80p for 500g)   **(L)**
A beat-the-brand buy. Gram for gram they are under half price and they taste better.

---

(9)   **TESCO** Frosted Flakes, 750g, £1.46 (98p for 500g)
Buy it. These beat the brand on price and equal it on all taste fronts.

---

(8)   **ASDA** Frosted Flakes, 500g, £1.07   **(GF)**
You're better off with Asda's Frosted Flakes. As good as, if not better than, Kellogg's.

---

(8)   **MORRISONS** Frosted Flakes, 500g, £1.09
A cheaper and better buy! A different colour from the brand, but the taste is better.

---

(8)   **SAINSBURY'S** Frosted Flakes, 500g, £1.09   **(GF) (L)**
A beat-the-brand buy. Indeed, even at the same price this would still be the better buy.

---

(8)   **WAITROSE** Frosted Flakes, 500g, £1.09   **(GF) (L) (N/S)**
Put it in the trolley. This cereal tastes less sweet than the brand although it has similar sugar levels.

---

(8)   **KWIK SAVE** Frosted Flakes, 500g, £1.15
Kwik Save has a winner here. It's Frosted Flakes are cheaper and better tasting (dry or with milk) than the brand.

---

(8)   **SOMERFIELD** Frosted Flakes, 500g, £1.29
Sweet, crisp and crunchy. Put them in the trolley unless you also shop at Kwik Save.

---

(7)   **CO-OP** Frosted Flakes, 500g, £1.45   **(L) (V)**
Still worth a punt for the Co-op shopper! Cheaper, and equals the brand for taste.

KELLOGG'S FROSTIES, 500g, £1.65

This is not the healthiest of breakfast cereals. Indeed, a 30g serving has around 33% of your recommended daily intake of added sugar, but it does contain 17% of your RDA of vitamins and iron.

---

(1)   **TESCO** Value Frosted Flakes, 500g, 54p   **(V)**
Leave it on the shelf. Even at this price these frosted flakes are difficult to swallow.

Kellogg's Bran Flakes

Salt, Sugar

(8) **WAITROSE** Bran Flakes, 500g, 99p (L)
A beat-the-brand buy. Much cheaper, and the brand's equal on all the flavour fronts.

KELLOGG'S BRAN FLAKES, 500g, £1.65

Promoted as the healthy cereal option. A 30g serving delivers 22% of your recommended daily intake of fibre, and 25% of your vitamins and iron. However, 13g of sugar is mingled in with all that healthy stuff.

(5) **SAINSBURY'S** Whole Grain Bran Flakes, 750g, £1.35 (89p for 500g) (L)
Just a flake below the brand, but it will satisfy the fibre lover.

(5) **KWIK SAVE** Bran Flakes, 750g, £1.35 (93p for 500g)
Stick it in the trolley. It's cheaper and you'll hardly taste the difference with milk.

(5) **TESCO** Healthyliving Bran Flakes, 500g, 93p
The brand just has the edge on flavour, but this is great value for money.

(5) **MORRISONS** Bran Flakes, 500g, 99p
Worth a punt! It's cheaper and tastes nearly as good as the brand.

(5) **SOMERFIELD** Bran Flakes, 500g, 99p
Just a tad less in quality, but if you require bran at below a quid this will hit the spot.

(5) **ASDA** Organic Bran Flakes, 500g, £1.26 (V)
An organic alternative! Cheaper than the brand, but it comes second taste-wise.

(3) **CO-OP** Bran Flakes, 500g, £1.35 (L) (V)
This does not compete taste-wise. Buy the brand if you want to finish the packet.

Kellogg's Fruit 'n Fibre

Iron, Salt, Sugar, Vitamins

(9) **SAINSBURY'S** Whole Grain Fruit & Fibre, 500g, £1.08 **(L)**
Buy it. Nearly half the price of the brand, and its equal in appearance and taste.

(9) **KWIK SAVE** Fruit & Fibre, 500g, £1.09
Great buy. A big saving and Kwik Save has not scrimped on the fruit or nuts.

(9) **MORRISONS** Fruit & Fibre, 500g, £1.19
Make room in your trolley. An enjoyable "own label" that competes well with the brand.

(9) **WAITROSE** Fruit & Fibre, 500g, £1.19 **(L)**
A beat-the-brand buy. It's cheaper and the mix and taste quality equal that of Kellogg's.

(9) **SOMERFIELD** Fruit & Fibre, 750g, £1.85 (£1.23 for 500g) **(V)**
With milk it is difficult to tell the difference between this and Kellogg's.

KELLOGG'S FRUIT 'N FIBRE, 500g, £1.98
An excellent balance between the wheat flakes, fruit and nuts that lasts right down to the bottom of the pack. Healthwise, a 30g serving delivers 19% of your RDA of vitamins and iron.

(5) **ALDI** Harvest Morn Fruit & Fibre, 500g, 95p **(L)**
A cheaper alternative, but the fruit and nut mix is not as good as the brand.

(5) **ASDA** Fruit & Fibre, 500g, £1.08
Cheaper than the brand, but the mix (too many large chunks) and taste come second.

(5) **TESCO** Fruit & Fibre, 500g, £1.08
There's nothing wrong with the quality, it's just that the added fruit and nuts are too big and too chunky.

(4) **CO-OP** Fruit & Fibre, 500g, £1.49 **(L)**
Where's the fruit? Too much fibre means that this is not as well mixed as Kellogg's.

Alpen Original

Lactose, Salt, Sugar, Sulphur dioxide (E220)

(10) **ALDI** Harvest Morn Swiss Style Muesli, 1kg, 99p (75p for 750g)
Grab it. Very similar to the brand, and gram for gram this is less than half price.

(10) **TESCO** Swiss Style Muesli, 2kg, £2.39 (90p for 750g)
You certainly get extra at Tesco with this! Cheap price with similar tastes to the brand.

(9) **ASDA** Swiss Style Muesli, 750g, £1.07
This is one to buy. Spoon for spoon there is little difference between Asda's and Alpen's.

(8) **WAITROSE** Swiss Style Muesli, 750g, £1.25
Cheaper. It looks the same in the bowl and tastes the same in the mouth.

(8) **SOMERFIELD** Swiss Style Muesli, 750g, £1.29
Buy it. Even regular Alpen buyers will not be disappointed with this one.

ALPEN ORIGINAL, 750g, £1.89
Alpen is a mix of wheat flakes, oats, raisins, hazelnuts and almonds. The front of the packet does not tell you that this cereal also contains a mountain of sugar and too much salt.

(2) **CO-OP** Swiss Style Muesli, 750g, £1.49
Forget it. A very poor "own label" that has been mean with the nuts and raisins.

Alpen Original (No Added Sugar or Salt)

Iron, Lactose, Salt, Sugar, Sulphur dioxide (E220), Vitamins

(9) **ASDA** No Added Sugar or Salt Swiss Style Muesli, 750g, £1.07
Be aware that no added sugar or salt does give a much drier taste than regular muesli.

(9) **WAITROSE** Swiss Style Muesli No Added Sugar or Salt, 560g, £1.09 (£1.46 for 750g)
A great beat-the-brand buy. Drier and more chewy, but not inferior in quality.

(9) **TESCO** Swiss Style Muesli No Added Sugar or Salt, 750g, £1.29
Buy it... unless you're passing Waitrose. Cheaper and as good as the brand.

ALPEN ORIGINAL NO ADDED SUGAR OR SALT, 750g, £1.89
Drier tasting than the regular Alpen. Sugar and salt watchers should note that this cereal does still contain some, and should check the nutrition label for their precise content.

Jordans Special Luxury Fruits & Nuts Muesli

Iron, Salt, Sugar, Sulphur dioxide (E220), Vitamins

(10) **ASDA** 55% Fruit & Nut Muesli, 500g, £1.34 (£2.01 for 750g) **(V)**
You'll want two bowls – this is so moreish. The perfect 10 is for its great taste.

(9) **ALDI** Harvest Morn Luxury Muesli, 500g, 99p (£1.49 for 750g)
Put it in the trolley – you can't tell the difference between this and the brand, and it's around a quid cheaper.

(8) **KWIK SAVE** Fruit & Nut Muesli, 500g, £1.15 (£1.73 for 750g) **(V)**
Cheaper and the brand's equal in quality. However, the peel fruits may be a little too spiky for some.

(7) **WAITROSE** Fruit & Nut Muesli, 1kg, £2.95 (£2.21 for 750g) **(L) (N/S) (V)**
An excellent alternative to the brand.

(7) **MARKS & SPENCER**, Luxury Fruit & Nut Muesli, 500g, £1.59 (£2.39 for 750g)
Gram for gram it's about the same price as Jordans, but the quality is another notch up.

JORDANS SPECIAL LUXURY FRUITS & NUTS MUESLI, 750g, £2.44

Not any healthier, but if you find the Swiss style muesli boring, then the extra flavours of dried fruits here maybe what's required to make your eyes sparkle.

(2) **MORRISONS** Luxury Fruit & Nut Muesli, 500g, £1.29 (£1.94 for 750g),
Don't! My five-year-old could have done a better job of mixing this one.

(2) **SAINSBURY'S** Fruit & Nut Muesli, 500g, £1.34 (£2.01 for 750g) **(L) (V)**
Forget it. Like the Morrisons above, the ingredient mix – with or without milk – is difficult to swallow.

Nestlé Shreddies

Gluten, Nuts, Salt, Sugar, Wheat

---

(10)   **ASDA** Malted Wheaties, 750g, £1.24 (83p for 500g)   **(V) (N/S)**
Buy it. Gram for gram this cereal is under half the price and similar in taste quality to the brand.

---

(10)   **SAINSBURY'S** Malties, 750g, £1.24 (83p for 500g)   **(L) (V)**
A beat-the-brand buy. Sainsbury's cereal has a comparable taste at under half the brand's price.

---

(8)   **CO-OP** Malt Crunchies, 500g, £1.29   **(L) (N/S) (V)**
A good buy. A tad darker in colour, otherwise it's difficult to tell them apart.

NESTLÉ SHREDDIES, 500g, £1.79
Popular cereal. Healthwise, a 30g serving will deliver at least 16% of your RDA of vitamins and iron, but don't forget to count the sugar and salt content!

---

(2)   **SOMERFIELD** Malted Wheats, 500g, 74p
Leave it on the shelf. These misshapen Malted Wheats taste even worse than they look.

Weetabix

Fibre, Iron, Salt, Sugar, Vitamins

(9) **SOMERFIELD** Wheat Biscuits, 24 biscuits, 64p **(V)**
No competition! Almost half the price and they taste as good as the brand.

(9) **ALDI** Wheat Bisks, 24 biscuits, 69p **(L)**
Make room in the trolley for at least one packet. There is little or no difference between this and the brand.

(7) **ASDA** Whole Wheat Bisks, 24 biscuits, 94p **(N/S) (V)**
This beats the brand. It's cheaper, and the colour, shape and taste are very similar.

(8) **TESCO** Healthyliving Wheat Biscuits, 24 biscuits, 94p **(V)**
Don't buy the brand: Tesco's "own label" delivers a similar flavour for less money.

(8) **MORRISONS** Wheat Biscuit, 24 biscuits, 95p
Buy Morrisons. You won't taste the difference, with or without milk.

(8) **SAINSBURY'S** Wholewheat Biscuits, 24 biscuits, 98p **(L) (V)**
Put it in the trolley. Taste-wise, it's difficult to tell this and the brand apart.

(7) **CO-OP** Wholewheat Biscuits, 24 biscuits, £1.05 **(L) (N/S) (V)**
A good buy. Slightly different in taste to the brand, but with milk, the flavour appears the same.

(7) **WAITROSE** Wholewheat Biscuits, 24 biscuits, 99p **(L) (N/S)**
Put it in the trolley. Taste-wise, there is no noticeable difference with or without milk.

WEETABIX, 24 BISCUITS, £1.24

Two Weetabix biscuits will deliver over 30% of your RDA of vitamins and iron and are a good source of fibre. However, like most cereals the salt and sugar content needs counting.

(1) **TESCO** Value Wheat Biscuits, 36 biscuits, 69p
Leave it on the shelf. Cheap – and you get 12 more biscuits – but the taste is bland and difficult to swallow.

Kellogg's Rice Krispies

Iron, Salt, Vitamins

(10) **MORRISONS** Rice Crackles, 600g, £1.19 (90p for 450g) **(GF)**
Buy it. It's under half price and is equal to the brand taste-wise.

(9) **ASDA** Rice Snap, 440g, 98p **(GF) (N/S)**
Snap it up – it's different, but just as good. Darker and less sweet than the brand.

(9) **ALDI** New Day Crispy Rice, 440g, 99p **(L)**
Darker and smaller, but with milk there was little difference on all taste fronts.

(9) **SOMERFIELD** Crisp Rice, 440g, £1.09 **(GF)**
A sound purchase. Not as sweet as the brand, but delivers comparable taste quality.

(9) **SAINSBURY'S** Rice Pops, 440g, £1.18 **(GF) (L) (N/S)**
A must-buy for the Sainsbury's shopper. It's almost identical to the brand's snap, crackle and pop.

(9) **TESCO** Kids Rice Snaps, 440g, £1.18 **(GF)**
In the cereal bowl, you can't tell the difference between this and Kellogg's.

(8) **KWIK SAVE** Rice Snaps, 440g, £1.19 **(L)**
Put it in the trolley. This beats the brand on price and equals it on taste.

(8) **WAITROSE** Rice Pops, 440g, £1.25 **(GF) (L) (N/S)**
A big saving for the Waitrose shopper! More toasty, but it's of a similar quality to the brand.

(7) **CO-OP** Crisp Rice, 440g, £1.49 **(GF) (L)**
If the Co-op is just around the corner, then this is a beat-the-brand buy.

KELLOGG'S RICE KRISPIES, 450g, £1.89

Certainly a healthier option than the sugar-coated Frosties for children – but they're expensive, even taking into account that the weight is 10g more than the "own labels". Fortunately, however, all the "own labels" here delivered the same quality at a much cheaper price.

Scott's Porridge Oats

Salt, Sugar

(9) **WAITROSE** Porridge Oats (rolled), 1kg, 79p **(L) (V)**
Buy it. For Waitrose shoppers this is cheaper and just as enjoyable as the brand.

(8) **SAINSBURY'S** Taste the Difference Whole Rolled Oats, **(N/S) (V)**
750g, 69p (92p for 1kg)
Give it a try. These enjoyable sweet-tasting oats more than compete with the brand.

SCOTT'S PORRIDGE OATS, 1kg, £1.48
One of the healthiest breakfasts you can eat. Moreover, all products were tasted dry, and
then made with water rather than milk to make it easier to detect the difference.

(5) **ASDA** Scottish Porridge Oats, 500g, 38p (76p for 1kg)
One notch down in quality, but will hit the spot for most.

(3) **SOMERFIELD** Porridge Oats, 1kg, 85p
Buy the brand. Poor quality, and it does not get close to the brand taste-wise.

(3) **CO-OP** Porridge Oats, 500g, 55p (£1.10 for 1kg) **(L) (N/S) (V)**
Leave it on the shelf. Pay the extra and buy the brand – it's three times better.

(2) **MORRISONS** Quick & Easy Porridge Oats, 1kg, 57p
Boring to the palate. You'll need to add plenty of supplements to get this off the spoon.

(2) **TESCO** Scottish Porridge Oats, 500g, 38p (76p for 1kg) **(N/S) (V)**
Has Tesco's buyer actually tasted this? Wallpaper glue has more appeal – leave it
on the shelf.

2
Bread, Pastries & Cakes

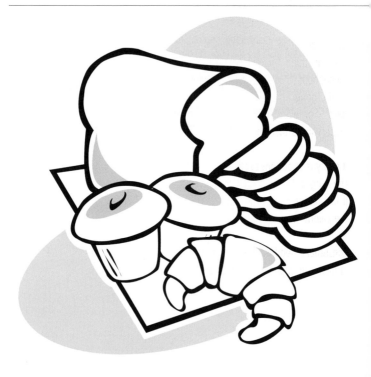

Obviously, good home baking tastes better and is generally healthier than anything bought from a supermarket. Today, however, as life's roundabout speeds up, most of us buy our bread, pastry and cakes ready made, generally weekly, confident that they will stay fresh for several days – or even weeks. Do we ignore the additives, flavourings and preservatives that ensure this prolonged life? It seems we do.

It really is important to check that nutrition label, check it again and keep checking it. Not that it's easy. What do all those E numbers mean? And if the cake and pastries aren't sold by weight, it's very difficult to assess the calorie intake.

Consumers need to be proactive, to take notice of additives and to protest – or approve – through their purchases.

Kingsmill Toastie White Medium Sliced Bread

Carbohydrate, Emulsifier, Iron, Salt, Soya, Sugar, Vitamins

---

(9) **SAINSBURY'S** Medium Sliced White Bread, 800g, 42p **(N/S) (V)**
Buy it. Almost half price, more toaster-friendly, and presents a similar taste to the brand.

---

(9) **TESCO** Premium Wholesome White Medium Sliced Bread, 800g, 55p **(V)**
A beat-the-brand buy. Tesco is much cheaper and better tasting than the brand.

---

(8) **KWIK SAVE** White Medium Sliced Bread, 800g, 46p
Put it in the trolley. Not as white as the brand, but still its equal taste-wise.

---

(8) **CO-OP** White Medium Sliced Bread, 800g, 47p **(L) (V)**
More toaster-friendly. More like Hovis in colour and texture than the brand.

---

(8) **MORRISONS** Best Loaf White Medium Sliced Bread, 800g, 47p
Morrisons and Kingsmill are so similar they could have come out of the same packet.

---

(8) **SOMERFIELD** White Bread Medium Sliced, 800g, 49p
A grey-white bread when compared to Kingsmill's whiter-than-white, but with little difference taste-wise.

---

(6) **MARKS & SPENCER** Premium White Medium Sliced Bread, 800g, 79p **(V)**
Buy it. A few pence cheaper, but that's the only difference between this and the brand.

KINGSMILL TOASTIE WHITE MEDIUM SLICED BREAD, 800g, 83p
Interestingly, Kingsmill Toastie bread is a little (about 4mm) too tall for regular toasters.
Check the nutrition label for sugar and salt content.

---

(5) **ASDA** Square Cut Medium Sliced Bread, 800g, 42p **(N/S) (V)**
One notch down in quality, but it fits in the toaster, and it's nearly half the brand price.

---

(2) **ALDI** Village Baker White Medium Sliced Bread, 800g, 25p **(L)**
Not bread as we know it. Leave it – unless the taste of the bread does not matter to you.

Hovis Classic White Thick Sliced Bread

Carbohydrate, Emulsifier, Iron, Salt, Soya, Sugar, Vitamins

(9) **SAINSBURY'S** White Thick Sliced Bread, 800g, 42p **(N/S) (V)**
Put it in the trolley. A few crumbs off half price and similar in quality to the brand.

(9) **TESCO** White Thick Sliced Bread, 800g, 44p **(V)**
A beat-the-brand buy. A whiter colour than the brand and little difference in taste.

(8) **KWIK SAVE** White Thick Sliced Bread, 800g, 46p
Buy it. More bread for your money, and a similar colour and taste to the brand.

(8) **MORRISONS** Best Loaf White Thick Sliced Bread, 800g, 47p
As good as and cheaper than the brand. However, it's more Kingsmill than Hovis.

(8) **ASDA** Square Cut Bakers Gold White Thick Sliced Bread, 800g, 48p **(N/S) (V)**
Buy it. Equal in taste to Hovis, but style-wise it is very similar to Kingsmill.

(8) **SOMERFIELD** White Thick Sliced Bread, 800g, 49p
Put it in the trolley. It is cheaper and tastes as good as the brand.

(6) **CO-OP** Gold White Thick Sliced Bread, 800g, 79p **(L) (V)**
This costs a few pennies more, but it's a much better bread than the brand.

HOVIS CLASSIC THICK SLICED WHITE BREAD, 800g, 72p

There is little difference in quality between Kingsmill and Hovis, but there is a variation in colour – Hovis is grey-white rather than white-white. Note the sugar and salt levels.

(2) **ALDI** Village Baker White Thick Sliced Bread, 800g, 25p **(L)**
Don't waste your money. This bread may be cheap, but you'll get more pleasure eating soggy tissue paper.

Hovis Hearty Wholemeal Medium Sliced Brown Bread

Carbohydrate, Emulsifier, Fibre, Iron, Salt, Soya, Sugar, Vitamins

(9) **ALDI** Village Green Medium Sliced Wholemeal Brown Batch Loaf, 800g, 59p **(L)**
Put it in the trolley. This is cheaper, healthier and much better tasting than the brand.

(8) **MORRISONS** Superlife Wholemeal Medium Sliced Brown Bread, 800g, 43p
Buy it. This "Superlife" bread is as good as the brand – even after seven days.

(8) **SAINSBURY'S** Wholemeal Medium Sliced Brown Bread, 800g, 47p **(N/S) (V)**
Grab the loaf. The wholemeal flavours compete well with the brand's – and it's much cheaper, too.

(8) **KWIK SAVE** Wholemeal Sliced Brown Bread, 800g, 48p
A wholemeal bargain! Cheaper, and it equals the quality and flavours of the brand.

HOVIS HEARTY WHOLEMEAL MEDIUM SLICED BROWN BREAD, 800g, 71p
Better tasting, better for you and 1p cheaper than its Hovis white brother! Unlike most products, where "better" normally means it costs more, that's not the case here.

(5) **ASDA** Square Cut Wholemeal Medium Sliced Brown Bread, 800g, 40p **(N/S) (V)**
Worth a punt! A similar style to Hovis, but the taste quality is a small step down.

(5) **TESCO** Wholemeal Medium Sliced Brown Bread, 800g, 40p **(N/S) (V)**
A cheaper alternative to the brand. The quality difference will hardly be noticed in a loaded sandwich.

(5) **MORRISONS** Stone Ground Wholemeal, Medium Sliced Brown Bread, 800g, 43p
Cheaper, but side by side, this is a small step down in flavour quality from the brand.

(5) **CO-OP** Medium Sliced Brown Bread, 800g, 47p **(L) (V)**
An alternative to the brand. Cheaper and a few crumbs off the brand's taste quality.

(5) **MARKS & SPENCER** Premium Wholemeal, Sliced Brown Bread, 800g, 89p **(V)**
Not a beat-the-brand buy. It costs more and is no better in quality. Buy elsewhere.

Kingsmill Wholemeal Thick Sliced Brown Bread

Carbohydrate, Emulsifier, Fibre, Iron, Salt, Soya, Sugar, Vitamins

(10) **ALDI** Village Bakery Premium Gold Thick Sliced Multigrain Bread, 800g, 54p **(L)**
Cheaper and better than the brand by several slices.

(8) **ASDA** Square Cut Wholemeal Thick Sliced Brown Bread, 800g, 40p **(N/S) (V)**
Put it in the trolley. Much cheaper and competes well with the brand in taste and quality.

(8) **CO-OP** Wholemeal Thick Sliced Brown Bread, 800g, 45p **(L) (V)**
Grab this loaf. Cheaper, and most shoppers will prefer the extra wholemeal taste.

(8) **SAINSBURY'S** Wholemeal Thick Sliced Brown Bread, 800g, 47p **(N/S) (V)**
A sound buy! Cheaper, and delivers an extra layer of flavour compared to the brand.

(8) **TESCO** Premium Wholemeal Thick Sliced Brown Bread, 800g, 52p **(V)**
Buy it. Tastier than the brand, and it will keep Hovis buyers happy too.

KINGSMILL WHOLEMEAL THICK SLICED BROWN BREAD, 800g, 69p
A healthier, cheaper and tastier option than Kingsmill's white sliced. However, if you compare it to the flavour of the equivalent Hovis loaf, it comes out second best.

New York Plain Bagels

Carbohydrate, Fibre, Lactose, Salt, Yeast

(7) **ASDA** 4 Plain Bagels, 78p (98p for 5)
Per bagel, Asda's are about 2p cheaper and deliver a similar quality to the brand.

(7) **TESCO** 5 Plain Bagels, 99p
As good – put them in the trolley. Taste-wise, they're very similar to the brand.

(7) **WAITROSE** 5 Plain Bagels, £1.09 **(L)**
A beat-the-brand buy for the Waitrose shopper. Just as good as the brand, and a few pence cheaper.

(7) **MARKS & SPENCER** 5 Plain Bagels, £1.09 **(V)**
Good purchase! The same price as the brand, but the taste quality is much better.

(6) **SAINSBURY'S** Bakery 4 Plain Bagels, £1.15 (£1.43 for 5)
Buy them! They are worth the extra cash as they're much better quality than the brand.

NEW YORK PLAIN BAGELS, £1.09 (FOR 5)
A solid doughy bun that tastes best toasted. However, anybody that has been to New York will know that these bear little comparison to the bagels freshly baked over there.

New York Cinnamon & Raisin Bagels

Carbohydrate, Fibre, Lactose, Salt, Yeast

(7) **ASDA** 4 Cinnamon & Raisin Bagels, 78p (98p for 5)
Grab a pack! Evenly baked, consistent cinnamon and raisin flavours – and they're cheaper.

(7) **TESCO** 5 Cinnamon & Raisin Bagels, 99p
Put it in the trolley. Better quality and more harmonious flavours than the brand.

(7) **WAITROSE** 5 Cinnamon & Raisin Bagels, £1.09 **(V)**
A beat-the-brand buy. Better flavoured, more enjoyable and you'll save a few pennies.

(6) **SAINSBURY'S** Bakery 4 Cinnamon & Raisin Bagels, £1.15 (£1.43 for 5)
Buy a pack. Much better quality than the brand and certainly worth the extra cash.

NEW YORK CINNAMON & RAISIN BAGELS, £1.09 (FOR 5)
Heady cinnamon notes can be smelt even through the plastic wrapping. Flavour-wise, they are America's equivalent to the British hot cross bun and taste best toasted.

Mr Kipling Exceedingly Good Bramley Apple Pies

Fibre, Lactose, Sugar, Sulphites (E221–E228)

(8) **ALDI** Crofters 6 Apple Pies, 69p
A beat-the-brand buy. Not identical in appearance, but they taste as good as the brand.

MR KIPLING EXCEEDINGLY GOOD 6 BRAMLEY APPLE PIES, £1.04
Mr Kipling's apple pies do have that "I want another bite" quality. However, the apple filling is not so good on its own. Count the sugar content!

(5) **KWIK SAVE** Simply 6 Apple Pies, 40p
No packaging frills and worth a punt. A notch down in quality, but value for money.

(5) **ASDA** 6 Apple Pies, 79p
A cheaper alternative to the brand, but the pastry does not have a crisp crunch.

(5) **MORRISONS** 6 Apple Pies, 79p
Worth a punt for the Morrison's shopper. Very similar to Asda's apple pies in appearance and taste.

(4) **SAINSBURY'S** 6 Bramley Apple Pies, 81p
They look good, and they beat the brand on price, but the bite quality is second rate.

(3) **SOMERFIELD** 6 Bramley Apple Pies, 85p
Not an alternative to the brand. Cheaper, but the pastry is too thick and dry.

(2) **TESCO** 6 Bramley Apple Pies, 78p
Leave them. Dry and pasty pastry, with an artificial-tasting apple filling.

(2) **CO-OP** 6 Apple Pies, 99p
Buy the brand. You'll get at least double the taste quality for just a few pence more.

Mr Kipling Exceedingly Good Real Fruit Jam Tarts

Egg, Lactose, Soya, Sugar, Sulphites (E221–E228)

---

(10) **ASDA** 6 Assorted Jam Tarts, 52p **(V)**
A very good buy. Different flavours to the brand, but the taste quality is similar.

MR KIPLING EXCEEDINGLY GOO 6 REAL FRUIT JAM TARTS, £1.04
Much better tasting than Mr Kipling's apple pies. The pack holds six tarts but just three flavours: two raspberry, two apricot and two blackcurrant and apple.

---

(5) **SAINSBURY'S** 6 Assorted Jam Tarts, 55p
Good value for money. These tarts are only a few crumbs below the brand.

---

(5) **TESCO** 6 Assorted Jam Tarts, 55p **(V)**
Again, cheaper than the brand, but the tarts and their jams are a step below the brand in terms of quality.

---

(5) **MORRISONS** 6 Jam & Lemon Curd Tarts, 59p
Acceptable pastry and filling flavours – and a cheaper alternative to the brand.

---

(4) **ALDI** Holly Lane 6 Assorted Jam Tarts, 45p **(L)**
A much cheaper price, but there is a big step down in taste quality.

---

(4) **SOMERFIELD** 6 Jam Tarts, 89p
Try another shop. Not cheap, and they are a good notch below the brand in quality.

---

(3) **KWIK SAVE** 10 Assorted Jam Tarts, 79p
Not the bargain the packet suggests. Plenty of tart, but just a scraping of jam!

McVitie's Original Jamaica Ginger Cake

Carbohydrate, Egg, Fibre, Lactose, Salt, Sugar, Soya

MCVITIE'S ORIGINAL JAMAICA GINGER CAKE, 280g, 99p

Moist, moreish ginger cake! Interestingly, there is no weight on the packet, which is not helpful if you are trying to compare prices or are on a diet.

(5) **TESCO** Ginger Slab Cake, 360g, 77p (60p for 280g)
Cheaper alternative. However, it does not have brand's ginger kick or irresistible flavours.

(5) **ALDI** Stonemill Ginger Cake, 300g, 79p (74p for 280g)
You get more cake for your money, but it's not as moist, nor is it of the same quality as the brand.

(3) **SOMERFIELD** Ginger Cake, 280g, £1.35
Don't bother! The brand's cake is cheaper and tastes very much better.

3
Marmalade, Jam & Honey

Anybody who has ever made jam or marmalade will be aware of the quantity of sugar it takes. Very roughly, equivalent amounts of fruit and sugar are used to make jam (according to the type), and double the amount of sugar for marmalade. But the extra quantity of sugar in bought jam or marmalade only really hits home when you read the ingredients label. Believe me, too often it's teeth-rottingly high. With nearly 300g of sugar in a jar, a few rounds of toast and marmalade would use up a high proportion of the recommended daily maximum of 60g of sugar.

We need help with these products, but we do not get it. With tiny unreadable print and jars of different sizes and weights, just how does the consumer compare prices and value for money? We shouldn't need a magnifying glass, calculator and science manual to work out how to buy the healthiest and best-value products in our supermarkets.

Robertson's Golden Shredless Marmalade

Sugar, Sulphur dioxide (E220)

---

(8) **ASDA** Shredless Marmalade, 454g, 75p   **(GF) (N/S) (V)**
A beat-the-brand buy. Put it in a Robertson's jar, and you wouldn't know the difference.

---

(7) **TESCO** No Peel Orange Jelly Marmalade, 340g, 60p (80p for 454g)   **(V)**
Buy it. Like for like, it's cheaper and delivers a comparable taste to the brand.

ROBERTSON'S GOLDEN SHREDLESS MARMALADE, 454g, 92p
No shreds of peel, but it still retains a biting orange flavour. Alas, it is seriously sweet: this 454g jar contains more than 286g of sugar – well over four times your 60g recommended daily intake of added sugar.

---

(5) **MORRISONS** Shredless Marmalade, 454g, 60p
Not for weight watchers. There's more sugar in this jar than the brand – and it certainly tastes like it.

---

(4) **SAINSBURY'S** Orange Shredless Marmalade, 454g, 80p
Cheaper than the brand, but you pay for it with a big step down in quality!

Robertson's Golden Shred Marmalade

Sugar, Sulphur dioxide (E220)

---

(10) **ASDA** Extra Special Orange Thin Cut Marmalade, **(GF) (N/S) (V)**
Reduced Sugar, 340g, 87p (£1.16 for 454g)
You'll love it, so buy it. It costs more than the brand, but the taste is fantastic.

---

(9) **ALDI** Citora Fine Cut Marmalade, 454g, 49p **(L)**
Grab a jar. Cheaper, more fruit and it competes with the brand in taste quality.

---

(8) **SAINSBURY'S** Orange Shred Fine Cut, Marmalade, 454g, 60p
Put it in the trolley. Similar to the brand taste-wise – but the price is much cheaper.

---

(8) **TESCO** Medium Cut Marmalade, 454g, 60p **(V)**
Darker colour, much more orange flavour and at least equal to the brand taste-wise.

---

(8) **KWIK SAVE** Thin Cut Orange Marmalade, 454g, 60p
A good buy for the Kwik Save shopper. Beats the brand on price and equals it on taste.

---

(7) **ASDA** Fine Cut Marmalade, 454g, 75p **(GF) (N/S) (V)**
Save yourself some cash and put it in the trolley – you can't tell the difference in taste.

---

(7) **CO-OP** Orange Marmalade Fine Cut, 454g, 85p **(GF) (L) (N/S) (V)**
Buy it. A tad more sugar, but taste-wise there's little difference from the brand here.

ROBERTSON'S GOLDEN SHRED MARMALADE, 454g, 92p
Although this contains identical sugar and fruit levels to the Shredless, the fine orange shreds help to reduce the sweet taste. But remember, it's mainly sugar you're spreading on your toast.

---

(5) **KWIK SAVE** Simply Medium Cut Orange Marmalade, 454g, 31p
One notch down in quality, but with toast and butter it is an acceptable alternative.

---

(5) **SOMERFIELD** Fine Cut Orange Marmalade, 454g, 68p
This is just a step below the brand in taste, but it's still good value for money.

---

(5) **SOMERFIELD** Makes Sense Medium Cut Orange Marmalade, 454g, 34p
This won't cut it if you normally buy the brand, but it's worth a punt at this price.

---

(4) **MARKS & SPENCER**, Medium Cut Seville Orange Marmalade **(GF) (N/S) (V)**
454g, £1.49
Don't waste your money. This is a tad better than the brand, but not this price better.

Robertson's
Thick Cut Marmalade

Sugar, Sulphur dioxide (E220)

---

(9) **ALDI** Citora Thick Cut Marmalade, 454g, 49p **(L)**
A bargain buy – at this price. Bigger chunks than the brand, but it is of equal quality.

---

(8) **SAINSBURY'S** Orange Shred Fine Cut Marmalade, 454g, 60p
Take it off the shelf. It's cheaper and delivers similar quality and citric bite to the brand.

---

(7) **WAITROSE** Thick Cut Seville Orange Marmalade, 454g, 89p **(GF) (L) (N/S) (V)**
Buy it. A more solid style, but it tastes just as good as the brand.

ROBERTSON'S GOLDEN SHRED CHUNKY, 454g, 92p
Chunky orange shreds give this marmalade a real citric bite, and you hardly notice the sugar. However, if you're on a diet, don't spread it on too thickly since the jar still contains over 286g of sugar.

---

(5) **CO-OP** Orange Marmalade Thick Cut, 454g, 99p **(GF) (L) (N/S) (V)**
If the brand's cheaper – buy it. A darker colour, but the taste quality is similar.

---

(4) **KWIK SAVE** Thick Cut Orange Marmalade, 454g, 60p
The chunks don't do it here. Cheaper, but real marmalade lovers won't care for it much.

---

(4) **TESCO** Thick Cut Orange Marmalade, 454g, 60p **(V)**
Not an alternative to the brand. The chunky chunks spoil the taste of the marmalade.

---

(4) **SOMERFIELD** Thick Cut Orange Marmalade, 454g, 68p
A good saving, but the chunks will be too chewy for most people's taste.

---

(4) **ASDA** Thick Cut Marmalade, 454g, 75p **(GF) (N/S) (V)**
The chunks are just too long, so you have a less balanced marmalade.

Hartley's Best Strawberry Jam

Sugar, Sulphur dioxide (E220)

(10)   **ASDA** Fine Strawberry Jam, 454g, 58p (43p for 340g)   **(GF) (V)**
Buy it. It does not have whole strawberries in it, but matches the brand for flavour.

(10)   **TESCO** Strawberry Jam, 454g, 58p (43p for 340g)   **(V)**
Make room in the trolley. It's as good as the brand, and under half the price.

(10)   **KWIK SAVE** Strawberry Jam, 454g, 60p (45p for 340g)
A bargain price! Not as chunky as the brand, but of a similar taste quality.

(10)   **MORRISONS** Strawberry Jam, 454g, 60p (45p for 340g)
As good as the brand, and at the same bargain price as Kwik Save and Sainsbury's.

(10)   **SAINSBURY'S** Strawberry Jam 454g, 60p (45p for 340g)
Buy it. A serious saving for a jam that delivers comparable quality to the brand.

(10)   **SOMERFIELD** Strawberry Jam, 454g, 65p (49p for 340g)
This is as good as the brand. It's less chunky, but just as palate pleasing.

(10)   **WAITROSE** Strawberry Jam, 454g, 65p (49p for 340g)   **(GF) (L) (N/S) (V)**
Although with similar fruit and sugar level, the taste is much better than the brand.

(9)   **CO-OP** Strawberry Jam, 454g, 75p (57p for 340g)   **(GF) (L) (N/S) (V)**
Stick it in the trolley if you normally buy the brand. As good, and almost half the price.

(6)   **SOMERFIELD** So Good Strawberry Conserve, 340g, £1.39   **(V)**
This tastes very much better than the brand and it is worth the extra premium.

HARTLEY'S BEST STRAWBERRY JAM, 340g, £1.08 (£1.44 for 454g)
Like most jams or conserves, this should be labelled "sugar with strawberries". Here the ingredients list 61g of sugar to 45g of fruit per 100g.

(5)   **ASDA** Smartprice Strawberry Jam, 454g, 35p (27p for 340g)   **(GF)**
A notch down from Hartley's, but it's still worth a punt.

(5)   **MARKS & SPENCER** Strawberry Conserve, 340g, £1.49   **(V)**
The shopper's choice. The taste is better than the brand, though price-wise perhaps not this much better.

Hartley's Best Raspberry Jam

Sugar, Sulphur dioxide (E220)

(10) **ASDA** Fine Raspberry Jam, 454g, 58p (43p for 340g)
Don't bother with the brand. This delivers a better taste, a bigger jar and a better price.

(10) **KWIK SAVE** Raspberry Jam, 454g, 60p (45p for 340g)
Too many seeds may spoil the enjoyment for some, but flavour-wise it's spot on.

(10) **KWIK SAVE** Seedless Raspberry Jam, 454g, 60p (45p for 340g)
Buy it. It tastes sweeter than the brand, even though the label says it is not!

(10) **SAINSBURY'S** Raspberry Jam, 454g, 60p (45p for 340g)
Put it in the trolley. Taste-wise, there is nothing no difference between this and the brand.

(10) **SOMERFIELD** Raspberry Jam, 454g, 65p (49p for 340g)
The only thing that really separates this and the brand is the price.

(10) **SOMERFIELD** Seedless Raspberry Jam, 454g, 65p (49p for 340g)
A silkily smooth, seedless jam that delivers pleasant sweet-and-sour flavours.

(10) **TESCO** Raspberry Jam, 454g, 58p (43p for 340g) **(V)**
Put it in the trolley. It's under half price and it tastes better than the brand.

(10) **WAITROSE** Raspberry Jam, 454g, 72p (54p for 340g) **(L)**
Very similar to Tesco's. It's not as cheap, but is still a big saving on the brand.

(8) **CO-OP** Raspberry Jam, 454g, 89p (67p for 340g) **(GF) (L) (N/S) (V)**
Most of the seeds have floated to the top, but the jam tastes far better than brand.

(7) **ALDI** Ouvertüre Raspberry Conserve with Vanilla Flavouring, **(GF) (L) (V)**
250g, 59p (81p for 340g)
Cheaper and much better than the brand – and the vanilla flavouring adds a nice twist.

HARTLEY'S BEST RASPBERRY JAM, 340g, £1.08 (£1.44 for 454g)
Like its Best Strawberry brother, it's too sweet, so watch the sugar. And as with all seeded raspberry jams, the seeds can spoil your enjoyment if they continually get stuck between your teeth.

(5) **MORRISONS** Raspberry Jam, 454g, 60p (45p for 340g)
A cheaper alternative, but flavour-wise this is one notch down from the brand.

(4) **MORRISONS** Seedless Raspberry Jam, 340g, 59p
Buy this if you want it sweet! No more sugar content than the brand, but the sweetness from this seedless jam dominates the taste.

Hartley's Best Apricot Jam

Sugar, Sulphur dioxide (E220)

---

(9) **ALDI** Grandessa Light Apricot Spread, 430g, 79p (63p for 340g)　　　　**(L)**
This may be too tart for some tastes. But it's cheaper and delivers better fruit quality.

---

(7) **ASDA** Extra Special Apricot Jam, 340g, 87p　　　　**(GF) (N/S) (V)**
Good buy for the Asda Shopper. It equals the brand's quality and has much less sugar.

---

(7) **KWIK SAVE** Apricot Conserve, 340g, 89p
A safe bet for the Kwik Save shopper. Cheaper, with a similar taste quality to the brand.

---

(7) **MORRISONS** Apricot Conserve, 340g, 95p
Put it in your trolley. A few pence cheaper, and the taste is better than the brand.

HARTLEY'S BEST APRICOT JAM, 340g, £1.08

Although the sugar quantity is very high – like the rest of Hartley's range – the fruit and acidity regulator present a more balanced taste.

---

(5) **ASDA** Apricot Jam, 454g, 58p (43p for 340g)　　　　**(GF) (N/S) (V)**
Worth a punt! Small step down in quality, but on toast you won't notice the difference.

---

(5) **SAINSBURY'S** Apricot Jam, 454g, 60p (45p for 340g)
A cheaper alternative. Not as good as the brand, but still excellent value for money.

---

(5) **TESCO** Apricot Jam, 454g, 58p (43p for 340g)
Good saving. Not the same quality as the brand, but still enjoyable on buttered toast.

---

(5) **CO-OP** Apricot Jam, 454g, 89p (67p for 340g)　　　　**(GF) (L) (N/S) (V)**
This is not the cheapest "own label", but it still costs a lot less than the brand.

---

(3) **SOMERFIELD** Apricot Jam, 454g, 65p (49p for 340g)
The apricot flavour is good, but several hard chewy apricot chunks spoil it.

---

(3) **WAITROSE** Apricot Conserve, 340g, £1.29　　　　**(GF) (L) (V)**
Leave it on the shelf. Buy the brand – it's much cheaper and tastes better.

---

(3) **SOMERFIELD** So Good Apricot Conserve, 340g, £1.39　　　　**(V)**
Not a good buy. This costs a lot more and does not beat the brand.

Frank Cooper's Blackcurrant Conserve

Sugar, Sulphur dioxide (E220)

---

(10) **MORRISONS** Blackcurrant Conserve, 340g, 59p
The one to buy. Not quite as chunky as the brand, but taste-wise it hits the spot.

---

(10) **SAINSBURY'S** Blackcurrant Jam, 454g, 60p (45p for 340g)
Fewer whole blackcurrants, but in a sandwich it has a similar taste quality to the brand.

---

(10) **SOMERFIELD** Blackcurrant Jam, 454g, 65p (49p for 340g)
Buy it. Much cheaper and not as chunky, but it delivers comparable quality to the brand.

---

(10) **TESCO** Blackcurrant Jam, 454g, 58p (43p for 340g)
Not as chunky, but on toast it is difficult to taste the difference.

---

(8) **ASDA** Extra Special Blackcurrant Jam, 340g, 87p   **(GF) (N/S) (V)**
Cheaper, less sugar and certainly the equal to the brand on all flavour fronts.

---

(7) **WAITROSE** Blackcurrant Conserve, 340g, £1.29   **(GF) (L) (N/S) (V)**
Put it in the trolley. It's cheaper, and looks and tastes the same as the brand.

---

(7) **SOMERFIELD** So Good Blackcurrant Conserve, 340g, £1.39
Buy it. Admittedly, it's only a few pence cheaper, but they all add up on a big shop.

FRANK COOPER'S BLACKCURRANT CONSERVE, 340g, £1.41
There is no doubt that this is blackcurrant jam! There are 67g of sugar per 100g of jam here, but the fruit is so prolific and chunky you hardly notice it. RDA sugar is 60g.

---

(5) **KWIK SAVE** Blackcurrant Jam, 454g, 60p (45p for 340g)
Does not have the blackcurrant "oomph" of the brand, but it still offers great value for money.

---

(5) **CO-OP** Blackcurrant Jam, 454g, 89p (67p for 340g)   **(GF) (L) (N/S) (V)**
A good, cheaper alternative. Not as chunky, but lots of berries and plenty of flavour.

---

(4) **ASDA** Blackcurrant Jam, 454g, 58p (43p for 340g)   **(GF) (N/S) (V)**
A cheaper alternative to the brand. But, if you are particular your blackcurrant jam, this won't do.

---

(4) **ALDI** Grandessa Light Blackcurrant Spread 430g, 79p (63p for 340g)   **(L)**
Worth a punt, but it does taste watery in comparison with the brand.

Wilkin & Sons Lemon Curd

Egg, Fat, Lactose, Sugar, Sulphur dioxide (E220)

---

(8) **MARKS & SPENCER** Lemon Curd, 325g, £1.19p (£1.25 for 340g)
Marks & Spencer beats the brand with this one. Much cheaper and similar quality.

---

(8) **TESCO** Finest Lemon Curd, 312g, £1.19 (£1.30 for 340g) **(N/S)**
Allowing for the gram difference this is much cheaper, and delivers comparable quality.

---

(7) **WAITROSE** Luxury Lemon Curd, 325g, £1.29 (£1.35 for 340g) **(GF) (N/S)**
This is much better than Waitrose's regular lemon curd, and it matches the brand
for taste.

WILKIN & SONS LEMON CURD, 340g, £1.65
Just as a leading brand should be. With its enjoyable taste balance between the lemon and
the acidity, you'll be keen for more. Like all curds, it will keep longer and better if stored
in the fridge.

---

(3) **ASDA** Extra Special Lemon Curd, 340g, £1.08 **(GF) (N/S)**
Not the worst, but even this leaves you with an unwanted egg-like taste in your mouth.

---

(2) **ASDA** Lemon Curd, 411g, 51p (42p for 340g)
Leave it. This tastes artificial and is a very poor example of a lemon curd.

---

(2) **SAINSBURY'S** Lemon Curd 411g, 56p (47p for 340g)
Buy the brand. This does not deliver a lemon curd taste as we know it.

---

(2) **CO-OP** Lemon Curd, 411g, 69p, (57p for 340g) **(L) (N/S)**
Forget it. The unnatural lemon taste will start to grate after a couple of mouthfuls.

---

(2) **WAITROSE** Lemon Curd, 411g, 75p (62p for 340g) **(GF) (L) (N/S)**
Don't bother. Just a thick gluey artificial lemon mixture that turns sour in the mouth.

Gales Set Honey

Sugar. Not suitable for children under 12 months.

(7) **ASDA** Set Honey, 454g, £1.58 **(GF) (N/S)**
Beats the brand price, and the taste is comparable, both from the jar and on toast!

(6) **SAINSBURY'S** Taste the Difference English Honey, 340g, £2.69 (£3.59 for 454g)
Worth the extra! This is at least a couple of notches up in flavour quality.

GALES SET HONEY, 454g, £1.76
A subtle, floral-tasting, solid honey that delivers a pleasant, natural sweetness.
Sugar – added or natural, still piles on the pounds. Your recommended daily intake
of added sugar is 60g.

(5) **MARKS & SPENCER** New Zealand Set Clover Honey, 340g, **(GF)**
£2.29 (£3.59 for 454g)
The extra hike in price does deliver an extra taste twist, but it's so subtle.

(5) **TESCO** Finest New Zealand Clover Honey, 454g, £2.69 **(N/S)**
The soft, moreish flavour of the clover raises this honey to a level slightly higher than
the brand.

(3) **MORRISONS** Pure Set Honey, 454g, £1.69
Don't. This has an unpleasant yeasty taste that lingers long after the honey has departed.

(2) **WAITROSE** Pure Set Honey, 454g, £1.79 **(GF) (L) (N/S)**
Leave it. Around the same price as the brand, but it delivers a strong yeasty twang.

Gales Clear Honey

Sugar. Not suitable for children under 12 months.

(8) **ASDA** Clear Honey, 454g, £1.58 **(GF) (N/S)**
This is the one to buy. You'll struggle to tell the difference between this and the brand.

(8) **TESCO** Finest Pure Clear Honey, 454g, £1.58 **(N/S)**
Put this in the trolley. It's cheaper and presents almost identical flavours to the brand.

(6) **SAINSBURY'S** Taste the Difference Acacia Clear Honey, 454g, £2.85
Expensive, but well worth it. It's so good you could just spoon the jar clean!

GALES CLEAR HONEY, 454g, £1.76
You might find this clear style of honey too runny for toast and sandwiches. However, for cooking or adding to porridge or yoghurts, it's perfect. Don't forget, your sugar RDA is 60g.

(3) **MORRISONS** Pure Clear Honey, 454g, £1.59
Grab the brand. The unrewarding yeasty twang is almost identical to the unpleasant flavour of Morrisons' set honey.

(2) **WAITROSE** Pure Clear Honey, 454g, £1.79 **(GF) (L) (N/S)**
The brand's the better buy. Like Waitrose's set honey, it's spoilt by a yeasty twang.

(1) **ALDI** Harvest Spread Clear Honey, 500g, £1.49 (£1.35 for 454g) **(GF) (L)**
Leave it – it's disgusting. The plastic bottle is 50g larger, but it looks like a shampoo container and delivers a plastic-tasting honey.

4
Dairy Products
& Cheese

On the whole, this book reveals that supermarket "own label" products are cheaper than, and often of a quality equal to (or even better than) well-known brands. Cheeses have, at least in part, refuted that finding. I was very surprised to discover several branded cheeses on the shelves and deli counters that were both better quality and less expensive. "Own labels" certainly dominate this area, but shoppers seem to be failing to check and compare prices with the big brands.

The supermarkets don't make checking very easy, though. So many front labels are priced per packet, rather than per kilo. Don't be fooled. Check the shelf or the back label for the price per kilo. Dairy products in particular are normally cheaper in large packs. Sometimes, two 250g packs of an own label are more expensive than one 500g pack of a competing brand, so don't be conned out of your hard-earned cash.

Warnings of nut or seed traces in unflavoured natural dairy products surprise some people. But there is good reason for such alerts: the merest trace can trigger a serious allergic reaction. It is essential that you check all the labels, confident that the best information is available.

Bird's Fresh Custard

Egg, Fat, Lactose, Sugar, Thickeners

---

(8) **ASDA** Fresh Custard, 500g, 98p **(GF)**
Put it in the trolley: it is cheaper and tastes much better than the brand.

---

(8) **MORRISONS** Fresh Custard, 500g, 99p
The sugar and fat content is a little higher, but it's cheaper and tastes better than the brand.

---

(8) **SAINSBURY'S** Fresh Custard, 500g, 99p **(GF) (N/S)**
Buy it. It's cheaper and very similar to the brand on all taste fronts.

---

(8) **SOMERFIELD** Fresh Custard, 500g, 99p
Put it in the trolley. The taste is comparable to the brand and at a cheaper price.

---

(8) **WAITROSE** Fresh Custard, 500g, 99p **(GF)**
Buy it if you normally purchase the brand. You pay less for a similar flavour.

---

(6) **ASDA** Extra Special Crème Anglaise, 500g, £1.38
Costs more, but tastes wonderful. Not for dieters – the pot contains 65g of saturated fats.

---

(6) **TESCO** Finest Custard, 500g, £1.49 **(GF)**
Well worth the extra money – buy it. You'll be rewarded with a heavenly white vanillin custard.

---

(6) **WAITROSE** Fresh Vanilla Custard, 500g, £1.59 **(GF) (N/S)**
Seriously good. This vanilla-speckled, creamy white custard will delight your taste buds.

---

(6) **SAINSBURY'S** Taste the Difference Custard, 500g, £1. 64 **(GF) (N/S)**
This is restaurant quality – treat yourself. It tastes even better than Asda's Crème Anglaise.

BIRD'S FRESH CUSTARD, 500g, £1.25
Much better than tinned custard! However, it does contain thickeners and has over 50g of sugar and 10g of saturated fats.

Bird's Low Fat Fresh Custard

Egg, Fat, Lactose, Sugar, Thickeners

(8) **ASDA** Good For You Fresh Custard, 500g, 98p **(GF)**
Better tasting than the brand, but the saturated-fat content is the same as Bird's regular!

BIRD'S LOW FAT FRESH CUSTARD, 500g, £1.35
Not as thick as the regular Bird's Fresh Custard, and not as enjoyable to taste. However, while the fat saturates are less than half, the makers have added Xanthan gum (E415) as a stabiliser and thickener, which has been associated with food intolerance.

Rachel's Organic Greek Style Yogurt

Fat, Lactose, Salt, Sugar

(7) **CO-OP** Greek Style Yogurt, 450g, £1.09.
Although it tastes sharp, next to the brand it has an extra layer of sweetness.

(6) **TESCO** Organic Greek Style Yogurt, 500g, £1.35 (£1.21 for 450g) **(GF) (N/S)**
It does not have the brand's natural acidic bite but, many shoppers may prefer this.

RACHEL'S ORGANIC GREEK STYLE YOGURT, 450g, £1.49
This thick, creamy yogurt has a cleansing acidic bite and works well as a substitute for crème fraîche, or mixed with honey. No added ingredients.

(5) **ASDA** Good for You Greek Style Yogurt, 450g, 83p **(GF)**
A cheaper alternative (not organic), but it lacks the brand's depth of flavour.

(5) **ASDA** Greek Style Yogurt, 450g, 83p **(GF)**
Worth a punt. But like Asda's Good for You, this is one step down in taste quality.

(4) **SAINSBURY'S** Greek Style Yogurt, 200g, 69p (£1.55p for 450g) **(GF)**
Not as good as the brand. Indeed, this small pot is gram for gram more expensive too.

(4) **SOMERFIELD** Greek Style Yogurt, 200g, 69p (£1.55p for 450g)
Buy the brand. This tastes very like Sainsbury's above, and it's expensive too.

Yeo Valley Organic Strawberry Yogurt

Carbohydrate, Fat, Lactose, Protein, Sugar

⑦ **MORRISONS** Organic Low Fat Strawberry Yogurt, 4 x 150g, £1.39 **(GF)**
As good as the brand, but this pack of four contains a carton of strawberry, raspberry, apricot and rhubarb.

YEO VALLEY ORGANIC STRAWBERRY YOGURT, 150G, 45P
It may surprise some buyers that this product also contains lemon juice, starch and colours – all organically approved of course.

⑤ **SAINSBURY'S** Organic Greek Style Strawberry Yogurt, 4 x 100g, £1.49 **(GF)**
Buy the brand. This mixed pack tastes as good, but, gram for gram, it costs more.

③ **MARKS & SPENCER** Organic Low Fat Strawberry Yoghurt, 3 x 170g, £1.50 **(GF)**
Like for like, this is a similar price to the brand, but the strawberries taste tinned.

Yeo Valley Organic Raspberry Yogurt

Carbohydrate, Fat, Lactose, Protein, Sugar

⑦ **MORRISONS** Organic Low Fat Raspberry Yogurt, 4 x 150g, £1.39 **(GF)**
As good as the brand, but this pack of 4 also contains strawberry, apricot and rhubarb.

YEO VALLEY ORGANIC RASPBERRY YOGURT, 150g, 45p
This contains similar ingredients to and is as enjoyable as Yeo Valley strawberry yogurt, unless you don't like raspberry seeds.

⑤ **TESCO** Organic Low Fat Raspberry Yogurt, 4 x 125g, £1.55 **(GF)**
Mysteriously, Tesco's yogurts work out more expensive than the brand, but are no better in quality.

Yeo Valley Organic Half Fat Crème Fraîche

Fat, Lactose, Sugar

---

(7) **MORRISONS** Reduced Fat Crème Fraîche, 200g, 65p
Beats the brand for fat content and price, and equals it on the taste front.

YEO VALLEY ORGANIC HALF FAT CRÈME FRAÎCHE, 200g, 69p
Crème fraîche became popular as a lower fat alternative to fresh cream. Today, however, Greek Style yogurt (with its even lower fat content) is becoming the preferred alternative.

---

(5) **SAINSBURY'S** Be Good to Yourself Crème Fraîche, 200g, 70p   **(N/S)**
Buy the Yeo Valley product if it is cheaper, otherwise put this one in your trolley.

---

(5) **SAINSBURY'S** Crème Fraîche, 200g, 72p
Similar flavours and quality, but a few pennies more, and a lot more fat content.

---

(5) **WAITROSE** Crème Fraîche, 200g, 72p   **(GF) (N/S)**
Similar style to Sainsbury's, and an alternative if Yeo Valley is not on the shelves.

---

(5) **MARKS & SPENCER** Crème Fraîche, 300g, £1.09 (73p for 200g)
Still worth a punt! A whisper away in quality, and just a tad more expensive.

---

(5) **CO-OP** Crème Fraîche Light, 200g, 89g   **(N/S)**
Equals the brand for taste and betters it with lower fat content; but it is 20p more.

---

(5) **CO-OP** Crème Fraîche, 200g, 89g   **(N/S)**
Equal in taste, but more expensive, and the fat content is 60g in this 200g tub.

---

(4) **ASDA** Crème Fraîche, 200g, 64p
This is a notch down in quality, delivering a thicker, more cloying taste. Buy the brand.

---

(3) **MORRISONS** Crème Fraîche, 200g, 65p
The fat content is over 70g and the taste quality is very poor, compared to the brand.

---

(3) **SOMERFIELD** Good Intentions Crème Fraîche, 200g, 89p
Don't waste your cash – buy the brand. It is cheaper and much better tasting.

---

(3) **SOMERFIELD** Crème Fraîche, 200g, 89p
Leave it on the shelf. The brand delivers far better taste and is a lot cheaper.

Country Life English Butter Freshly Churned (sweet cream style)

Fat, Lactose, Salt

---

(8) **ALDI** Greenvale Blended Butter, 250g, 53p
Good value and quality. Next to the brand it tastes a little more salty, but contains no more salt.

---

(8) **ASDA** Smartprice Butter, 250g, 53p
The colour and taste are very similar to Aldi's, although the salt level is slightly lower.

---

(7) **ASDA** English Creamy Butter, 250g, 64p
Although this compares well with the brand, Asda's Smartprice is the better buy.

---

(7) **MORRISONS** English Butter, 250g, 69p
Put it in the trolley. Besides the wrapper, there's no difference in colour or taste.

---

(7) **SAINSBURY'S** English Creamy Butter, 250g, 69p   **(GF) (N/S)**
Pick this one – if you normally buy the brand you won't be able to tell the difference.

COUNTRY LIFE ENGLISH BUTTER FRESHLY CHURNED, 250g, 72p
Country Life is a sweet cream rather than sour cream butter (Lurpak is the UK's leading brand of sour cream style, *see* page 60). The saturated fat content is very high at 50g.

---

(5) **SOMERFIELD** So Good West Country Butter, 250g, £1.15
This is just a tad better tasting than the brand, but it's not worth this much more.

---

(5) **SOMERFIELD** English Butter, 250g, 79p
Only buy it if it's cheaper than the brand. Taste-wise there's little to choose between two.

---

(5) **CO-OP** Creamy Butter, 250g, 82p   **(GF) (N/S)**
Buy whichever is cheaper, as this "own label" is of a similar quality to the brand.

---

(4) **MARKS & SPENCER** Freshly Churned Butter, 250g, 92p
Shop elsewhere for your butter. It costs more, and is no better tasting than the brand.

---

(4) **WAITROSE** English Butter, 250g, 92p   **(GF) (N/S)**
Of equal quality to the brand. However, Waitrose is not the shop for bargain butter.

---

(3) **WAITROSE** Dairy Butter, 250g, 78p   **(GF) (N/S)**
Although 30 days within its use-by date, this butter revealed an unusual nutty tang.

Country Life Unsalted English Butter Freshly Churned (sweet cream style)

Fat, Lactose, Salt

(7) **SAINSBURY'S** Unsalted English Butter, 250g, 79p **(GF) (N/S)**
Buy it. Tastes as good as the brand. More expensive than Sainsbury's salted butter.

(7) **SOMERFIELD** Unsalted English Butter, 250g, 79p
Put it in the trolley. It's cheaper and of comparable quality to the brand.

COUNTRY LIFE UNSALTED ENGLISH BUTTER FRESHLY CHURNED, 250g, 89p
The producers have made sure you won't mix the two up! Unsalted Country Life displays blue wrapping and lettering rather than the gold and green of the salted.

Yeo Valley Organic Butter (sweet cream style)

Fat, Lactose, Salt

(8) **ASDA** Organic Slightly Salted Butter, 250g, 88p **(GF)**
Buy it. This tastes as good as the brand, although it does contain a little more salt.

(8) **TESCO** Organic Lightly Salted Butter, 250g, 88p **(N/S)**
Put it in the trolley. More of a salty tang, but the quality is comparable to the brand.

(8) **SAINSBURY'S** Organic Slightly Salted Butter, 250g, 89p **(GF) (N/S)**
It's cheaper, tastes as good, spreads better and is less salty than the brand.

(8) **MORRISONS** Organic Salted Butter, 250g, 89p
This has no more salt than Tesco's lightly salted, and tastes no saltier than the brand.

YEO VALLEY ORGANIC BUTTER, 250g, £1.09
Organic butter may be better for you than regular, but it still contains over 80% fat. And it will still pile on the pounds if you spread it too thickly. The recommended daily intake of fat is 70g for women and 95g for men.

Lurpak Slightly Salted Butter (sour cream style)

Fat, Lactose, Salt

---

(8) **ALDI** Greenvale Slightly Salted Butter, 250g, 69p
There's a big saving here for a butter that delivers a similar quality to the brand.

LURPAK SLIGHTLY SALTED BUTTER, 250g, 97p
Lurpak is made using sour cream. A lactic culture is added to the cream to turn it sour, so this style is known as lactic butter.

Lurpak Spreadable

Fat, Lactose, Rapeseed oil, Salt

---

(7) **TESCO** Spreadable, 500g, £1.59 (80p for 250g)
Buy it. On or off bread, this is as good as Lurpak, and a lot cheaper.

---

(6) **MARKS & SPENCER** Naturally Spreadable Butter, 250g, £1.19
More expensive, but churned from 100% cream, and will be preferred by butter lovers.

LURPAK SPREADABLE, 250g, 97p
This contains around 80% fat but, unlike regular butters, is a mix of butter and vegetable oil. However, this blending reduces the clean lactic taste for which regular Lurpak is famed.

---

(4) **ALDI** Greenvale Spreadable, 250g, 35p
A low price, and fine for a loaded sandwich, but the brand tastes much better.

---

(4) **CO-OP** Spreadable, 250g, 89p   **(GF) (N/S)**
Cheaper than the brand, but the drawback is that you can taste the added rapeseed oil.

I Can't Believe It's Not Butter Vegetable Spread

Fat, Lactose, Salt

(7) **ASDA** You'd Butter Believe it Vegetable Spread, 500g, 71p **(GF)**
You get a real hit of butter, and it beats the brand for taste and price.

(7) **TESCO** Butter Me Up Vegetable Spread, 500g, 71p **(N/S)**
Buy it. Tastes as good as Asda's, and is much better than the brand.

I CAN'T BELIEVE IT'S NOT BUTTER VEGETABLE SPREAD, 500g, 82p
The butter taste doesn't last long. Not surprising when 94.5% is made up of vegetable oils, salt, emulsifiers, preservatives and colouring.

(3) **ALDI** Beautifully Butterfully Vegetable Spread, 500g, 59p
Don't. This tastes like margarine, not butter, and like the brand has a metallic twang.

Bertolli Lucca Olive Spread

Fat (high in monounsaturates and low in saturated fats), Lactose, Salt

---

(9) **ALDI** Summerlite Olive Spread, 500g, 69p
Grab it. This is an olive off half price and delivers similar flavours and quality.

---

(8) **MORRISONS** Olive Spread, 500g, 92p **(GF)**
Taste-wise, this works as well as the Bertolli, although the olive notes are not as pronounced.

---

(8) **SAINSBURY'S** Olive Spread, 500g, 92p **(GF) (N/S)**
Put it in the trolley. This is cheaper and it mirrors the tastes of the brand.

---

(8) **TESCO** Olive Spread, 500g, 92p
An excellent buy! Similar to the brand in fat, olive oil levels and taste quality.

---

(7) **WAITROSE** Olive Spread, 500g, 99p **(GF) (N/S)**
A beat-the-brand buy for Waitrose shoppers. It's cheaper and tastes much better.

BERTOLLI LUCCA OLIVE SPREAD, 500g, £1.17
Although presented as a healthier option to butter, it may surprise people that the vegetable fat content is 59% and the olive-oil content is as little as 21%.

---

(4) **ASDA** Olive Spread, 500g, 92p **(GF)**
A notch down in quality. More olive oil in this pack, but you'd never know it.

---

(4) **CO-OP** Olive Reduced Fat Spread, 500g, £1.15 **(N/S)**
Buy the brand. Only a few pence more, and it's another step up in quality.

---

(4) **SOMERFIELD** Olive Spread, 500g, £1.19
It is more expensive and the quality is not as good. Buy the brand, unless you live near an Aldi store!

Original Flora Spread

Emulsifiers, Fat, Lactose, Salt. Not suitable for pregnant and breastfeeding women, and children under five.

(10) **ASDA** Sunflower Spread, 500g, 46p
A beat-the-brand buy. Half the price; contains more sunflower oil and tastes as good.

(10) **SAINSBURY'S** Sunflower Spread, 500g, 46p
Grab it. More sunflower oil, with a similar fat content and comparable taste to the brand.

(9) **SAINSBURY'S** Be Good To Yourself Light Sunflower Spread, 500g, 48p
Buy it. Cheaper than the brand, with half the fat content and the taste is comparable.

ORIGINAL FLORA SPREAD, 500G, 92P
This is promoted as a healthy spread that includes sunflower oil. However, a product containing emulsifiers, preservatives and colouring can't really be called healthy.

(1) **TESCO** Only 5% Fat Sunflower Spread, 500g, 79p **(N/S)**
Yuk! Better to go without if this is the only option.

(1) **ALDI** Summerlite Low Fat Sunflower Spread, 500g, 39p
I think that 10p would be too much to pay for this! The strong chemical taste would spoil a sandwich.

Kraft Philadelphia Full Fat Soft Cheese

Fat, Lactose, Salt, Sugar

---

(8) **ASDA** Soft & Creamy Cheese, 200g, 77p **(GF) (N/S)**
Buy it. Higher fat, but beats the brand on price and equals it for quality.

---

(8) **SAINSBURY'S** Smooth & Creamy Full Fat Soft Cheese, 200g, 84p
This matches the brand for quality, but be aware that the fat content is higher.

KRAFT PHILADELPHIA FULL FAT SOFT CHEESE, 200g, £1.14
Philadelphia is a very popular soft cheese brand. However, it does have a high saturated fat content of 32g. Nutritionists recommend an upper daily limit for saturated fat of 20g for women and 30g for men.

---

(5) **TESCO** Full Fat Soft & Creamy Cheese, 200g, 77p **(GF)**
Worth a punt. Much cheaper than the brand and tastes nearly as good alone or on toast.

---

(4) **WAITROSE** Full Fat Soft Cheese, 200g, £1.15 **(GF) (N/S)**
Buy the brand. Its cream-cheese taste is better and it's around the same price.

Kraft Light Philadelphia Low Fat Soft Cheese

Fat, Fibre, Lactose, Salt, Sugar

(10) **ALDI** Westacre Medium Fat Soft Cheese, 200g, 45p **(GF)**
Buy it. Under half price, with similar taste and fat levels and slightly less salt.

(7) **CO-OP** Extra Light Soft Creamy Cheese, 200g, £1.05 **(GF)**
Put it in the trolley. The taste level is similar, fat content is lower and it's cheaper.

KRAFT LIGHT PHILADELPHIA LOW FAT SOFT CHEESE, 200g, £1.14
A healthier option, but it will still put on the pounds if you over-indulge. The saturated fat content is lower at 21g, but it's still high.

(5) **TESCO** Light Medium Fat Soft & Smooth Cheese, 200g, 77p
A cheaper option, but, side by side, the brand just beats it on taste.

(5) **KWIK SAVE** Medium Fat Soft Creamy Cheese, 200g, 78p
Worth a punt. Although it is very much cheaper, it doesn't taste quite as good.

(5) **SAINSBURY'S** Light Medium Fat Soft Creamy Cheese, 200g, 84p **(GF) (N/S)**
A cheaper alternative to the brand. However, the cheese flavour is a notch down.

(5) **SOMERFIELD** Half Fat Soft Creamy Cheese, 200g, 89p
This does not quite match the brand for taste, but, at this price, it's an option.

(5) **CO-OP** Light Soft Creamy Cheese, 200g, £1.05 **(GF)**
The brand has a tad more flavour, but this is cheaper, and has similar fat levels.

(3) **ASDA** Good for You Soft Creamy Cheese, 200g, 77p **(GF) (N/S)**
Leave it on the shelf. Very low fat content, but the taste is bland and boring.

(3) **SOMERFIELD** Good Intentions Reduced Fat Natural Soft Cheese, 200g, 89p
Don't! By reducing the fat content to this level the maker has removed the taste too.

(3) **WAITROSE** Light Low Fat Soft Cheese, 200g, £1.15 **(GF) (N/S)**
Buy the brand. This has very low fat content, but it lacks any pleasing flavour.

(2) **SAINSBURY'S** Be Good to Yourself Soft Creamy Cheese, 200g, 84p **(GF) (N/S)**
You won't "be good to yourself" by buying this. It's low in fat, but it tastes terrible.

Longley Farm
Natural Cottage Cheese

Fat, Lactose, Salt, Sugar

LONGLEY FARM NATURAL COTTAGE CHEESE, 250g, 49p
Longley Farm is a very tasty cottage cheese and the only brand that has survived in our supermarkets. If it's not on the shelves, try the deli counter or buy from Morrisons.

(5) **MORRISONS** Natural Cottage Cheese, 500g, 89p (45p for 250g) **(GF)**
Buy the brand. It's a few pence more, but it has that extra edge on flavour.

(5) **SAINSBURY'S** Natural Cottage Cheese, 650g, £1.23 (48p for 250g) **(GF) (N/S)**
Buy it if your local Sainsbury's or its deli counter does not have the brand.

(5) **SOMERFIELD** Natural Cottage Cheese, 250g, 52p
A few pence more, but in flavour it's just a nudge away and a good alternative.

(5) **WAITROSE** Natural Cottage Cheese, 250g, 62p **(GF) (N/S)**
More money, but it equals the brand for taste. Buy it if the brand is not available.

(5) **TESCO** Natural Cottage Cheese 300g, 64p (54p for 250g) **(GF) (N/S)**
A whisper away in quality, but no cheaper. Buy it if the brand is not available.

(4) **CO-OP** Natural Cottage Cheese, 300g, 85p (71p for 250g) **(GF)**
The brand beats this for taste and price. Try Morrisons if the brand is not available here.

(3) **KWIK SAVE** Natural Cottage Cheese, 250g, 55p
No match for the brand, but it's much better than Kwik Save's low fat cottage cheese.

(2) **ASDA** Natural Cottage Cheese, 454g, 78p (43p for 250g) **(GF) (N/S)**
Leave it on the shelf. Taste-wise it's very poor and does not come close to the brand.

Longley Farm Virtually Fat Free Cottage Cheese

Fat, Lactose, Salt, Sugar

LONGLEY FARM VIRTUALLY FAT FREE COTTAGE CHEESE, 250g, 49p

Compared to Longley Farm's regular this is whiter-coloured and cleaner tasting. The fat level has been reduced to 0.25g from 15g. Again, if it's not on the shelves, try the deli counter or buy from Morrisons.

---

(4) **TESCO** Healthy Living Natural Cottage Cheese, **(N/S)**
300g, 58p (49p for 250g)
Comparable price, but it comes second to the brand on all flavour fronts.

---

(4) **SAINSBURY'S** Be Good to Yourself Natural Cottage Cheese, **(GF) (N/S)**
450g, £1.15 (64p for 250g)
Gram for gram this is more expensive and less tasty than the brand.

---

(4) **SOMERFIELD** Good Intentions Cottage Cheese, 250g, 69p
Buy it only if the brand is not available. In flavour and price, this comes second.

---

(4) **CO-OP** Half Fat Natural Cottage Cheese, 300g, 85p (71p for 250g) **(GF)**
Buy the brand. This is more expensive and the brand still beats it hands down for taste.

---

(4) **ASDA** Good For You Natural Cottage Cheese, 227g, 44p (48p for 250g) **(GF) (N/S)**
It might be better for you than their regular, but it is not better than the brand.

---

(3) **ALDI** Westacre Balanced Lifestyle Low Fat Cottage Cheese, 200g, **(GF)**
39p (49p for 250g)
Side by side with the brand, this tastes bland, and it is only a tad cheaper.

---

(2) **KWIK SAVE** Low Fat Natural Cottage Cheese, 250g, 55p
Leave it on the shelf. The brand is five times better, and costs less.

Mevgal Greek Feta Cheese

Fat, Lactose, Salt

(8) **CO-OP** Greek Feta Cheese, 200g, £1.39 **(GF) (N/S)**
The quality is equal to the brand, but it has more of a salty flavour (this pack contains 7g of salt – 1g more than the recommended daily intake).

(7) **ASDA** Greek Feta Cheese, 200g, £1.47 **(GF) (N/S)**
Put it in the trolley. It's difficult to distinguish between Asda's feta and the brand in taste.

MEVGAL GREEK FETA CHEESE, 200g, £1.58

Feta is a tangy, crumbly Greek cheese with a salt twist, made from sheep and goat's milk. A 200g pack contains 42g of fat; and although it's not mentioned, the salt content will be high.

(5) **SAINSBURY'S** Slightly Sharp & Crumbly French Feta Cheese, **(GF) (N/S)**
200g, £1.83
A softer style when compared to the brand, but it comes at an added premium.

(5) **TESCO** Feta Cheese Made in France from Sheep's Milk, 200g, £1.66 **(N/S)**
Worth a punt! This French feta reveals the same salty tang as found in the brand.

(5) **TESCO** Mild Feta Cheese Made in Demark from Cow's Milk, 200g, £1.24 **(N/S)**
Smooth rather than tangy. Tastes more like Cheshire cheese than feta.

Société Roquefort Cheese

Fat, Lactose, Salt

(8) **TESCO** French Roquefort, 100g, £1,54
A big saving – put it in the trolley. Very similar flavours and quality to the brand.

SOCIÉTÉ ROQUEFORT CHEESE, 100g, £2.14

Roquefort is a strong, blue-veined French cheese that is made from unpasteurised sheep's milk. Don't over indulge as it is high in fat (30g per 100g) and salt (4g per 100g).

(5) **SOMERFIELD** So Goo Roquefort, 150g, £1.39 (93p for 100g) **(GF) (N/S)**
Well worth a punt. A step down in flavour compared with the brand, though.

Frico Dutch Edam Cheese

Colour (E160B Annatto), Fat, Lactose, Nitrates (E252 and E253), Salt

FRICO DUTCH EDAM CHEESE, £3.29–£3.49/kg

You'll find the Frico brand at the deli cheese counter; the supermarket's "own label" Dutch Edam occupies the shelf space in the cheese section. Fat content is high.

---

(5) **ALDI** Emporium Edam Cheese, £3.79/kg **(GF)**
There is little difference in the taste, but the price is high compared to the brand.

---

(5) **ASDA** Dutch Edam Cheese, £3.68/kg **(GF) (N/S)**
More expensive than the brand, and no better quality.

---

(5) **KWIK SAVE** Dutch Edam Cheese, £3.87/kg **(GF) (N/S)**
This similar tasting Edam is fine, but you're paying more for it than the brand.

---

(5) **CO-OP** Dutch Edam Cheese, £3.99/kg **(N/S)**
Buy the brand if it's available. This "own label" is more expensive and no better tasting.

---

(5) **SAINSBURY'S** Dutch Edam Cheese, £4.15/kg **(GF) (N/S)**
Go to Sainsbury's deli counter, and you'll find the brand sitting there at £3.49/kg!

---

(5) **SOMERFIELD** Dutch Edam Cheese, £4.31/kg **(GF) (N/S)**
More expensive, though like Kwik Save's, this mirrors the flavours of the brand.

---

(5) **TESCO** Dutch Edam Cheese, £4.39/kg
Buy the brand at the deli counter. Frico tastes as good, and is a lot cheaper.

---

(5) **SAINSBURY'S** Organic Dutch Edam Cheese, £8.55/kg **(GF) (N/S)**
Organic and a tad better tasting than the brand, but at over £5 more per kilogram!

Castelli Organic Italian Mozzarella

Fat, Lactose, Salt

---

(8) **ASDA** Italian Mozzarella, 125g, 78p   **(GF) (N/S)**
A beat-the-brand buy. Not organic, but raw or cooked, there is very little difference in flavour between this and the brand.

---

(8) **TESCO** Italian Fresh Mozzarella, 150g, 94p (79p for 125g)   **(GF)**
Even this bigger pack is still cheaper. A more milky taste, but no less quality.

---

(8) **SAINSBURY'S** Italian Mozzarella, 150g, 95p (79p for 125g)   **(GF) (N/S)**
Put it in the trolley. Compared to the brand it has a more milky flavour.

---

(7) **CO-OP** Italian Style Mozzarella, 125g, 99p   **(N/S)**
Made in Italy, but the milk could be from elsewhere. Equal in quality and a softer taste.

CASTELLI ORGANIC ITALIAN MOZZARELLA, 125g, £1.09
Mozzarella is a milky, soft, white curd cheese that is eaten both raw and cooked. The packet's 22g saturated fat content is high. The RDA is 20g for women and 30g for men.

Butlers Red Leicester Cheese

Colour (E160B Annatto), Fat, Lactose, Nitrates (E252 and E253), Salt

(9) **WAITROSE** Red Leicester Cheese, £5.95/kg **(GF) (N/S)**
Buy it – it's so much cheaper. Plenty of flavour, but without the brand's sharp bite.

(8) **SOMERFIELD** Organic Farmhouse Red Leicester Cheese, £7.50/kg
Different from the brand: the taste is less sharp, but it still reveals plenty of flavour.

(8) **ASDA** Extra Special Farmhouse Red Leicester Cheese, £7.76/kg
Buy it. It is made by Butlers and delivers similar flavours and quality.

(8) **TESCO** Finest Handmade Extra Mature Red Leicester Cheese, £8.15/kg
Made by the brand, and delivers similar quality and taste at a much cheaper price.

(7) **CO-OP** Rothbury Red Leicester Non GM Rennet Cheese, £8.79/kg **(GF) (N/S)**
This is cheaper and it tastes better than the brand, although Butlers do make it.

BUTLERS RED LEICESTER CHEESE, £8.95/kg

All Red Leicester cheese has a high fat content and most contains annatto (E160B),
the colour additive that has been associated with food intolerance.

(5) **TESCO** Red Leicester Cheese, £4.68/kg
A notch down on flavour, but you'd expect that from a cheese that's over £4 cheaper.

(5) **SAINSBURY'S** Red Leicester Cheese, £4.97/kg **(GF) (N/S)**
Worth a punt. The Red Leicester flavours are not as pronounced or as sharp as the brand.

(5) **CO-OP** Red Leicester Non GM Rennet Cheese, £5.50/kg **(GF) (N/S)**
It does not have the brand's depth of flavour, but it is more than just a red cheese.

(4) **ALDI** Westacre Red Leicester Cheese, £3.89/kg
if you just want a red cheese buy it. However, it does not have the brand's quality.

(4) **MORRISONS** Red Leicester Cheese, £3.89/kg
Good value for a red cheese. However, it does not have the brand's flavour or bite.

(3) **ASDA** Red Leicester Cheese, £4.68/kg **(GF) (N/S)**
Leave it. This is just a red cheese with "Red Leicester" on the Label.

(3) **KWIK SAVE** Red Leicester Cheese, £4.95/kg **(GF) (N/S)**
Similar colour to the brand, but that's it. It should be labelled "Red Cheese".

(3) **SOMERFIELD** Red Leicester Cheese, £5.96/kg **(GF) (N/S)**
Tasted blind, you'd never know this was Red Leicester. At this price it should be obvious.

Cathedral City Mature White Cheddar Cheese

Fat, Lactose, Salt

---

(6) **MORRISONS** Extra Mature Davidstow White Cheddar, £7.48/kg
If you like strong cheese, buy it. An extra step up in flavour from the brand.

---

(6) **WAITROSE** Davidstow Mature Cheddar Cheese, £8.35/kg
Beats the brand for taste. Includes an extra-mature flavour without being too strong.

---

(6) **CO-OP** Truly Irresistible Farmhouse White Cheddar Cheese, £10.49/kg **(N/S)**
A good quality, strong cheddar cheese; well worth the extra premium.

CATHEDRAL CITY MATURE WHITE CHEDDAR CHEESE, £4.74/kg
The taste is mellow with a salty bite. Like all white cheddar cheese, this is high in fat, saturates and salt, but does not contain the colour annatto!

---

(5) **TESCO** Medium Mature White Cheddar Cheese, £4.68/kg
Beats the brand for price, but the taste is a small step down.

---

(4) **SAINSBURY'S** British Mature White Cheddar Cheese, £5.28/kg   **(GF) (N/S)**
Save money and buy the brand. It beats this on price and taste.

---

(4) **CO-OP** Farmhouse Mature White Cheddar Cheese, £7.70/kg   **(N/S)**
Buy the brand. This is almost £3 more and it's a good notch down in quality.

---

(3) **SOMERFIELD** Mature English Cheddar Cheese, £5.25/kg   **(GF) (N/S)**
Save money and buy the brand. It's cheaper and much better than this "own label".

---

(2) **KWIK SAVE** Farmhouse Cheddar, £5.66/kg   **(GF) (N/S)**
More expensive and it tastes sour. Don't waste your money. Buy the brand.

---

(2) **ALDI** Westacre Mature White Cheddar Cheese, £4.79/kg   **(GF**
Don't spoil a sandwich. Cheaper than the brand, but it's not half the quality.

Wensleydale Creamery White Cheshire Cheese

Colour (E160B Annatto), Fat, Lactose, Salt

WENSLEYDALE CREAMERY WHITE CHESHIRE CHEESE, £4.69/KG

This superb mild white Cheshire cheese is only found at the supermarkets' deli counters. Shelf space in the cheese aisle is saved for their "own label" Chesires.

(5) **ASDA** Coloured Cheshire Cheese, £4.68/kg **(GF) (N/S)**
A similar price, but a small step down in quality. Moreover, it contains the colouring annatto, which has been associated with food intolerance.

(5) **TESCO** Cheshire Cheese, £4.68/kg
Can't wait for the deli counter? This is just a whisper away in taste quality.

(5) **MORRISONS** Cheshire Crumbly & Tangy Cheese, £4.69/kg
Buy the brand from the deli counter. The same price, but not quite the same quality.

(5) **SAINSBURY'S** Cheshire Cheese, £4.97/kg **(GF) (N/S)**
Buy the brand from the deli, since it just beats this in price and taste.

(5) **SAINSBURY'S** Organic Cheshire Cheese, £5.99/kg **(GF) (N/S)**
Organic, and more expensive, but it still does not match the brand for taste.

(4) **CO-OP** White Cheshire Non GM Rennet Cheese, £5.50/kg **(GF) (N/S)**
Buy the brand: it's cheaper and much better quality. Unfortunately, the Co-op does not sell it.

(4) **MORRISONS** White Cheshire Cheese, £4.76/kg
More expensive and not as good as the brand or Morrisons' Crumbly & Tangy.

(2) **SOMERFIELD** Cheshire Cheese, £5.96/kg **(GF) (N/S)**
Leave it on the shelf. This is not a good example of Cheshire cheese.

5
Tinned Products

The tinned products in this section are the mainstay of most kitchen cupboards, and many shopping trolleys will contain at least one of the products reviewed in this chapter. You can imagine, then, just how fiercely brands and "own labels" wage war on these shelves. The retailers' strategy is to steal the brand's market share and erode our automatic purchase of the big name. At the moment, the supermarkets are gaining ground.

Nevertheless, there are plenty of problems for the tinned product shopper to solve. Many of the salt and sugar levels are high, and labels are massively unhelpful, as manufacturers and retailers try to hide these facts behind science. It is recommended that we reduce our salt intake to 6g per day and in a 415g tin of baked beans, there could well be 4g. However, this information is often displayed as levels of sodium, which *looks* much less, and therefore appears healthier. Just remember that 1g of sodium is equal to 2.5g of salt. Don't be deceived!

Heinz Baked Beans in Tomato Sauce

Fibre, Salt, Sugar

---

(10) **MORRISONS** Baked Beans in Tomato Sauce, 420g, 19p
Beat-the-brand shoppers at Morrisons can put these baked beans in their trolley with confidence.

---

(9) **SAINSBURY'S** Baked Beans in Tomato Sauce, 420g, 24p   **(GF) (L**
Grab the tin! Sainsbury's won't disappoint here. The beans taste just as good at nearly half the price.

---

(9) **SOMERFIELD** Baked Beans in Tomato Sauce, 420g, 26p   **(GF) (N/S) (V**
Buy them. Both the sauce and beans are of a similar quality to the brand.

---

(7) **MARKS & SPENCER** Baked Beans in Tomato Sauce, 420g, 38p   **(GF) (N/S) (V**
Put them in your basket. The taste is as good, and they are a few pence cheaper.

HEINZ BAKED BEANS IN TOMATO SAUCE, 415g, 44p

A very successful brand by which all others are judged! However, shoppers should be aware that baked beans have around 4g of salt per tin. The RDA is 6g.

---

(5) **TESCO** Baked Beans in Tomato Sauce, 420g, 24p   **(GF**
Nearly as good as Heinz, but extra added sugar makes the sauce taste sweeter.

---

(5) **KWIK SAVE** Baked Beans in Tomato Sauce, 420g, 24p   **(GF) (L) (N/S) (V**
The flavour is comparable, but the beans are a little more chewy.

---

(5) **WAITROSE** Baked Beans in Tomato Sauce, 420g, 25p   **(GF) (L**
Buy Waitrose's Perfectly Balanced Baked Beans instead (*see* opposite); they are better for you and taste better.

---

(5) **CO-OP** Baked Beans in Tomato Sauce, 420g, 27p   **(GF) (L) (N/S) (V**
The beans and sauce look very similar to the brand, but the taste is a small step down.

---

(4) **ASDA** Baked Beans in Tomato Sauce, 420g, 24p   **(GF) (N/S) (V**
The beans are fine, but the sauce's paprika and spice are just a little too spiky.

---

(3) **ALDI** Corale Premium Quality Baked Beans in Tomato Sauce, 420g, 17p   **(L**
Cheap, but not good enough. The sweet tomato sauce has an unusual, unrewarding tang

---

(1) **ASDA** Smartprice Baked Beans in Tomato Sauce, 410g, 15p   **(GF) (N/S) (V**
Don't. Even at this price, grey beans in a disgusting sauce will take some swallowing.

Heinz Weight Watchers Baked Beans in Tomato Sauce

ibre, Salt, Sugar

---

(9) **SOMERFIELD** Good Intentions Reduced Sugar & Salt Baked Beans **(GF) (N/S) (V)** in Tomato Sauce, 420g, 25p

Buy it. Less salt and sugar, and they taste as good as their regular baked beans.

---

(9) **WAITROSE** Perfectly Balanced Baked Beans **(GF) (L) (N/S) (V)** in Tomato Sauce, 420g, 26p

This beats the brand in beans. Much cheaper, less salt and they taste as good.

HEINZ WEIGHT WATCHERS BAKED BEANS IN TOMATO SAUCE, 415g, 44p

The taste is as good as the regular Heinz beans, so these are a good healthy alternative. Less sugar per tin, but the salt level still remains at around 4g.

---

(5) **ASDA** Reduced Sugar & Salt Baked Beans in Tomato Sauce, **(GF) (N/S) (V)** 420g, 25p

Better tasting than Asda's regular beans, but the paprika is still too dominant.

---

(2) **SAINSBURY'S** Reduced Sugar & Salt Baked Beans in Tomato Sauce, **(GF) (L)** 420g, 25p

Don't. There is no eating pleasure here whatsoever. Buy Sainsbury's regular beans and eat less!

---

(2) **TESCO** Healthy Living Baked Beans in Tomato Sauce, 420g, 25p **(GF) (N/S) (V)**

Much less sugar and salt than the brand, but taste-wise these are difficult to swallow!

Heinz Spaghetti in Tomato Sauce

Fibre, Salt, Sugar

(8) **TESCO** Spaghetti in Tomato Sauce, 410g, 26p   (V
Buy it. Cheaper and just as good as the brand. Indeed, the best "own label" tasted.

HEINZ SPAGHETTI IN TOMATO SAUCE, 400g, 41p
As with baked beans, consumers need to be aware of the high sugar and salt content. But on the positive side this tin also contains 2g of fibre and 30% of your RDA of vitamins and iron.

(4) **ASDA** Spaghetti in Tomato Sauce, 414g, 26p   (N/S) (V
Cheaper, with more salt and sugar, and it does not taste as good as the brand.

(4) **SAINSBURY'S** Spaghetti in Tomato Sauce, 410g, 26p
On toast this tastes fine but, straight from the tin, the brand is the better.

(3) **SOMERFIELD** Spaghetti in Tomato Sauce, 410g, 26p
Buy the brand. Chew this spaghetti and you're left with a nasty taste of chlorine.

(3) **KWIK SAVE** Spaghetti in Tomato Sauce, 410g, 26p
Put the brand in the trolley. Strong dried spaghetti flavours overpower the tomato sauce.

(2) **ASDA** Smartprice Spaghetti in Tomato Sauce, 410, 11p   (N/S) (V
You get your money's worth, but taste-wise they are not an alternative to the brand.

(1) **MORRISONS** Spaghetti in Tomato Sauce, 410g, 27p
Leave it on the shelf. This is competing with the Co-op for the worst "own label" tinned spaghetti.

(1) **CO-OP** Spaghetti in Tomato Sauce, 410g, 30p   (GF) (L) (N/S) (V
With 6.6g of salt and 20g of sugar, it is fortunate that this tastes so disgusting.

Green Giant Sweetcorn

Fibre, Salt, Sugar

(8)   **WAITROSE** American Crisp & Sweet Sweetcorn, 330g, 45p   **(GF) (L) (N/S) (V)**
Buy it. Similar quality to the brand, and you get more sweetcorn for your money.

(7)   **SAINSBURY'S** Naturally Sweet Sweetcorn No Added Sugar or Salt,   **(L)**
272g, 45p (56p for 340g)
A good buy. Cheaper and not as sweet as the brand, but it is of similar quality.

GREEN GIANT SWEETCORN NIBLETS ORIGINAL, 340g, 60p
Moreish and enjoyable on their own or with a salad. In fact, they taste almost as if they are straight from the cob! This tin does contain 22g of sugar – your recommended daily intake of added sugar is 60g.

(5)   **TESCO** Sweetcorn, 325g, 28p
A cheaper alternative, but the quality of the corn is not as sweet or as tasty.

(4)   **ASDA** No Added Sugar or Salt Sweetcorn, 326g, 28p   **(V)**
Less sugar and salt, but the taste is at least a notch below the brand.

(3)   **KWIK SAVE** Sweetcorn, 325g, 29p   **(L)**
Forget the saving and buy the brand. The taste of this corn is second rate.

(2)   **SOMERFIELD** Sweetcorn, 326g, 36p   **(V)**
Poor quality. Chewy and stringy sweetcorn makes eating this an unpleasant experience.

(1)   **ALDI** Sweet Harvest Sweetcorn, 340g, 23p   **(L)**
Try another shop. This sweetcorn has a strong sour taste that is very unappetising.

(1)   **CO-OP** Sweetcorn, 325g, 45p   **(L) (N/S) (V)**
Don't waste your money! This corn tastes disgusting and should not be on the shelf.

Crosse & Blackwell Garden Peas in Water

Fibre, Salt, Sugar

---

(10) **ASDA** Garden Peas in Water, 300g, 25p (GF) (N/S) (V)
Put them in the trolley. Under half the brand price and similar in taste.

---

(10) **KWIK SAVE** Garden Peas in Salted Water, 300g, 25p (L)
Kwik Save beats the brand in garden peas. Similar in quality and less than half the price.

---

(10) **MORRISONS** Garden Peas in Water, 300g, 25p (GF)
A wallet pleaser! Colour and taste are similar to the brand; the only difference is the price.

---

(10) **SAINSBURY'S** Garden Peas in Sugar and Salted Water, (GF) (L) (N/S) (V)
300g, 25p
This easily beats the brand. It's half the price and delivers a similar taste quality.

---

(10) **SOMERFIELD** Garden Peas in Mint, Sugar and Salted Water, 300g, 25p
Buy these. The mint in the water delivers an extra flavour twist, and they're cheaper.

---

(10) **TESCO** Garden Peas in Sugar and Salted Water, 300g, 25p (GF) (N/S) (V)
They taste so similar to the brand, they could have come out of the same pod!

---

(9) **CO-OP** Garden Peas in Water, 400g, 37p (28p for 300g) (GF) (L) (N/S) (V)
Beat-the-brand shoppers will find a winner at the Co-op. Cheaper than the brand and similar in taste.

CROSSE & BLACKWELL GARDEN PEAS IN WATER, 300g, 55p
Like most tinned peas, the colour is a bleached khaki green. They are rich in fibre (15g per 300g of peas) and the salt and sugar levels are relatively low.

Batchelors Original Mushy Processed Peas

Fibre, Salt, Sugar

---

(8) **KWIK SAVE** Mushy Processed Peas, 300g, 27p
Buy this tin. Slightly more mushy, but equal to the brand on the flavour front.

---

(7) **SOMERFIELD** Mushy Processed Peas, 300g, 33p
Buy it. Unless you are passing Kwik Save, this is your beat-the-brand purchase.

BATCHELORS ORIGINAL MUSHY PROCESSED PEAS, 300g, 45p
As good as mushy peas from the fish and chip shop. Indeed, you get more per gram than you would from a tin of regular processed peas that come swimming in water.

---

(5) **ASDA** Smartprice Mushy Processed Peas, 300g, 14p **(GF) (N/S) (V)**
Smartprice delivers value and quality here. Taste-wise the brand is just slightly better in quality.

---

(5) **ALDI** Sweet Harvest Mushy Processed Peas, 400g, 19p (14p for 300g) **(L)**
Worth a punt at this price! A very mushy style and a small step down in quality.

---

(4) **CO-OP** Mushy Processed Peas, 300g, 31p **(L) (N/S) (V)**
Visually, the odd grey-green pea will be offputting, but taste-wise they are acceptable.

---

(4) **MORRISONS** Chip Shop Style Mushy Processed Peas, 300g, 39p **(GF)**
The overall taste is similar to the brand, but there are too many grey-brown peas.

---

(3) **SAINSBURY'S** Chip Shop Style Mushy Processed Peas, 300g, 34p **(L)**
Pay the extra and buy the brand: the taste and appearance is much better.

---

(3) **TESCO** Mushy Processed Peas 400g, 26p (20p for 300g) **(GF) (N/S) (V)**
A cheap price, but they're so watery it should say "pea soup" on the label.

Napolina Peeled Plum Tomatoes

Lypocene (an antioxidant found in tomato, pink grapefruit and palm oil, which is also used as a food colour)

---

(7) **MARKS & SPENCER** Chopped Tomatoes, 400g, 49p   **(GF) (N/S) (V)**
Put them in the trolley. They are chopped rather than whole, but deliver a similar taste quality.

---

(7) **WAITROSE** Italian Peeled Plum Tomatoes in Natural Juice,   **(GF) (L) (N/S) (V)**
400g, 45p
A sound buy! Not as sweet as the brand, but they're cheaper and of equal quality.

NAPOLINA PEELED PLUM TOMATOES, 400g, 58p
Napolina tomatoes are ripe and sweet, and ideal for any dish that requires peeled plum tomatoes. Only Waitrose and Marks & Spencer beat this brand.

---

(5) **MORRISONS** Peeled Plum Tomatoes, 400g, 29p
Under half price and good value for money, but there is a step down in quality.

---

(4) **SAINSBURY'S** Premium Peeled Plum Tomatoes, 400g, 45p   **(L)**
Side by side with the brand they are more acidic and a notch down in quality.

---

(3) **TESCO** Italian Peeled Plum Tomatoes, 400g, 35p   **(GF) (V)**
Variable quality, so buy the brand. There can be a sharp tangy taste, caused by half-ripe fruit.

---

(3) **ASDA** Peeled Plum Tomatoes, 400g, 35p   **(GF) (N/S) (V)**
There is a big saving here, but the tomatoes' tart flavour could spoil a delicate dish.

---

(1) **CO-OP** Peeled Plum Tomatoes, 400g, 37p   **(L) (N/S) (V)**
Don't ruin your cooking; buy the brand. The taste can be best described as vinegary.

---

(1) **ALDI** Carlini Peeled Plum Tomatoes, 400g, 15p
Leave them on the shelf and let somebody else ruin their pasta. They taste disgusting.

Heinz Vegetable Soup

Lactose, Salt, Sugar

---

(9) **MORRISONS** Thick Country Vegetable Soup, 400g, 35p
Put a couple in the trolley. Cheaper and much better tasting than the brand.

---

(8) **CO-OP** Creamy Golden Vegetable Soup, 400g, 45p   **(N/S)**
Buy it. Cream in colour rather than orange-brown, but it is cheaper and better tasting.

---

(8) **ALDI** Soupreme Chicken & Vegetable Chunky Soup, 400g, 49p   **(L)**
A sound buy for non-vegetarians. Cheaper and you get better tasting vegetables, with
flavoursome lumps of chicken.

HEINZ VEGETABLE SOUP, 400g, 59p
A poor substitute for freshly made vegetable soup, but the taste is passable. The salt content
is similar to Heinz's Cream of Chicken Soup (*see* page 85), and it also contains wheat flour.

---

(5) **SAINSBURY'S** Vegetable Soup, 400g, 35p   **(GF)**
Good value. Similar colour and vegetable mix to the Heinz soup, although the brand
edges it on taste.

---

(5) **KWIK SAVE** Vegetable Soup, 400g, 43p   **(N/S)**
This is cheaper, and in similar style to the brand, but is a small step down in quality.

---

(5) **SOMERFIELD** Vegetable Soup, 400g, 43p   **(N/S)**
Somerfield and the brand look similar, but the brand beats it on taste.

---

(5) **WAITROSE** Vegetable Soup, 425g, 43p   **(L) (N/S)**
Waitrose is similar to the brand in appearance, but it does not match it for flavour.

---

(4) **ASDA** Vegetable Soup, 400g, 35p   **(GF) (N/S)**
This is one notch down in quality. The vegetables are smaller and less flavoursome.

---

(1) **TESCO** Vegetable Soup, 400g, 35p
Buy the brand; this is disgusting. (I tasted another tin just in case the first was faulty.)

Heinz Cream of Tomato Soup

Lactose, Salt, Sugar

HEINZ CREAM OF TOMATO SOUP, 400g, 59p
Not as good as freshly made soup, but it does deliver a pleasant tomato flavour.
There are nearly 3g of salt and 20g of sugar in this tin. Soup for thought!

(5) **MORRISONS** Cream of Tomato Soup, 400g, 35p
It's much cheaper, but its tomato flavour is not good enough to beat this brand.

(5) **SAINSBURY'S** Cream of Tomato Soup, 400g, 35p **(GF)**
Similar to Morrisons and, likewise, not quite up to the taste quality of the brand.

(5) **TESCO** Cream of Tomato Soup, 400g, 35p **(GF)**
A cheaper option. You save money, but it's not as good as the brand.

(4) **KWIK SAVE** Cream of Tomato Soup, 400g, 43p **(N/S)**
It won't impress the Heinz lovers, but it's cheaper and delivers acceptable quality.

(4) **SOMERF!ELD** Cream of Tomato Soup, 400g, 43p **(N/S)**
Not for the purists! A more spicy tomato soup with mustard and paprika added to it.

(3) **ALDI** Soupreme Cream of Tomato Soup, 400g, 33p
Try somewhere else. Half price, but taste-wise it is at least two steps below the brand.

(2) **CO-OP** Cream of Tomato Soup, 400g, 45p **(N/S)**
Buy the brand. Tasting this blind you would struggle to recognise it as tomato soup.

(1) **ASDA** Cream of Tomato Soup, 400g, 35p **(GF) (N/S)**
Leave it on the shelf. The metallic taint is horribly strong in this soup.

Heinz Cream of Chicken Soup

Lactose, Salt, Sugar

(7) **ALDI** Thai Style Chicken Soup, 400g, 59p
Different from the brand, but if you want a spicy chicken soup then this is it.

HEINZ CREAM OF CHICKEN SOUP, 400g, 59p
This is healthier for you than Heinz Cream of Tomato Soup, with a tad less salt and much less sugar. It's worth noting that one of the ingredients is wheat flour.

(5) **ALDI** Soupreme Cream of Chicken Soup, 400g, 33p
This is worth a punt. It's much cheaper and just a whisper away in quality.

(5) **SAINSBURY'S** Cream of Chicken Soup, 400g, 35p
Cheaper than the brand, and just a small step down in taste quality.

(5) **TESCO** Cream of Chicken Soup, 400g, 35p
A cheaper option. However, the bits of chicken are less flavoursome than the brand's.

(5) **CO-OP** Cream of Chicken of Soup, 400g, 45p　　　　　　　　**(N/S)**
Cheaper and almost as good as the brand, but it does have a higher salt content.

(4) **ASDA** Cream of Chicken Soup, 400g, 35p　　　　　　　　**(N/S)**
Big step down in taste compared to the brand. Be prepared to add your own flavour.

(3) **MORRISONS** Cream of Chicken Soup, 400g, 35p
Leave it. The taste is artificial and is not an alternative to the brand.

(2) **KWIK SAVE** Cream of Chicken Soup, 400g, 43p　　　　　　　　**(N/S)**
Buy the brand. This recipe needs a rethink; the taste is more milk than chicken.

(2) **SOMERFIELD** Cream of Chicken Soup, 400g, 43p　　　　　　　　**(N/S)**
Don't waste your money. Like Kwik Save's chicken soup, this requires a recipe change.

John West Wild Red Salmon

Protein, Salt

---

(9) **ALDI** Ocean Rise Red Salmon, 213g, 99p **(L)**
This beats the brand. Almost half the price, it matches the brand for colour and flavour.

---

(8) **ASDA** Wild Pacific Red Salmon, 213g, £1.36 **(GF) (N/S)**
Make room in the trolley. This delivers equal quality and a similar colour to the brand.

---

(8) **TESCO** Wild Pacific Red Salmon, 212g, £1.36 **(GF)**
If you're shopping in Tesco, this competes with the colour and taste of the brand.

---

(7) **WAITROSE** Red Sockeye Salmon, 213g, £1.69 **(GF) (L) (N/S)**
Red salmon for Waitrose shoppers. Not as red as the brand, but matches it for flavour.

---

(6) **WAITROSE** Skinless & Boneless Red Salmon, 180g, £2.69 **(GF) (N/S)**
Expensive, but top quality, and it beats the taste of the brand (and Marks & Spencer).

JOHN WEST WILD RED SALMON, 213g, £1.99
This is classified as red and, certainly, next to pink salmon it is darker. But it is no better for you than pink salmon, it just tastes better, hence the extra hike in price.

---

(5) **MORRISONS** Red Salmon, 418g, £2.49 (£1.27 for 213g)
Nearly as good! Bigger is nearly always cheaper and here you get great value for money.

---

(5) **CO-OP** Sockeye Wild Pacific Red Salmon, 213g, £1.58 **(L) (N/S)**
It's cheaper and worth buying. However, side by side, the brand edges it for flavour.

---

(5) **MARKS & SPENCER** Wild Canadian Red Salmon, **(GF) (N/S)**
180g, £2.99 (£3.54 for 213g)
You pay extra for it being skinless and boneless, but it's no better tasting than the brand.

---

(4) **SAINSBURY'S** Wild Canadian Red Pacific Salmon, **(L)**
418g, £2.31 (£1.18 for 213g)
Like Sainsbury's pink salmon, straight from the tin this is a notch down in taste quality.

---

(4) **SOMERFIELD** Wild Pacific Red Salmon, 213g, £1.55
The brand has an extra layer of flavour, but this will work fine in a sandwich.

Princes Tuna Steak in Brine/Spring Water

Protein, Salt

---

(8) **SAINSBURY'S** Tuna Chunks in Brine, 185g, 57p (62p for 200g) **(L)**
Buy it. The colour is a slightly darker pink, but there is little difference in taste.

---

(8) **TESCO** Tuna Chunks in Brine, 185g, 57p (62p for 200g) **(GF)**
Buy Tesco over the brand: it's cheaper, and the flavour is at least as good.

---

(8) **MORRISONS** Skipjack Tuna Chunks in Brine, 185g, 58p (63p for 200g)
Put it in the trolley. This "own label" delivers similar quality to the brand for less money.

---

(7) **SOMERFIELD** Skipjack Tuna Chunks in Brine, 185g, 63p (68p for 200g) **(GF) (N/S)**
A beat-the-brand buy for the Somerfield shopper. Cheaper and of a similar quality.

---

(7) **ASDA** Tuna Steaks, in Brine, 200g, 67p **(GF) (N/S)**
Asda tuna is good for the beat-the-brand shopper. Similar in taste and a cheaper price.

---

(6) **MARKS & SPENCER** Tuna Steak in Spring Water, **(GF) (N/S)**
198g, 89p (90p for 200g)
This is well worth the extra few pence, as it delivers an extra layer of flavour.

PRINCES TUNA STEAK IN BRINE/SPRING WATER, 200g, 82p
Named tuna "steak", but the appearance is strand-like rather than solid. As with salmon, tuna is a healthy tinned product, rich in protein.

---

(5) **CO-OP** Tuna Steak in Brine, 198g, 73p (74p for 200g) **(L) (N/S)**
A deeper pink in colour and cheaper, but the brand's tuna edges it in flavour.

---

(4) **ALDI** Ocean Rise Tuna Chunks in Brine, 185g, 35p (38p for 200g) **(L)**
A good step down in quality. Although labelled "chunks", the appearance is more strand-like.

6
Tinned Fruits
& Puddings

Once again, the message is: read the label. You can't always trust your tastebuds to assess the hidden problems there might be with a food product. Who would think that a tin of mouthwateringly sharp fruit like grapefruit could mask a whole mountain of sugar? But it can. A 410g tin may well contain more than the recommended daily allowance of 60g of added sugar per day.

Del Monte is without doubt the biggest brand in this section, which makes the inadequacy of its nutritional labelling a complete disgrace. The labels are so incomprehensible that you need to go to one of the supermarket's websites to get a clearer picture of what the food levels actually mean. There is, for instance, no mention of the word "sugar". Instead, it is included under the umbrella term of "carbohydrates". You can't help thinking that such obscurity is intended to mislead.

Del Monte Apricot Halves in Light Syrup

Fibre, Sugar

(8) **SAINSBURY'S** Apricot Halves in Light Syrup, 411g, 50p   **(GF) (L) (V)**
A healthier buy. More than 20g less sugar than Del Monte and the apricots taste better.

(8) **ASDA** Apricot Halves in Light Syrup, 411g, 55p   **(GF) (N/S) (V)**
Buy it. Lighter coloured and slightly bigger apricots, but with a more pleasing taste.

(8) **TESCO** Apricot Halves in Light Syrup, 411g, 55p   **(V)**
This is a beat-the-brand buy. Better tasting, with a lot less sugar and much cheaper.

(8) **KWIK SAVE** Apricot Halves in Light Syrup, 411g, 56p
Put it in the trolley. Kwik Save's apricots beat the brand on taste and price.

(8) **MORRISONS** Apricot Halves in Juice, 410g, 59p
Cheaper and of equal quality to the brand. The fruit in juice, as opposed to syrup, delivers less sugar and a cleaner taste.

(8) **SOMERFIELD** Apricot Halves in Apple Juice, 411g, 59p
Competes on all the taste fronts. If you're calorie-counting, these have much less sugar.

(8) **SOMERFIELD** Apricot Halves in Light Syrup, 411g, 59p
A sound buy for the sweeter-toothed. This is cheaper and of similar quality to the brand.

(7) **WAITROSE** Apricot Halves in Fruit Juice, 410g, 65p   **(GF) (L) (N/S) (V)**
Buy Waitrose – it equals the brand for taste, has less sugar, and is still cheaper.

(7) **CO-OP** Apricots Halves in Juice, 411g, 68p   **(GF) (L) (N/S) (V)**
Buy it. Co-op's apricots in juice contain less sugar and taste better than the brand.

DEL MONTE APRICOT HALVES IN LIGHT SYRUP, 420g, 72p (70p for 410g)

The nutritional labelling is so vague, it might as well be in double Dutch. No stated sugar levels, but the carbohydrate (which you can guarantee is 99.9% sugar) is more than 60g for the tin. Note that this tin gives you around 10g more than the "own labels".

(5) **CO-OP** Apricots Halves in Light Syrup, 411g, 65p   **(N/S) (L) (V)**
These apricots are of a similar quality to the brand, but the syrup is not as good.

Del Monte Fruit Cocktail in Light Syrup

Fibre, Sugar

(9) **ALDI** Sweet Valley Fruit Cocktail in Light Syrup, 410g, 35p **(L)**
One for your trolley. Much cheaper and a similar quality to the brand; no cherries though.

(9) **MORRISONS** Fruit Cocktail in Pear Juice, 410g, 49p
Beats the brand for price, it has less sugar and the quality of the fruit mix is as good.

(8) **WAITROSE** Fruit Cocktail in Fruit Juice, 410g, 59p **(GF) (L) (N/S) (V)**
The fruit juice is a healthier option. It's also cheaper and the mix of fruit is as good.

(6) **MARKS & SPENCER** Exotic Fruit Salad in Light Syrup, 425g, 99p **(GF) (N/S) (V)**
(96p for 410g)
No cherries. The fruit is in large chunks, but tastes very much better than the brand.

DEL MONTE FRUIT COCKTAIL IN LIGHT SYRUP, 420g, 72p (70p for 410g)

This fruit cocktail contains peaches, pears, pineapple, grapes and cherries. The sugar count is around 60g: which is your entire recommended daily intake of added sugar. Note that this tin gives around 10g more than the "own labels".

(5) **ASDA** Fruit Cocktail in Light Syrup, 411g, 46p **(GF) (N/S) (V)**
A cherry off the quality of the brand. But it's cheaper and good value for money.

(5) **TESCO** Fruit Cocktail in Light Syrup, 410g, 46p **(N/S) (V)**
It's cheaper and there are plenty of cherries. But taste-wise it comes second to the brand.

(5) **SOMERFIELD** Fruit Cocktail in Pear Juice, 411g, 52p **(GF) (V)**
Although it's cheaper and has less sugar, it's not quite the same quality as the brand.

(5) **KWIK SAVE** Fruit Cocktail in Light Syrup, 400g, 49p (50p for 410g) **(V)**
Similar to Somerfield (though a smaller tin) and, likewise, a small step down in quality to the brand.

(4) **SAINSBURY'S** Fruit Cocktail in Light Syrup, 411g, 42p **(GF) (L) (V)**
The fruit mix and quality is at least one step down, and this tin contains more sugar.

(2) **ASDA** No added Sugar Fruit Cocktail in Light Syrup, 411g, 42p **(GF) (N/S) (V)**
Buy Asda's regular. Don't touch this one – the fruit and juice taste like vinegar.

Del Monte Grapefruit Segments in Light Syrup

Fibre, Sugar

(9) **ASDA** No Added Sugar Grapefruit Segments in Fruit Juice, **(GF) (N/S) (V)**
540g, 53p (41p for 420g)
The taste is very sharp, even though the tin contains 26g of sugar. But quality is good.

(9) **SAINSBURY'S** Grapefruit Segments in Syrup, 539g, 64p (50p for 420g)**(GF) (L) (V)**
Buy it. Cheaper and the grapefruit taste and quality are comparable to the brand.

(7) **TESCO** Grapefruit Segments in Natural Juice, 410g, 58p (59p for 420g) **(V)**
A beat-the-brand buy for the Tesco shopper. Better quality, low sugar and not too tart.

(7) **CO-OP** Grapefruit Segments in Light Syrup, 411g, 59p (60p for 420g)**(L) (N/S) (V)**
This is cheaper and a similar style and quality to the brand – but it has more sugar.

(7) **WAITROSE** Grapefruit Segments in Fruit Juice, 540g, **(GF) (L) (N/S) (V)**
79p (62p for 420g)
Buy it. Gram for gram, this is cheaper. The taste is mouth-watering, and not too sharp.

(7) **CO-OP** Grapefruit Segments in Grapefruit Juice, **(GF) (L) (N/S) (V)**
411g, 63p (64p for 420g)
Less sugar than the brand, but be prepared for some serious mouth-watering acidity.

(6) **MARKS & SPENCER** Grapefruit Segments, 540g, £1.09 (83p for 420g)**(GF) (N/S) (V)**
Superb – buy it! This mix of red, pink and white grapefruit segments is worth the extra.

DEL MONTE GRAPEFRUIT SEGMENTS IN LIGHT SYRUP, 420g, 67p **(V)**
This canned grapefruit delivers a really mouth-watering taste. But don't let those sharp
flavours fool you – there is over 40g of sugar in this tin.

(5) **ASDA** Smartprice Grapefruit Pieces in Light Syrup, **(GF) (N/S) (V)**
540g, 44p (34p for 420g)
Not as mouth-watering as the brand, and a little more chewy, but great value for money.

(5) **ALDI** Sweet Valley Grapefruit Segments in Light Syrup, 540g, **(L)**
49p (38p for 420g)
Does not have the zingy pungency of the brand, but at this price it's a sound buy.

(3) **SAINSBURY'S** Organic Grapefruit in Own Juice, **(GF) (L) (V)**
410g, 99p 411g, 63p (£1.01 for 420g)
OK, so it's organic. But it costs more and it doesn't taste anywhere as good.

Del Monte Mandarin Oranges Whole Segments in Own Juice

Fibre, Sugar

(9) **ASDA** No Added Sugar Mandarin Segments in Orange Juice, **(GF) (N/S) (V)**
298g, 27p
A much lower price, less sugar and the taste is the equal to the brand.

(9) **ALDI** Sweet Valley Mandarin Segments in Light Syrup, **(L)**
312g, 29p (28p for 298g)
As good as the brand. The fruit is a better shape and the taste is slightly sweeter.

(9) **ASDA** Mandarin Segments in Light Syrup, **(GF) (N/S) (V)**
312g, 30p (29p for 298g)
Cheaper and of similar quality. There's more sugar and sweeter-tasting segments though.

(8) **MORRISONS** Orange Segments in Natural Juice, 298g, 30p
Morrisons is cheaper and has a similar mandarin bite to the brand – buy it.

(8) **KWIK SAVE** Mandarin Orange Segments in Orange Juice, 298g, 31p
Buy it. Much smaller segments than the brand, but with similar tangy orange tastes.

(8) **SOMERFIELD** Mandarin Orange Segments in Orange Juice, 298g, 32p
Good saving, and it delivers similar quality, although the segments taste slightly sweeter.

(8) **CO-OP** Mandarin Orange Segments in Mandarin Juice, **(GF) (L) (N/S) (V)**
298g, 34p
Beats the brand. The segments are slightly smaller, but they and the juice taste similar
to the brand.

(7) **WAITROSE** Mandarin Oranges in Fruit Juice, **(GF) (L) (N/S) (V)**
295g, 39p (39p for 298g)
Waitrose shoppers, this is the one to buy. It's clean and tangy, just like the brand.

**DEL MONTE MANDARIN ORANGES WHOLE SEGMENTS IN OWN JUICE,
298g, 47p**
These Mandarin oranges reveal a tangy orange flavour that works well on its own or as an
ingredient in a trifle or pudding. Note that the sugar content is around 30g.

(4) **TESCO** Mandarin Segments in Light Syrup, 312g, 30p (28p for 298g) **(N/S) (V)**
The brand is better. The flavour of the syrup has spoilt the clean tangy orange flavours.

Del Monte Peach Slices in Juice

Fibre, Sugar

(8) **ASDA** No Added Sugar Peach Slices in Fruit Juice, 411g, 42p   **(GF) (N/S) (V)**
Grab it. A slightly darker colour than the brand, but the taste is spot on!

(8) **SAINSBURY'S** Peach Slices in Fruit Juice, 411g, 42p   **(GF) (L) (V)**
Buy it. These peaches are more orange in colour than the ones from the brand.

(8) **TESCO** Peach Slices in Fruit Juice, 410g, 42p   **(V)**
Grab a couple for the cupboard. They are cheaper, and better tasting than the brand.

(8) **KWIK SAVE** Peach Slices in Pear Juice, 411g, 45p
A better buy. Less sugar and they taste at least as good as the brand.

(8) **WAITROSE** Peach Slices in Fruit Juice, 410g, 45p   **(GF) (L) (N/S) (V)**
A beat-the-brand buy for the Waitrose shopper. Cheaper, and the taste is similar.

DEL MONTE PEACH SLICES IN JUICE, 415g, 72p (71p for 410g)
Peaches in juice rather than syrup have less sugar. Moreover, not only are they healthier, they taste better. Your recommended daily intake of added sugar is 60g. Note that this tin is around 5g heavier than most "own labels".

(3) **CO-OP** Peach Slices in Pear Juice, 411g, 51p   **(GF) (L) (N/S) (V)**
This juice spoils the peach flavours here. What's wrong with canning them in peach juice?

(2) **MORRISONS** Peach Slices in Juice, 410g, 42p
Buy the brand. I tasted two cans from different batches, and both had a fusty flavour.

John West Pear Halves in Fruit Juice

Fibre, Sugar

---

(9) **SOMERFIELD** Pear Halves in Grape Juice, 411g, 34p
You won't be disappointed with these: they're around half price, and of a similar quality.

(9) **SAINSBURY'S** Pear Halves in Fruit Juice, 411g, 38p **(GF) (L) (V)**
A Sainsbury's beat-the-brand purchase. The taste is as good as the brand and there's less sugar.

(8) **TESCO** Pear Quarters in Juice, 822g, 79p (40p for 411g) **(V)**
This big tin is worth it. Quarters rather than halves, but the taste is first class.

(7) **WAITROSE** Pear Halves in Fruit Juice, 410g, 59p **(GF) (L) (N/S) (V)**
Not the cheapest "own label", but it's less than the brand, and at least as good.

(6) **MARKS & SPENCER** Pear Halves in Grape Juice, 420g, £1.49 **(GF) (N/S)**
(£1.46 for 410g)
Expensive, but the premium taste is worth it. They come in a glass jar rather than a tin.

JOHN WEST PEAR HALVES IN FRUIT JUICE, 410g, 65p
Nearly 30g less sugar in this tin compared with John West's Pear Halves in Syrup. The fruit is not as sweet, but the taste is much cleaner and it's the healthier option.

(4) **MORRISONS** Pear Halves in Fruit Juice, 410g, 34p
Ripe pears, but their flavour is spoilt by the use of a poor quality fruit juice.

(4) **CO-OP** Pear Halves in Pear Juice, 411g, 48p **(GF) (L) (N/S) (V)**
It's difficult to understand why these are half the taste quality of Co-op's pears in syrup.

Del Monte Sliced Pineapple in Own Juice

Fibre, Sugar

---

(7) **WAITROSE** Pineapple Slices in Fruit Juice, **(GF) (L) (N/S) (V)**
425g, 69p (70p for 432g)
Buy it – it tastes as good. Just a few pence cheaper, but they all add up.

---

(6) **MARKS & SPENCER** Hawaiian Pineapple Slices **(GF) (N/S) (V)**
in Pineapple Juice, 567g, £1.29 (98p for 432g)
Well worth the extra premium: healthier, less sugar, and better tasting than the brand.

DEL MONTE SLICED PINEAPPLE IN OWN JUICE, 432g, 72p
Pineapples are naturally rich in sugar and this tin contains at least 60g. However, you'd need to go to a supermarket's website to find that out. Your recommended daily intake of added sugar is 60g.

---

(5) **ASDA** No Added Sugar Pineapple Slices in Pineapple Juice, **(GF) (N/S) (V)**
425g, 53p (54p for 432g)
Worth a punt. Cheaper and with less sugar, but a small step down on the taste front.

---

(5) **SOMERFIELD** Pineapple Slices in Pineapple Juice, 432g, 69p
Much better tasting than Somerfield's Pineapple Slices in Light Syrup (*see* below), but still not as good as the brand.

---

(5) **CO-OP** Pineapple Slices in Pineapple Juice, 420g, 75p (77p for 432g) **(L) (N/S) (V)**
Similar taste quality, but only buy this product if it is cheaper than the brand. (Brands tend to be more expensive in the Co-op.)

---

(4) **SAINSBURY'S** Pineapple Slices in Natural Juice, 432g, 53p **(GF) (L) (V)**
Cheaper, but at least one step down in quality, and the juice has a metallic flavour.

---

(4) **SOMERFIELD** Pineapple Slices in Light Syrup, 432g, 69p
Pay the extra for the brand. Here, there is more sugar, and less taste satisfaction.

---

(3) **MORRISONS** Pineapples Slices in Juice, 425g, 62p (63p for 432g)
Buy the brand. The pineapples are of variable quality; some are hard and chewy.

---

(2) **TESCO** Pineapple Slices in Natural Juice, 432g, 53p
Don't waste your money. Slightly better than Aldi's, but they're still bland and tasteless.

---

(1) **ALDI** Sweet Valley Pineapple Slices in Natural Juice, 432g, 39p **(GF) (L) (V)**
Don't buy it – 39p is far too much for these blanched and tasteless pineapple slices.

Del Monte Prunes in Juice

fibre, Sugar. Contains stones.

(9)   **SAINSBURY'S** Californian Prunes in Fruit Juice, 410g, 46p   **(GF) (L) (V)**
Put it in your trolley. Contains loads of fibre and it matches the brand for taste.

(9)   **SAINSBURY'S** Californian Prunes in Syrup, 420g, 46p (45p for 410g)   **(GF) (L) (V)**
Not as healthy as the ones in fruit juice (*see* above). But there is little difference in taste and the tin is 10g heavier.

(9)   **TESCO** Prunes in Fruit Juice, 410g, 46p
A beat-the-brand buy. Cheaper, and the taste is very similar to the brand.

(8)   **ASDA** Prunes in Light Syrup, 420g, 51p (50p for 410g)   **(GF) (N/S) (V)**
Buy it. The taste is comparable to the brand, and it is much cheaper – particularly since you get 10g more than the brand.

(7)   **CO-OP** Prunes in Syrup, 410g, 69p   **(L) (N/S) (V)**
You can't fault the prune taste, but the tin's 94g of sugar could be an issue.

(7)   **WAITROSE** Prunes in Juice, 410g, 72p   **(GF) (L) (N/S) (V)**
Grab it. Cheaper, with an easy to open ring-pull tin, revealing comparable tastes.

DEL MONTE PRUNES IN JUICE, 410g, 89p

Most tinned prunes are high in sugar, rich in iron and contain at least 8g of fibre. Like all tinned fruits, it's worth straining the highly sugared juice off – especially if you're on a diet.

(3)   **MORRISONS** Prunes in Apple Juice, 410g, 51p
Not so good. The fruit is mushy and the taste is like watery black treacle.

Ambrosia Devon Custard

Fat, Lactose, Sugar

AMBROSIA DEVON CUSTARD, 425g, 61p
This thick, creamy, yellow custard is enjoyable cold or hot. The complete tin contains 7g of fat and 30g of sugar. Your recommended daily intake of added sugar is 60g.

(5) **SOMERFIELD** Good Intentions Low Fat Custard, 425g, 40p
A good buy! The taste is just a tad off the brand's, but it does have more sugar.

(4) **ASDA** Smartprice Ready to Serve Custard, 396g, 20p (22p for 425g) **(GF) (N/S)**
At this price it's good value for money, but the taste is a good notch down.

(4) **SAINSBURY'S** Basics Custard, 396g, 20p (22p for 425g)
An alternative! It won't impress the brand lovers, but it is well worth the money.

(4) **TESCO** Value Ready to Serve Custard, 396g, 20p (22p for 425g)
Similar in quality to Asda's & Sainsbury's and, like them, it's worth a punt at this price.

(3) **KWIK SAVE** Creamy Ready to Serve Custard, 425g, 40p
Buy the brand or try another shop. A strong metallic taste spoils the custard.

(3) **SOMERFIELD** Creamy Ready to Serve Custard, 425g, 40p
Leave it. Like Kwik Save's custard, this has a metallic tang that ruins the flavour.

(3) **CO-OP** Healthy Living Ready to Serve Low Fat Custard, **(GF) (N/S)**
396g, 49p (53p for 425g)
This is better tasting than Co-op's regular custard, but is still not up to the standard of Ambrosia.

(2) **CO-OP** Ready to Serve Custard, 396g, 49p (53p for 425g) **(GF) (N/S)**
Don't buy it. This is such poor quality that it makes Asda's Smartprice version taste heavenly.

Ambrosia Creamed Rice

Fat, Lactose, Sugar

(10) **ALDI** Sweet Valley Creamed Rice Pudding, 624g, 39p (24p for 425g) **(GF)**
Buy it. This tastes as good as the brand, and it works out at less than half price.

(9) **ASDA** Creamed Rice Pudding, 425g, 30p
Put a couple of tins in the trolley. It provides a similar taste and is very much cheaper.

(9) **SAINSBURY'S** Creamed Rice Pudding, 425g, 30p
Leave the Ambrosia on the shelf and buy this. It's cheaper and of a similar quality.

(9) **TESCO** Creamed Rice Pudding, 425g, 30p **(GF) (N/S)**
Put the Tesco and Ambrosia rice pudding in two bowls, and it's difficult to tell them apart.

(8) **SOMERFIELD** Creamed Rice Pudding, 425g, 40p
Somerfield beats the brand by delivering a comparable quality more cheaply.

(8) **SOMERFIELD** Good Intentions Low Fat Rice Pudding, 425g, 40p
Cheaper and of an equal quality, but with a lower fat content and slightly more sugar.

(7) **CO-OP** Organic Rice Pudding, 425g, 49p **(N/S)**
Buy this one. This equals Co-op's Thick & Creamy for taste, and it has less fat.

(6) **CO-OP** Thick & Creamy Rice Pudding, 425g, 52p **(N/S)**
Creamier and better tasting than the brand, but it does contain more sugar and fat.

(6) **SAINSBURY'S** Luxury Creamed Rice Pudding, 425g, 55p
It costs one penny more, but it's far more palate pleasing than the brand's creamed rice.

AMBROSIA CREAMED RICE, 425g, 54p
Enjoyable, but not as good as freshly made rice pudding! Moreover, the sugar content is just over 30g and it contains 8g of fat, of which 4.6g are saturates.

(5) **ASDA** Smartprice Rice Pudding, 425g, 15p **(GF) (N/S)**
Not of the quality of the brand, but it delivers a great 15p bargain.

(5) **KWIK SAVE** Simply Rice Pudding, 624g, 22p (15p for 425g)
A cheaper alternative to the brand! A big can that delivers an acceptable rice pudding.

(3) **MORRISONS** Creamed Rice Pudding, 425g, 35p
Buy the brand. Admittedly, this is a much cheaper in price, but it tastes overpoweringly metallic.

7
Pizzas, Fresh Soups, Pork Pies, Cold Meats & Pâtés

Most of us have placed a fast food in the shopping trolley, and more and more of us, because we are busy or too tired, are doing so more and more often. This brings its own problems, since prepared foods contain shedloads of additives – often those associated with food intolerances and unhealthy diets – even when they are labelled "fresh" or for special diets. If shoppers read back labels more carefully – and if they were easier to understand – I suspect much more home cooking would be done.

Supermarkets' charcuterie products are either found pre-wrapped on the aisle shelves or freshly sliced at the deli counter. Unfortunately, most shoppers don't bother to wait their turn at the deli counter. Now, that's a big mistake! I've checked prices and found that some of the pre-wrapped cold meats in this section are astonishingly more expensive than the ones from Harrods' Charcuterie!

Where there is not a competitive brand in this section, I've used one of the supermarket deli products to demonstrate the price differential. These products, of course, don't have ingredient labels, so you must ask the counter assistant if you have special dietary requirements.

Pizza Express Margherita Pizza

Emulsifiers, Fat, Fibre, Lactose, Salt, Sugar, Yeast

---

(10) **TESCO** Italiano Margherita Pizza, 382g, £2.49 (£1.76 for 270g) **(N/S)**
Buy this. It's under half the price of the brand, and it tastes as good.

---

(10) **MARKS & SPENCER** Cheese & Tomato Stonebake Pizza, 340g,
£2.99 (£2.38 for 270g)
Outstanding quality. This is as good as, and better than you'd get in most restaurants.

---

(10) **TESCO** Finest Margherita Pizza, 489g, £3.79 (£2.10 for 270g)
This beat-the-brand pizza is cheaper and two notches up on Pizza Express.

---

(10) **ASDA** Extra Special Margherita with Basil Pesto Pizza, 385g, **(N/S)**
£3.48 (£2.44 for 270g)
Bigger, cheaper and better than the brand. Before you buy, make sure you like pesto.

---

(8) **SAINSBURY'S** Pizzeria Style Margherita Pizza, 429g, £3.49 (£2.20 for 270g)
Put it in the trolley. It tastes as good as the brand, and it's cheaper.

PIZZA EXPRESS MARGHERITA PIZZA, 270g, £3.85
This is not as good as one which has been freshly made in a Pizza Express restaurant.
If you eat the whole pizza your intake of saturated fats and salt would be around half
your recommended daily intake.

---

(5) **ASDA** Good For You Stonebaked Margherita Pizza, **(N/S)**
290g, £1.88 (£1.75 for 270g)
A healthier option and around half the price of the brand. It's not as tasty, though.

---

(4) **CO-OP** Thin & Crispy Cheese & Tomato Pizza, **(N/S)**
300g, £2.39 (£2.15 for 270g)
Not as tasty and it's crammed with ingredients that have been associated with food
intolerance.

---

(3) **ALDI** Carlos Four Cheese Stone Baked Pizza, 330g, 99p (81p for 270g)
Very cheap! But tastewise it does not compare, and uses tomato purée rather than
tomatoes in the topping.

---

(3) **MORRISONS** Four Cheese Pizza, 385g, £2.49 (£1.75 for 270g)
Leave it on the shelf. It has better ingredients than Aldi's, but it's no better tasting.

Pizza Express American Hot Pepperoni & Chilli Pizza

Emulsifiers, Fat, Fibre, Lactose, Salt, Soya, Sugar, Yeast

---

(8) **SAINSBURY'S** Hot & Spicy Pizza, 376g, £2.99 (£2.35 for 295g)
Put it in the trolley. This is as good as the brand, and it's much cheaper.

---

(7) **MARKS & SPENCER** Double Pepperoni Stonebake Pizza,
370g, £3.79 (£3.02 for 295g)
Beats the brand for price and at least matches it in quality.

PIZZA EXPRESS AMERICAN HOT, PEPPERONI & CHILLI PIZZA, 295g, £3.85

This delivers exactly what it says on the packet. However, the salt level is high at 4.4g.
(It is recommended that you reduce your salt intake to 6g.)

---

(5) **CO-OP** Italian Style Pepperoni Pizza, 385g, £2.99 (£2.29 for 295g)   **(N/S)**
This tastes fine. However, it does have a high salt level and contains many flavour-enhancing ingredients.

---

(4) **ALDI** Carlos Pepperoni Stone Baked Pizza, 330g, 99p (89p for 295g)
Good value. A chilli or two would have helped to spice up the flavour here.

---

(3) **TESCO** Pepperoni Pizza, 387g, £2.49 (£1.89 for 295g)
Leave it on the shelf. Bitter pepperoni sits on a very boring pizza base.

---

(2) **ASDA** American Stuffed Crust Pepperoni Pizza, 490g,   **(N/S)**
£2.78 (£1.67 for 295g)
Leave it. This tastes too salty – not surprising, as it contains 6.6g of salt.

New Covent Garden Fresh Tomato Soup

Celery, Maize, Lactose, Salt, Sugar, Yeast

(9) **ALDI** Soupreme Tomato & Pepper Soup, 500g, 89p (£1.06 for 600g)   **(GF) (L)**
No basil in it, but it offers an equal taste at nearly half the brand price.

(8) **TESCO** Tomato & Basil Soup, 600g, £1.18
Beats the brand on price. Different, but the taste on the spoon is just as enjoyable.

(8) **SAINSBURY'S** Gluten Free Tomato & Basil Soup, 600g, £1.29   **(GF)**
Ten times the quality of Sainsbury's Dietary Special, and very comparable to the brand.

(7) **MARKS & SPENCER** Tomato & Basil Soup, 600g, £1.79   **(GF) (N/S) (V)**
Put it in the basket. Beats the brand for price and presents equal quality in taste.

(7) **WAITROSE** Tomato & Fresh Basil Soup, 600g, £1.79   **(GF) (L)**
Buy it. This tastes different, but it's of equal quality and cheaper than the brand.

NEW CONVENT GARDEN PLUM TOMATO & SWEET BASIL, 600g, £1.95
A beautifully crafted soup with pronounced tomato flavours, enhanced with basil. However be careful: the product is labelled as nut free – but nuts are used in the factory.

(5) **ASDA** Good For You Tomato & Basil Soup, 500g, 98p (£1.18 for 600g)
A healthier option, but a step down in taste quality when compared to the brand.

(3) **CO-OP** Tomato & Basil Soup, 600g, £1.75   **(N/S)**
Don't. This tub has more salt then the RDA, and it tastes like it.

(3) **MORRISONS** Tomato & Basil Soup, 600g, £1.19
Cheaper, but too much salt, and the taste is a long way down from the brand.

(2) **ASDA** Creamy Tomato Soup, 500g, 98p (£1.18 for 600g)
Don't bother. It beats the brand for price, but delivers very poor taste quality.

(2) **TESCO** Tomato Soup, 500g, 98p (£1.18 for 600g)
Leave it on the shelf. Buy Tesco's Tomato & Basil or trade up to the brand.

(1) **SAINSBURY'S** Dietary Specials Creamy Tomato & Basil Soup, 515g, £1.79 (£2.08 for 600g)
This tastes disgusting! It is aimed at shoppers with food intolerances, yet it contains milk, celery, yeast and maize, all of which can be a problem.

New Covent Garden Fresh Carrot & Coriander Soup

Celery, Maize, Lactose, Salt, Sugar, Yeast

NEW COVENT GARDEN FRESH CARROT & CORIANDER SOUP, 600g, £1.95

This is so nice you could easily finish a whole carton yourself. But beware! If you do, you'll have consumed your entire recommended daily intake of salt.

---

(5) **SAINSBURY'S** Carrot & Coriander, 600g, £1.29 **(GF)**
Buy it. Very good quality and it beats the brand on price, though not on taste.

---

(5) **WAITROSE** Carrot & Fresh Coriander, 600g, £1.69 **(GF)**
Good quality, but next to the brand it is a good notch down in quality.

---

(4) **CO-OP** Carrot & Coriander Soup, 600g, £1.75 **(N/S)**
Less salt, but that's it. The brand tastes better and is the one to buy.

---

(2) **MARKS & SPENCER** Carrot & Coriander Soup, 600g, £1.79 **(N/S)**
Very disappointing indeed. It's cheaper and looks similar, but tastes seriously second rate.

---

(2) **MORRISONS** Carrot & Coriander Soup, 600g £1.19
Don't. The taste is poor. And why is there concentrated orange juice in it?

Bells Steak & Gravy Pies

Egg, Emulsifiers, Fat, Lactose, Salt, Soya, Sugar, Sulphites (E221–E228), Yeast

(8) **TESCO** Shortcrust Pastry Steak Pie, 250g, £1.28 (£1.03 for 200g) **(N/S)**
Different pastry, but it's cheaper and it presents a similar quality to the brand.

(8) **SAINSBURY'S** Shortcrust Pastry Steak Pie, 250g, £1.39 (£1.11 for 200g)
A beat-the-brand buy for the Sainsbury's shopper. It's bigger, tastes as good as the brand and is cheaper.

(7) **CO-OP** Shortcrust Pastry Steak Pie, 520g, £3.25 (£1.25 for 200g) **(L) (N/S)**
This is too big for one person. However, it's better tasting and, like for like, it's cheaper.

(7) **SOMERFIELD** Puff Pastry Deep Fill Steak Pie, 210g, £1.59 (£1.52 for 200g) **(N/S)**
The meat and pastry are of comparable quality and, like for like, it is cheaper.

(6) **MARKS & SPENCER** Shortcrust Pastry Steak Pie, 250g, £1.99 (£1.59 for 200g)
Much better quality and, gram for gram, it works out at only a few pennies more.

BELLS 2 STEAK AND GRAVY PIES, 200g, £1.53

The pies cook well and taste good. The base pastry is crisp and the top is flaky. The sugar, salt and saturated fat levels for one 100g pie are not high, but nor are they particularly low.

(4) **ASDA** Shortcrust Pastry Steak Pie, 200g, £1.02 **(N/S)**
Just one 200g pie instead of two 100g pies, and a notch down in taste quality.

Ginsters Cornish Pasties

Celery, Egg, Emulsifiers, Fibre, Fat, Lactose, Mustard, Salt, Soya, Sugar, Sulphites (E221–E228), Yeast

(6) **WAITROSE** Hand Crimped Cornish Shortcrust Pasty, **(L)**
200g, £1.55 (£1.16p for 150g)
Buy it. Gram for gram, it's more expensive, but it beats the brand for taste.

GINSTERS 2 CORNISH PASTIES, 454g, £2.09 (70p for 150g)
Just what you expect from a Cornish pasty: a mix of beef, potatoes, swede and seasoning wrapped in puff pastry. Saturated fats are very high – this is not a dieter's snack!

(5) **MORRISONS** 4 Cornish Pasties, 600g, £1.59 (40p for 150g)
Better than Sainsbury's, but it comes second to the brand on all taste fronts.

(5) **ASDA** Cornish Pasty, 150g, 47p **(N/S)**
The brand beats this. However, if just one pasty is required, then it's worth buying.

(5) **TESCO** Cornish Pasty, 150g, 47p
Similar to Asda's and, likewise, it is a notch down on the brand's quality and seasoning.

(5) **SOMERFIELD** Cornish Pasty, 150g, 69p **(N/S)**
Worth a punt if you want just one pasty, however the quality is a small step down.

(4) **ASDA** Smartprice Cornish Pasty, 160g, 27p (25p for 150g) **(N/S)**
Compared to the brand, it's two notches down in quality, but it's still great value.

(4) **SAINSBURY'S** Basics Cornish Pasty, 150g, 27p
Not as good as the brand, but it delivers plenty of pasty for your money.

(4) **SAINSBURY'S** 4 Cornish Pasties 600g, £1.91 (48p for 150g)
Buy the brand. You'll get two less pasties and fewer grams, but it'll taste better.

(2) **ALDI** Crestwood 3 Corned Beef Pasties, 450g, 99p (33p for 150g)
Leave it on the shelf. Asda's Smartprice tastes better and is cheaper.

Pork Farms Pork Pie

Celery, Egg, Fat, Fibre, Lactose, Monosodium glutamate (MSG), Mustard, Salt, Soya, Sugar, Sulphites (E221–E228), Yeast

(8) **ASDA** Melton Mowbray Small Pork Pie, 140g, 68p **(N/S)**
Put it in your trolley. It tastes much better and is cheaper than the brand.

(8) **MORRISONS** Melton Mowbray Pork Pie, 300g, £1.49 (71p for 142g)
A big, moist and moreish pork pie that beats the brand for flavour and price.

(8) **TESCO** Melton Mowbray Pork Pie, 140g, 72p **(N/S)**
Buy it. The filling and pastry taste at least as good and it costs less.

(8) **SAINSBURY'S** Melton Mowbray Pork Pie, 140g, 76p
Put it in the trolley – it won't disappoint. Sainsbury's pie tastes better and is cheaper.

(8) **SOMERFIELD** Melton Mowbray Pork Pie, 300g £1.59 (76p for 142g)
This beats the brand for price and taste. And you get better value from bigger pies.

(7) **WAITROSE** Melton Mowbray Pork Pie, 140g, 89p **(L) (N/S)**
Beats the brand for taste. Little difference in the price, but a more enjoyable flavour.

(6) **MARKS & SPENCER** Pork Pie,150g, 99p (94p for 142g)
Better than the brand. A few pence more, but it delivers a more flavoursome mouthful.

(6) **CO-OP** Melton Mowbray Pork Pie, 135g, 99p (£1.04p for 142g) **(L) (N/S)**
More expensive, but the pastry bite and the pork taste is better than the brand.

PORK FARMS PORK PIE, 142g, 90p
An enjoyable and easy-eating pork pie. However, if you're weight-watching, there is nearly 40g of fat in this two mouthful pie!

(5) **ALDI** Crestwood 4 Melton Mowbray Pork Pies, 200g, 89p (63p for 142g)
Worth a punt! Cheaper and a similar style, but they don't match the brand for taste.

(5) **KWIK SAVE** 6 Mini Melton Pork Pies, 300g, £1.49 (71p for 142g) **(N/S)**
Side by side, the brand just edges it on the filling and pastry flavour.

Pork Farms Sausage Rolls

Celery, Egg, Fat, Fibre, Lactose, Mustard, Monosodium glutamate (MSG), Salt, Soya, Sugar, Sulphites (E221–E228), Yeast

PORK FARMS 6 SAUSAGE ROLLS, 450g, £1.54

Spicily seasoned sausage surrounded by pastry. Not a dieter's snack though – the fat content for one sausage roll is 17.9g. The RDA is 70g for women and 95g for men.

(5) **ASDA** 6 Sausage Rolls, 400g, £1.28 (£1.44 for 450g) **(N/S)**
Still worth a punt! Cheaper, but the brand has better tasting pastry and sausage.

(5) **KWIK SAVE** 6 Sausage Rolls, 420g, £1.39 (£1.49 for 450g) **(N/S)**
Cheaper alternative! The brand just edges it on the pastry and the sausage quality.

(5) **MORRISONS** 6 Pork Sausage Rolls, 420g, £1.39 (£1.49p for 450g)
This is a notch down from the brand. Moreover, the sausage is not as tasty.

(5) **SOMERFIELD** 2 Sausage Rolls, 145g, 69p (£2.15 for 450g) **(N/S)**
Buy the brand if you want six. The sausage rolls are tastier and cheaper.

(5) **MARKS SPENCER** 6 Mini Sausage Rolls, 200g, £1.29 (£2.91 for 450g)
Too expensive! No better tasting than the brand and, gram for gram, almost double the price.

(4) **TESCO** 2 Sausage Rolls, 134g, 50p (£1.68 for 450g) **(N/S)**
This works out more expensive than the brand and doesn't taste as good.

(4) **SAINSBURY'S** 2 Sausage Rolls, 132g, 55p (£1.88 for 450g)
Sainsbury's works out more expensive and a step down in quality from the brand.

(4) **ALDI** 5 Crestwood Sausage Rolls, 350g, 99p (£1.27 for 450g)
Although cheaper, here there is a big step down in quality when compared to the brand.

Fiorucci Parma Ham

Fat, Salt

---

(6) **WAITROSE** Riserva Parma Ham, 80g, £3.49   **(GF) (L) (N/S)**
Buy it. Eighteen months of ageing has produced an extra layer of flavour over the brand.

FIORUCCI PARMA HAM, 80g, £3.15
Very tasty – it's not difficult to eat up to 80g of this finely sliced Parma Ham. It's worth
noting then that it does contain very high levels of saturated fat and salt.

---

(5) **ASDA** Deli Parma Ham, 80g, £1.34
Flavour-wise this is a slice away from the brand, but it's well under half the price.

---

(5) **ALDI** Deli Continental Original Italian Ham, 100g, £1.39 (£1.12 for 80g)   **(L)**
A much cheaper alternative to the brand! However, it's a step down in taste quality.

---

(5) **TESCO** Finest Parma Ham, 85g, £1.99 (£1.88 for 80g)
Beats the brand on price, but does not reward the palate with as much flavour
as the brand.

---

(5) **ASDA** Extra Special Parma Ham, 60g, £1.68 (£2.24 for 80g)   **(GF)**
An alternative. This beats the brand for price and is nearly there on flavour quality.

---

(5) **MARKS & SPENCER** Parma Ham, 85g, £2.99 (£2.82 for 80g)   **(GF) (N/S)**
A cheaper alternative, but the brand just edges it as a palate-pleaser.

---

(5) **SAINSBURY'S** Taste the Difference Parma Ham, 85g, £2.99 (£2.82 for 80g)
Beats the brand for price. But even though it looks the same, it comes second taste-wise.

---

(5) **SOMERFIELD** Parma Ham, 80g, £2.99
An alternative to the brand but, slice for slice, this is a small step down on flavour.

Bernard Matthews
Wafer Thin Cooked Ham

Salt

---

(10) **ALDI** Courtway Wafer Thin Cooked Ham, 400g, £1.69 (43p for 100g) **(L)**
Aldi's beat-the-brand buy. Under half price and much better tasting than the
Bernard Matthews.

---

(10) **MORRISONS** Wafer Thin Cooked Ham, 400g, £1.89 (48p for 100g) **(GF)**
Grab a pack. This equals the brand on all flavour fronts and is less than half the price.

---

(9) **ASDA** Wafer Thin Cooked Ham, 200g, £1.04 (52p for 100g) **(GF) (N/S)**
Put a pack in the trolley. This beats the brand on taste and price.

---

(9) **TESCO** Honey Roast Wafer Thin Ham, 200g, £1.04 (52p for 100g)
If you're looking for wafer thin ham with an extra layer of flavour, then buy this.

---

(9) **TESCO** Wafer Thin Cooked Ham, 200g, £1.04 (52p for 100g) **(N/S)**
Leave the brand on the shelf, and buy this: it's cheaper and tastes just as good.

---

(9) **CO-OP** Wafer Thin Cooked Ham, 400g, £2.29 (58p for 100g) **(GF) (L) (N/S)**
Grab a pack. This tastes as good as the brand and, gram for gram, it's much cheaper.

---

(9) **ASDA** Honey Roast Thin Sliced Ham, 125g, 74p (60p for 100g) **(GF) (N/S)**
Slightly thicker than wafer thin, but better tasting and it's nearly half the brand's price.

---

(8) **CO-OP** Honey Roast Ham Wafer Thin, 200g, £1.49 (75p for 100g) **(GF) (L) (N/S)**
Like for like, this beats the brand on price and it has more "wafer thin" flavour.

BERNARD MATTHEWS WAFER THIN COOKED HAM, 100g, 99p
This wafer thin ham lacks the flavour of thicker cuts and requires the added flavour of a
loaded sandwich to be eaten with relish. The salt content is high.

Mattessons Baked Ham

Salt

---

(7) **KWIK SAVE** Gammon Ham, 125g, £1.29 **(L)**
Buy it. This beats the brand for the price and equals it on taste.

---

(6) **SAINSBURY'S** Taste the Difference Dry Cured Ham, 160g, £2.49 (£1.95 for 125g)
More money, but double the taste pleasure! Try the deli if you want it cheaper.

---

(6) **MARKS & SPENCER** Danish Roast Ham, 120g, £2.29 (£2.39 for 125g) **(GF) (N/S)**
Well worth the extra quid. Compared to the brand this has much more flavour.

MATTESSONS BAKED HAM, 125g, £1.38
This does not have the depth of flavour of the ham on the bone, but it's better than the
Bernard Matthews wafer thin ham. Beware: both the salt and saturated fat content is high.

---

(5) **MORRISONS** Carvery Dry Cured Ham, 150g, £1.69 (£1.41 for 125g)
Buy the brand or try the deli counter. This tastes no better, but it's more expensive.

---

(5) **SOMERFIELD** So Good Dry Cured Gammon Ham, 160g, £2.49 (£1.95 for 125g)
Not a big step up in quality from the brand, and there should be at this high price.

---

(5) **CO-OP** Mild Cured Ham, 125g, £2.05 **(GF) (L) (N/S)**
Like Somerfield's, this is only slightly better than the brand and not worth the extra cash.

Bernard Matthews Wafer Thin Turkey Ham

Salt

---

(7) **TESCO** Value Wafer Thin Turkey Ham, 200g, 99p (85p for 170g)
Pick it up. Slightly thicker turkey slices, but it's cheaper and of comparable taste.

BERNARD MATTHEWS WAFER THIN TURKEY HAM, 170g, 97p
Certainly better tasting and better value than Bernard Matthews' Wafer Thin Ham. However,
this pack contains over 4g of salt – and that's very high.

---

(3) **KWIK SAVE** Wafer Thin Turkey, 200g, £1.29 (£1.10 for 170g) **(L)**
Leave it. Gram for gram this is more expensive and not as tasty as the brand.

Bernard Matthews Honey Roast Ham

Emulsifiers, Lactose, Salt, Yeast extract

---

(8) **ALDI** Courtway Honey Roast Ham, 113g, 79p (£1.40 for 200g) **(GF) (L)**
The taste is not great, but it's as good as the brand and a lot cheaper.

(6) **TESCO** Healthy Living Honey Roast Ham, 100g, £1.04 (£2.08 for 200g) **(N/S)**
It's worth the extra few pennies. Less fat, less salt and better tasting than the brand.

(6) **MORRISONS** Dry Cured Honey Roasted Ham, 150g, £1.69 (£2.26 for 200g) **(GF)**
Buy it. A bit more cash, but you do get the taste of ham with a honey twist.

(6) **MARKS & SPENCER** Honey Roast Lean Ham, 113g, £1.29 (£2.29 for 200g) **(GF)**
It costs more than the brand, but the flavour is at least double the quality.

(6) **ASDA** Extra Special Honey Roast Wiltshire Ham, **(GF)**
144g, £2.56 (£3.56 for 200g)
Buy it – it's worth it. Yes, it is more expensive, but it's several leagues above the brand taste-wise.

(6) **SAINSBURY'S** Taste the Difference Honey Roast Ham Slices, **(GF)**
270g, £3.59 (£2.66 for 200g)
This beats the brand for taste, but it is a couple of slices more expensive.

(6) **WAITROSE** British Honey Roast Ham, **(GF) (L) (N/S)**
170g, £2.49 (£2.93 for 200g)
Much better tasting than the brand, and even at this higher price it's a better buy.

(6) **SOMERFIELD** So Good Dry Cured Honey Roast Ham, **(N/S)**
160g, £2.49 (£3.12 for 200g)
Not as good as Somerfield's Wiltshire ham but, next to the brand, it's several steps up.

(6) **SOMERFIELD** So Good Honey Roast Wiltshire Ham,
140g, £2.59 (£3.70 for 200g)
This is almost double the price of the brand, but it is well worth it.

BERNARD MATTHEWS HONEY ROAST HAM, 200g, £1.99
Lacks the flavour of ham on the bone, but has more than Bernard Matthews' wafer thin ham.
This honey roast ham does contain a lot of salt however.

Mattessons Roast Chicken

Salt

---

(8) **KWIK SAVE** Roast Chicken Breast, 100g, 99p (£1.24 for 125g)
Pluck it from the shelf. It tastes as good as the brand and it's cheaper.

MATTESSONS ROAST CHICKEN, 125g, £1.38
Not as popular as "own label" turkey or ham on the supermarket shelves. You still need to note the amount of salt and saturated fat on the nutrition label.

---

(5) **SAINSBURY'S** Roast Chicken Breast, 100g, £1.69 (£2.12 for 125g)
This costs more, but it's only a tad better. You'll get better value at Sainsbury's deli.

Herta Beechwood Smoked Frankfurters

Fat, Salt

---

(7) **SAINSBURY'S** 10 Beechwood Smoked Frankfurters, 350g, £1.49
Put a pack in the trolley. A cheaper price and a similar taste to the brand.

HERTA 10 BEECHWOOD SMOKED FRANKFURTERS, 350g, £1.57
Popular hot dog sausages. However, the saturated fat and salt content are seriously high, so it's not food for weight watchers and healthy eaters.

---

(5) **WAITROSE** 10 Beechwood Smoked Frankfurters, 350g, £1.57 **(GF) (N/S)**
If these are cheaper than the brand in Waitrose, buy them, for they taste very similar.

---

(5) **MARKS & SPENCER** 20 Mini Pork Frankfurters, 200g, £1.09 (£1.91 for 350g)
Not as smoky or flavoursome as the brand but, as cocktail sausages, they're fine.

---

(4) **ASDA** 10 Smoked Danish Pork Hot Dogs, 350g, 98p
These are a good notch down from the brand taste-wise, but they're a lot cheaper.

Bernard Matthews
Butter Basted Turkey Breast

Lactose, Salt

---

(8) **SAINSBURY'S** Taste the Difference Butter Roast Turkey Breast, **(GF)**
150g, £1.99 (£1.60 for 120g)
Pick this up. It beats the brand for taste and, gram for gram, on price.

(6) **ASDA** Extra Special Butter Roast Turkey, 142g, £2.56 (£2. 17 for 120g) **(GF)**
This is a few pence more than the brand, but it's a big step up in taste.

(6) **MARKS & SPENCER** Butter Basted Roast Turkey Breast,
130g, £2.49 (£2.30 for 120g)
Well worth it. The taste is almost as good as a turkey straight from the oven.

(6) **WAITROSE** Free Range Butter Oil Basted Turkey Breast,
140g, £3.08 (£2.64 for 120g)
Very much better quality than the brand, and you won't mind paying the extra.

BERNARD MATTHEWS BUTTER BASTED TURKEY BREAST, 120g, £1.99
Turkey is an excellent alternative to ham. Although the salt and saturated fat content is still high, it does contain less than most hams.

---

(5) **SOMERFIELD** So Good Butter Basted Turkey Breast,
150g, £2.49 (£2.00 for 120g)
Take your pick. Price and taste-wise there's little to choose between this and the brand.

(5) **CO-OP** Premium Butter Basted British Turkey, **(N/S)**
143g, £3.27 (£2.75 for 120g)
It looks better than the brand in the pack. But in reality it's more expensive and it tastes no better.

Co-op Deli Ham on the Bone

Fat, Salt

---

(6) **ASDA** Extra Special Pre-Packed Roast Ham Carved from the Bone, **(GF) (N/S)**
Pre-Packed, £18.00/kg
This will be cheaper at Asda's deli! And it's much better tasting than the Co-op deli.

---

(6) **SAINSBURY'S** Taste the Difference Thick Cut Ham Cooked on the Bone, **(GF)**
£18.50/kg
Check the Sainsbury's deli first. Better quality and far more tasty than the Co-op deli.

---

(6) **WAITROSE** Free Range Hand Carved Baked Gammon Ham **(GF) (L) (N/S)**
Pre-Packed, £19.50/kg
The best ham tasted. However, if your Waitrose has a deli counter, check that out first.

CO-OP DELI HAM ON THE BONE, £12.90/kg (GF) (L) (N/S)
Ham cooked on the bone will generally deliver more flavour, but due to the bone wastage
it is usually more expensive. The average salt content will be around 2g per 100g.

---

(5) **MORRISONS** The Best Pre-Packed Thick Sliced baked Gammon, £16.00/kg
Try the deli counter! Dry and meaty, this competes well on the flavour front.

---

(5) **CO-OP** Premium Thick Cut Ham on the Bone Pre-Packed, £18.90/kg **(L) (N/S)**
Co-op shoppers should buy it from the deli – it's £6 cheaper and a similar quality.

---

(4) **TESCO** Finest Wiltshire Cured Ham on the Bone Pre-Packed, **(GF) (N/S)**
£19.90/kg
You'll get better value at Tesco's deli. This pack is £7 more than Co-op's deli per
kilogram, and it's no better.

---

(4) **MARKS & SPENCER** Pre-Packed Breaded Wiltshire Gammon
Matured on the Bone, £23.06/kg
Too pricey! This wafer thin ham is the most expensive – and nowhere near the best.

Asda Deli Corned Beef

Fat, Salt

---

(6) **MARKS & SPENCER** Pre-Packed Lean Corned Beef, £7.84/kg **(GF) (N/S)**
This is very much better tasting than Asda's deli corned beef, and worth the extra.

ASDA DELI CORNED BEEF, £3.20/KG (GF)

Freshly sliced from the deli counter! Corned beef works well in a sandwich or with a salad.
However, the salt and saturated fat content are both high here.

---

(5) **ASDA** Pre-Packed Corned Beef, £6.17/kg
Queue at the deli counter. Just the price separates Asda deli and Asda off-the-shelf.

(5) **TESCO** Corned Beef Pre- Packed, £6.17/kg **(GF)**
Check out Tesco's deli counter. Similar taste quality to the corned beef from Asda deli.

(5) **SAINSBURY'S** Pre-Packed Corned Beef, £6.76/kg
Check out the deli counter! Slightly better tasting than the corned beef from Asda deli.

(5) **WAITROSE** Pre-Packed Corned Beef, £7.82/kg **(GF) (L) (N/S)**
Taste-wise it's a tad better quality, but it's certainly not over £4 per kilogram better.

(4) **ALDI** Hydale Corned Beef, £1.70/kg **(L)**
Seriously cheap, but it's big step down when you compare it to Asda's deli corned beef.

(4) **MORRISONS** Pre-Packed Corned Beef, £5.52/kg
It will be cheaper at Morrisons deli, but this is not as tasty as Asda's deli corned beef.

(4) **CO-OP** Corned Beef Pre-Packed, £8.29/kg **(L) (N/S)**
Co-op shoppers should try the deli. This costs £5 more – and not as good.

(2) **CO-OP** Everyday Pre-Packed Corned Beef, £3.56/kg **(GF) (N/S)**
Don't. This is very poor quality, and it's more money than Asda deli corned beef.

Asda's Deli Pastrami

Salt

ASDA'S DELI PASTRAMI, £9.40/kg
Meats from the deli counter are generally fresher, tastier and cheaper than ones from the aisle shelves. However, the salt content will still be high.

---

(5) **ALDI** Courtway Premium Pre-Packed Carvery Pastrami, £11.58/kg **(GF) (L)**
An alternative if there's no deli counter, but it's more expensive and no better quality.

---

(5) **ASDA** Pre-Packed Pastrami, £11.84/kg
Buy it from the deli counter where it's cheaper with a similar taste quality.

---

(5) **CO-OP** Continental Selection Pre-Packed Pastrami, £14.90/kg **(L) (N/S)**
The taste is a tad better quality than Asda's deli pastrami, but not this much more.

---

(5) **SAINSBURY'S** Taste the Difference Pre-Packed Pastrami, £18.25/kg **(GF)**
Try the deli counter. A very high price and only a small step up in quality.

---

(4) **TESCO** American Pastrami, £12. 29/kg
This is not as tasty as Asda's deli pastrami, and it's a lot more cash.

---

(4) **MORRISONS** American Style Pre-Packed Pastrami, £13.90/kg **(GF)**
Try another shop. This does not beat the Asda' deli pastrami for taste or price.

---

(4) **MARKS & SPENCER** Wafer Thin Pre-Packed Pastrami, £27. 87/kg **(GF) (N/S)**
Don't buy! It's three times the price, yet only a touch better in quality than Asda's deli pastrami.

Sainsbury's Deli Brussels Pâté

Egg, Emulsifiers, Fat, Lactose, Salt

SAINSBURY'S DELI BRUSSELS PÂTÉ, 175g, £1.14 (GF)

Brussels is a smooth pork and liver pâté. Health and weight watchers should be aware that all pâté is high in salt and saturated fat.

(5) **TESCO** Value Pre-Packed Pork & Liver Pâté, 300g, 82p (48p for 175g)
Good value! This pâté is from France rather than Brussels and is a cheaper alternative.

(5) **ASDA** Pre-Packed Smooth Brussels Pâté, 175g, 68p (GF) (N/S)
A cheaper alternative to the Sainsbury's deli pâté, but it's a small step down taste-wise.

(5) **KWIK SAVE** Pre-Packed Brussels Pâté, 175g, 75p
Beats the Sainsbury's deli pâté for price, but it's edged into second place on taste.

(5) **MORRISONS** Pre-Packed Brussels Pâté, 175g, 75p
Next to Sainsbury's deli pâté it doesn't taste as good, but it's still good value.

(5) **TESCO** Pre-Packed Brussels Pâté with Herbs, 170g, 98p (£1.01 for 175g)
The herbs present an extra flavour here, but it still does not beat the deli pâté.

(5) **MARKS & SPENCER** Pre-Packed Brussels Pâté, 170g, 99p (£1.02 for 175g)
M & S beats the deli pâté on price, but not on flavour.

(4) **ASDA** Smart Price Pre-Packed Smooth Brussels Pâté, 175g, 49p
Cheap and on a loaded sandwich – maybe! But if taste matters, try another shop.

(4) **ALDI** Courtway Pre-Packed Deli Brussels Pâté, 175g, 59p (L)
Nearly half price – but not as tasty or as palate-pleasing as the brand.

(4) **CO-OP** Half-Fat Pre-Packed Brussels Pâté, 175g, £1.79 (GF) (L) (N/S)
Expensive and still not as good as the deli pâté. The fat content is high too.

8
Sauces, Salad Dressings, Pickles & Olive Oil

Supermarkets know all about optical illusions, so don't be fooled by the long thin bottle standing next to the little dumpy one. Check and compare the gram weights or millilitre volumes. To make a true value for money calculation you really need to know the specific gravity of the product and therefore you need a calculator and... well, forget it! The point is it shouldn't be this difficult. Shoppers are entitled to labelling that is both simple and quickly and truthfully informative. Anyway, to help in making your choices, I've calculated the equivalent volume or weight for beat-the-brand shoppers.

Just a couple of gherkins, a pickled onion or two, a spoonful of pickle, dollop of mayonnaise, a dash of French dressing and "hey presto", your healthy salad suddenly contains half your recommended daily intake of salt, sugar and fat. And if you're calorie counting, even the reduced-fat versions of salad cream and mayonnaise are high in sugar, salt and fat. The pickles you savour rarely taste salty but they do actually have high levels of salt, just as the sweet versions have high levels of sugar. As an example, a small jar (310g) of Branston Pickle contains double the advised daily intake of salt. So if you care: check the label.

Heinz Tomato Ketchup

Maize, Salt, Sugar, Thickeners

---

(9) **ALDI** Colway Squeezy Tomato Ketchup, 750g, 69p (31p for 342g) **(L)**
Buy it. A similar quality to the brand and, gram for gram, it's almost half the price.

---

(9) **ASDA** Tomato Ketchup, 340g, 38p **(N/S) (V)**
This contains 60g more tomatoes than the brand, and it shows in the taste.

---

(9) **TESCO** Tomato Ketchup, 340g, 38p **(GF) (N/S)**
An excellent purchase. Cheaper, and it offers a similar sweet-and-sour taste to the brand.

---

(9) **CO-OP** Tomato Ketchup, 550g , 69p (43p for 342g) **(GF) (L) (N/S) (V)**
This is no less quality. However, the taste is sweeter and more redolent of tomatoes.

---

(8) **SAINSBURY'S** Squeezy Tomato Ketchup, 500g, 80p (55p for 342g) **(L)**
Buy it. Sweeter tasting, although the sugar levels are no higher than the brand's.

---

(7) **MORRISONS** Squeezy Tomato Ketchup, 445g, 79p (61p for 342g)
Put it in the trolley. Darker in colour and spicier, with more tomatoes in the ketchup.

---

(6) **MARKS & SPENCER** Tomato Ketchup, 300g, 79p (90p for 342g) **(GF) (N/S) (V)**
It's worth it. A quality ketchup that beats the brand for taste, but not for price.

HEINZ TOMATO KETCHUP, 342g, 64p
A brand by which all other ketchups are judged! Don't shake too much on your plate,
for this bottle contains over 60g of sugar and 9g of salt. This is more than your
recommended daily intake for both.

---

(5) **KWIK SAVE** Squeezy Tomato Ketchup, 500g, 68p (47p for 342g)
Gram for gram it's cheaper, but side by side, the brand just beats it in taste.

---

(4) **ASDA** SmartPrice Squeezy Tomato Ketchup, 483g, 41p (30p for 342g) **(N/S)**
Buy Asda's regular ketchup. A keen price, but it contains less tomatoes and has
a spiky taste.

---

(2) **TESCO** Value Tomato Ketchup, 570g, 34p (21p for 342g) **(GF) (V)**
Don't. It has an odd flavour that makes it difficult to swallow, even at this price.

HP Brown Sauce

Maize, Salt, Soya, Sugar, Thickeners

(7) MORRISONS Squeezy Brown Sauce, 440g, 79p (82p for 454g)
Put it in the trolley. This mirrors the tastes of the brand and it's cheaper.

HP BROWN SAUCE, 454g, 95p

Brown sauce with a moreish tangy taste. You'll need to check a supermarket's website to see that this bottle contains 13g of salt (it is recommended that you have no more than 6g daily).

(5) ASDA Brown Sauce, 340g, 42p (56p for 454g)   **(N/S) (V)**
At this price it's well worth a punt, but the brand beats it for taste.

(5) SAINSBURY'S Squeezy Brown Sauce, 500g, 89p (81p for 454g)   **(L)**
A different taste to the brand, but it's cheaper and just a shake away in quality.

(5) MARKS & SPENCER Brown Sauce, 300g, 79p (£1.20 for 454g)   **(N/S) (V)**
As good as the brand, but not better, and gram for gram it costs more.

(4) ASDA SmartPrice Brown Sauce, 535g, 23p (20p for 454g)
Cheap and passable, but not in the same league as the brand taste-wise.

(3) TESCO Brown Sauce, 340g, 67p (89p for 454g)   **(N/S) (V)**
This sauce is two notches down in taste and not that much cheaper. Buy the brand.

(3) KWIK SAVE Brown Sauce, 340g, 75p (£1.00 for 454g)
Buy the brand – it's at least double the taste quality for a similar price.

(2) ALDI Colway Squeezy Brown Sauce, 710g, 75p (48p for 454g)   **(V)**
Don't bother. The taste is so poor it will ruin, rather than complement, your food.

Colman's Horseradish Sauce

Egg, Gums, Milk, Mustard, Salt, Sugar, Sulphites (E221–E228), Thickeners

COLMAN'S HORSERADISH SAUCE, 250ml or 260g, 78p

It's very difficult for shoppers to compare prices when the brand is in millilitres and the "own label" in grams. But don't worry, I've done the calculations.

---

(5) **MORRISONS** Creamed Horseradish Sauce, 210g, 65p (81p for 260g)
More expensive and without the kick of the brand, but it's a less fiery alternative.

---

(5) **SAINSBURY'S** Horseradish Sauce, 185g, 67p (95p for 260g)   **(GF) (L)**
Looks cheaper, but when you do the calculations the brand beats it on price – and taste.

---

(5) **CO-OP** Hot Horseradish Sauce, 185g, 71p (£1.00 for 260g)   **(L) (N/S)**
Buy the brand. This almost matches the brand's flavour but, like for like, it costs a lot more.

---

(5) **TESCO** Finest Horseradish Sauce, 165g, £1.29 (£2.04 for 260g)   **(GF) (V)**
This is more subtle and a tad better in quality than the brand; but not £1.26 better.

---

(4) **KWIK SAVE** Horseradish Sauce, 185g, 55p (78p for 260g)
This milder horseradish does not beat the brand for taste, but the per gram price
is comparable.

---

(4) **SOMERFIELD** Horseradish Sauce, 185g, 69p (97p for 260g)   **(GF)**
Buy Colman's. This is not as hot, as tasty, or as cheap as the brand.

---

(4) **ASDA** Extra Special Horseradish Sauce, 190g, £1.18 (£1.62 for 260g)   **(N/S)**
Buy Colman's. An "extra special" hike in price for a horseradish sauce that's not as good.

---

(3) **ALDI** Bramwells Horseradish Sauce, 170g, 59p (91p for 260g)   **(GF)**
Buy your horseradish from somewhere else. This does not beat the brand on any front.

Colman's Tartare Sauce

Egg, Gums, Maize, Milk, Mustard, Salt, Sugar, Thickeners, Yeast

(6) **MORRISONS** Tartare Sauce, 205g, 72p (88p for 250g)
Buy it. This tastes much better than the brand and is well worth the extra premium.

(4) **KWIK SAVE** Tartare Sauce, 180g, 59p (82p for 250g)
Buy the brand. Like for like, this does not beat it for taste or price.

COLMAN'S TARTARE SAUCE, 250g or 250ml, 78p
Dieters should be aware that tartare sauce has high levels of salt, sugar and fat. It's not labelled so, but this 250ml sauce calculates out to 250g.

(3) **TESCO** Finest Tartare Sauce, 160g, £1.29 (£2.02 for 250g)   **(GF)**
Don't waste your hard-earned cash. Not as good as the brand in any way.

(2) **SAINSBURY'S** Tartare Sauce, 250g or 250ml, 89p   **(GF) (L)**
Don't! Even if the brand doubled in price it would still be a better buy than this.

(1) **ALDI** Bramwells Tartare Sauce, 165g, 59p (90p for 250g)   **(GF)**
Forget it – 10p would be too much to pay for this. A very poor example of tartare sauce.

Wilkin & Sons Redcurrant Jelly

Sugar

WILKIN & SONS REDCURRANT JELLY, 340g, £1.59   **(V)**
This sweet redcurrant jelly complements both cold and hot meats. But note that this jar contains 227g of sugar and it is recommended that you consume no more than 60g daily.

(5) **TESCO** Redcurrant Jelly, 340g, £1.00   **(GF)**
The most expensive and best tasting "own label", but it still comes second to the brand.

(4) **SOMERFIELD** Redcurrant Jelly, 340g, 54p
Worth a punt. Not as good as the brand, but it is much, much cheaper.

(4) **SAINSBURY'S** Redcurrant Jelly, 227g, 54p (81p for 340g)   **(L)**
A cheaper alternative to the brand. However, it's a big step down on the taste front.

(4) **MORRISON** Redcurrant Jelly, 260g, 69p (90p for 340g)
Cheaper, but the redcurrant flavours are a couple of notches down from the brand.

(2) **ASDA** Redcurrant Jelly, 227g, 67p (£1.00 for 340g)
Leave it, or try another shop. This tastes more like wine gums than redcurrants.

Colman's Bramley Apple Sauce

Maize, Salt, Sugar, Sulphur dioxide

(7) **ASDA** Bramley Apple Sauce, 280g, 63p (62p for 275g)   **(GF) (V)**
Buy it. Similar flavour and quality, though the apples are more crunchy than the brand's.

(7) **MORRISONS** Bramley Apple Sauce, 280g, 72p (71p for 275g)
Tastes better than the brand, but there were unwelcome bits of apple core in this jar.

(6) **SOMERFIELD** Bramley Apple Sauce, 280g, 79p (78p for 275g)
Buy it; it will not disappoint! A few pence more, but tatses much better than the brand.

(6) **CO-OP** Bramley Apple Sauce, 270g, 83p (86p for 275g)   **(GF) (L) (N/S) (V)**
A tad more expensive, but for many that extra sharpness will be worth the extra cost.

COLMAN'S BRAMLEY APPLE SAUCE, 250ml or 275g, 78P
Apple sauce is popular as an accompaniment to pork and goose. Dieters, note that this jar contains more than the 60g of sugar – which is the total recommended daily intake.

(5) **TESCO** Smooth Bramley Apple Sauce, 280g,   **(GF) (N/S) (V)**
£1.04 (£1.02 for 275g)
More expensive, no smoother and still with unwanted chewy core bits. Buy the brand.

(4) **SAINSBURY'S** Bramley Apple Sauce, 280g, 75p (73p for 275g)   **(GF) (L)**
Put the brand in your trolley. This is a chunky style that does not compare taste-wise.

(3) **KWIK SAVE** Bramley Apple Sauce, 270g, 71p (73p for 275g)
Buy the brand. Little saving and it does not get close to Colman's for taste.

(1) **ALDI** Bramwells Apple Sauce, 270g, 55p (56p for 275g)   **(GF) (L) (V)**
It's cheaper, but it tastes artificial and would spoil the food rather than complement it.

Colman's Mint Sauce

Colours, Gums, Salt, Sugar

COLMAN'S MINT SAUCE, 250g or 250ml, 78p

A mint sauce that delivers a blast of vinegar and mint. However, these two powerful favours mask the jar's high sugar (61.25g) and salt content (6.25g).

---

(4) **MORRISONS** Garden Mint Sauce, 205g, 72p (88p for 250g)
Buy Colman's. Gram for gram, the brand beats it both on price and taste.

---

(4) **SAINSBURY'S** Fresh Mint Sauce, 195g, 78p (£1.00 for 250g)   **(L)**
No better than Morrisons and, likewise, the brand beats it on taste and price front.

---

(4) **TESCO** Finest Mint Sauce with Balsamic Vinegar, 185g, £1.29 (£1.75 for 250g)
Phew! This is over double the price of the brand, and it's no better quality.

---

(4) **CO-OP** English Mint Sauce, 185g, 71p (96p for 250g)   **(GF) (L) (N/S) (V)**
Side by side and gram for gram, the brand is much better tasting and cheaper.

---

(2) **ASDA** Smartprice Mint Sauce, 165g, 17p (26p for 250g)   **(GF) N/S) (V)**
Buy the brand. This tastes better than Asda's regular, but not by much.

---

(1) **ALDI** Bramwells Mint Sauce, 280g, 45p (41p for 250g)   **(GF) (L)**
Don't even think about it. This is dreadful – if you've already bought a jar, take it back.

---

(1) **ASDA** Mint Sauce, 280g, 49p (44p for 250g)   **(GF) (V)**
This is as bad as Aldi's above. Just what was the buyer thinking of?

Colman's English Mustard

Colours, Fat, Salt, Sulphites (E221–E228), Thickeners, Wheat, Yeast

(8) **KWIK SAVE** English Mustard, 100g, 36p
Put it in the trolley. Cheaper, and the colour and taste are similar to the brand.

(8) **TESCO** English Mustard, 100g, 36p **(V)**
Great value for money. Slightly thinner consistency, but it delivers a similar taste quality.

(7) **WAITROSE** English Mustard, 180g, 79p (44p for 100g) **(GF) (L) (N/S) (V)**
Buy it. Waitrose's excellent ready-made tastes similar to Colman's powdered mustard!

(7) **MARKS & SPENCER** Hot English Mustard, **(GF) (N/S) (V)**
205g, 99p (49p for 100g)
Buy it if you like it hot. Similar quality, but more fiery than the brand.

COLMAN'S ENGLISH MUSTARD, 100g, 58p
Although not as fiery as Colman's powdered mustard, this ready-made is still hot, so you don't need too much of it. Remember, the profits are built on what's left on the plate!

(5) **SAINSBURY'S** English Mustard, 100g, 39p **(L)**
An alternative. Similar colour, though the flavour mix is not as good as the brand.

(5) **SOMERFIELD** English Mustard, 100g, 39p
Similar to Sainsbury's in taste and price, and likewise comes second to the brand.

(4) **ASDA** English Mustard, 100g, 36p
A lot cheaper, but the brand beats this for taste by at least a notch.

(4) **CO-OP** English Mustard, 180g, 76p (43p for 100g) **(L) (N/S) (V)**
This is much cheaper than the brand, but the mustard is spoilt by a floury flavour.

(2) **ALDI** Bramwells Hot English Mustard, 185g, 49p (26p for 100g) **(L) (V)**
Don't waste your money. The taste and mouthfeel of this mustard is very poor.

Bovril

Celery, Maize, Salt, Sugar, Yeast extract

(8) **TESCO** Beefy, 240g, £1.68
This contains beef stock. Provided you're not a vegetarian or vegan, this is the better buy.

(7) **CO-OP** Beefy, 240g, £2.19 **(GF) (L) (N/S)**
Not an alternative if you're a vegetarian. Cheaper and it tastes as good as the brand.

BOVRIL, 250g, £2.57 (£2.47 for 240g)
Bovril is mainly used for hot drinks and stocks. Rich in yeast and vitamins, it is a useful jar
to have in the cupboard. The brand jar is 10g heavier than the similar size "own labels".

Marmite

Celery, Maize, Salt, Sugar, Yeast extract

(8) **ASDA** Yeast Extract, 240g, £1.68 **(GF) (N/S) (V)**
Buy it. Beats the brand for price, and equals it in taste on all fronts.

(8) **TESCO** Yeast Extract, 240g, £1.68
A great purchase for the Tesco shopper: it looks and tastes the same as the brand,
and is cheaper.

(8) **MORRISONS** Yeast Extract, 240g, £1.69
Put it in the trolley. Cheaper and very similar to the brand in taste quality.

MARMITE, 250g, £1.98 (£1.90 for 240g)
Marmite has similar ingredients to Bovril, but it is less runny and is used mainly as
a spread. Suitable for most vegetarians. As with Bovril, the brand jar is 10g heavier
than the similar size "own labels".

(4) **CO-OP** Yeast Extract, 240g, £2.09 **(GF) (L) (N/S) (V)**
Leave it on the shelf. It does not beat the brand in taste or price.

Heinz Salad Cream

Colours, Egg, Fat, Mustard, Salt, Stabilisers, Sugar, Thickeners

(10) **ASDA** Salad Cream, 285g, 33p **(GF)**
Buy it. It's well under half the price and delivers a similar creamy texture and quality to the brand.

(10) **MORRISONS** Salad Cream, 285g, 33p
Next to the brand it's lighter in colour, but it tastes similar.

(10) **TESCO** Salad Cream, 285g, 33p **(GF)**
Buy it. This equals the brand on quality and beats it on price.

(10) **KWIK SAVE** Salad Cream, 260g, 35p (39p for 285g)
Kwik Save beats the brand with a bargain price and a competitively good taste.

(9) **ALDI** Colway Squeezy Salad Cream, 465g, 69p (43p for 285g) **(L)**
Buy it. Although yellower in colour, it is of a similar quality and nearly half the price of the brand.

(9) **SAINSBURY'S** Squeezy Salad Cream, 460g, 74p (46p for 285g) **(L)**
A beat-the-brand buy. Slightly thicker consistency, but similar taste and nearly half price.

(8) **SOMERFIELD** Salad Cream, 270g, 55p (58p for 285g)
This is a good buy, beating the brand on price and equalling it on taste.

HEINZ SALAD CREAM, 285g, 85p
A flavoursome dressing delivering a cleansing vinegar bite that is popular with salads. However, consumers should be aware that the sugar, salt and fat levels are very high.

(4) **CO-OP** Salad Cream, 283g, 55p **(GF) (N/S)**
Leave it on the shelf. The cream flavour is fine, but the after-taste is too vinegary.

(3) **ASDA** Smartprice Salad Cream, 283g, 23p
Buy Asda's regular. This comes a very poor third when compared to the brand.

Heinz Light Salad Cream

Colours, Egg, Fat, Mustard, Salt, Stabilisers, Sugar

(10) **TESCO** Healthy Eating Salad Cream, 283g, 33p **(V)**
Put it in the trolley. It's better for you and tastes as good as the brand.

(10) **ASDA** Reduced Fat Salad Cream, 285g, 33p **(V)**
Not as creamy but much cheaper, and it tastes as good with less fat, sugar and salt.

(8) **SAINSBURY'S** Be Good to Yourself Salad Cream, 285g, 49p **(L)**
Put it in the trolley. It's cheaper, of similar quality and a healthier option than the brand.

HEINZ LIGHT SALAD CREAM, 285g, 85p
Almost as tasty as the regular Heinz salad cream. This light version does have less salt, fat and sugar, but this jar still has plenty of fat (55g), sugar (28g) and salt (9g).

(3) **MORRISONS** Better for You Salad Cream, 285g, 33p
Compared to the brand, the taste is poor. Dieters should buy Morrisons' regular and use less.

Hellmann's Real Mayonnaise

Colours, Egg, Fat, Maize, Mustard, Salt, Stabilisers, Sugar, Thickeners, Yeast

---

(8) **WAITROSE** Mayonnaise, 500ml, 82p (70p for 428ml) **(GF) (L)**
Buy it. The taste is similar to the brand and it's a whole lot cheaper.

---

(6) **MARKS & SPENCER** Mayonnaise, 230g, 99p (£1.72 for 428ml) **(GF) (N/S)**
Better quality and worth the extra premium, but it lacks the mustard bite of the brand.

HELLMANN'S REAL MAYONNAISE, 400g or 428ml, £1.28
This moreish mayonnaise with a mustard twist is used as an accompaniment or dip.
Take note: this pot contains 316g of fat and 6g of salt.

---

(5) **ASDA** Real Mayonnaise, 500ml, 58p (50p for 428ml) **(GF) (N/S)**
This does not quite match the brand for taste, but it's still a great buy.

---

(5) **TESCO** Mayonnaise 500ml, 58p (50p for 428ml) **(GF)**
Buy it. This delivers top value for money, but the brand still edges it flavour-wise.

---

(5) **MORRISONS** Mayonnaise, 550ml, 59p (50p for 428ml)
This is under half the price of the brand, and it's not far off taste-wise.

---

(5) **CO-OP** Mayonnaise, 500ml, 79p (68p for 428ml) **(GF) (N/S)**
An alternative. The brand just beats the Co-op mayonnaise for taste, but not on price.

---

(5) **SAINSBURY'S** French Mayonnaise, 500ml, £1.19 (£1.02 for 428ml) **(GF) (L)**
A sound buy. Cheaper and, side by side, almost as good as the brand.

---

(4) **TESCO** Value Mayonnaise, 500ml , 37p (32p for 428ml)
In a loaded sandwich you'll hardly notice the difference, but alone, you certainly do.

---

(4) **SOMERFIELD** Mayonnaise 500ml, 64p (55p for 428ml)
Somerfield's new improved mayonnaise; but it still comes second on the taste front.

---

(3) **KWIK SAVE** Mayonnaise, 500ml, 79p (68p for 428ml)
Try another shop. Cheaper, but the dominant flavour of rapeseed oil spoils the taste.

---

(3) **ALDI** Kim Squeezy Mayonnaise, 500ml, 69p (59p for 428ml) **(L)**
It's not worth getting fat on this. It is cheaper, but taste-wise it's three steps below
the brand.

Hellmann's Light Mayonnaise

Colours, Egg, Fat, Mustard, Salt, Stabilisers, Sugar, Yeast

(8) **MORRISONS** Reduced Fat Mayonnaise, 550ml, 59p (44p for 406ml)
Grab it. This healthy alternative is much cheaper and it tastes better than the brand.

(10) **ASDA** Reduced Fat Mayonnaise, 500ml, 58p (47p for 406ml)
This is under half price, much better tasting and with only a tad more fat content.

(10) **TESCO** Reduced Calorie Mayonnaise 500ml, 58p (47p for 406ml)   **(GF)**
Buy it. Tesco's new and improved recipe, which certainly tastes as good as the brand.

(10) **SOMERFIELD** Good Intentions Mayonnaise, 500ml, 64p (52p for 406ml)
Beat the brand buy. Great price and it tastes at least as good as the brand.

(9) **KWIK SAVE** Reduced Fat Mayonnaise, 500ml, 79p (65p for 406ml)
Buy it. A big saving on the brand, and delivers a similar taste quality.

(9) **CO-OP** Reduced Fat Mayonnaise, 500ml, 79p (65p for 406ml)   **(GF) (L) (N/S)**
A good buy for the Co-op shopper. Beats the brand for price and is comparable in taste.

(8) **WAITROSE** Reduced Calorie Mayonnaise, 500ml, 82p (67p for 406ml)   **(GF) (L)**
An excellent buy for the Waitrose shopper. This is much cheaper and of a comparable quality to the brand.

(7) **SAINSBURY'S** Be Good to Yourself French Mayonnaise,   **(GF)**
500ml, £1.19 (97p for 406ml)
If you're a Sainsbury's shopper – buy it. It tastes better and is cheaper than the brand.

HELLMANN'S LIGHT MAYONNAISE, 400g or 406ml, £1.28
If you want taste pleasure, the regular mayonnaise is hard to beat. This contains less fat (119g – the regular contains 316g), but the salt content has increased from 6g to 9g.

(5) **ALDI** Kim Squeezy Light Mayonnaise, 500ml, 69p (56p for 406ml)   **(L)**
This is a cheaper alternative to the brand, but the taste is a squeeze below.

Hellmann's French Dressing

Celery, Colours, Egg, Milk, Mustard, Salt, Soya, Stabilisers, Sugar, Thickeners, Yeast

---

(10) **WAITROSE** French Dressing, 250ml, 99p **(GF) (L) (N/S) (V)**
Superb – the perfect 10! This is cheaper, tastier and much better quality than the brand.

---

(8) **TESCO** Healthy Living French Dressing, 250ml, 99p **(GF) (V)**
Put it in the trolley. It's healthier, cheaper and it equals the taste of the brand.

---

(7) **CO-OP** French Dressing, 250ml, £1.15 **(GF) (L) (N/S) (V)**
Put it in the trolley. The taste is better than the brand and it's cheaper.

---

(7) **MARKS & SPENCER** Classic French Dressing, 330g, £1.69 (£1.28 for 250ml)
A beat-the-brand buy. Like for like, it's cheaper and much better than the brand.

HELLMANN'S FRENCH DRESSING, 235ml, £1.27 (£1.35 for 250ml)

This popular dressing is used to deliver an extra twist of flavour to salads. However, this bottle contains 60g of fat, 13g of sugar and 4.7g of salt.

---

(5) **MORRISONS** French Style Dressing, 450ml, 79p (44p for 250ml)
Much cheaper, a thicker consistency, but the taste is just a shake off the brand.

---

(5) **SAINSBURY'S** Be Good to Yourself French Dressing, 250ml, 89p **(L)**
A good alternative for the Sainsbury shopper. Cheaper and healthier, but not as tasty as the brand

---

(5) **KWIK SAVE** French Dressing, 250ml, 99p
A cheaper alternative to the brand. However, taste-wise the quality is not as good.

Filippo Berio Extra Virgin Olive Oil

Fat

---

(10) **ALDI** Carlini Extra Virgin Olive Oil, 750ml, £1.95 (£1.30 for 500ml) **(GF) (L) (V)**
Buy it. It's cheap and good value, beating the brand on price and equalling it on flavour.

---

(10) **TESCO** Extra Virgin Olive Oil, 500ml, £1.58
This is a real beat-the-brand purchase. Under half the price and similar in quality.

---

(10) **ASDA** Extra Virgin Olive Oil, 500ml, £1.58 **(GF) (N/S) (V)**
Not as tasty as Asda's organic, but at least as good as the brand.

---

(10) **ASDA** Organic Extra Virgin Olive Oil, 500ml, £2.67 **(GF) (N/S) (V)**
Perfect 10 for superior quality! Cheaper, organic and extra layers of flavour on the swallow.

---

(9) **SAINSBURY'S** Extra Virgin Oil, 500ml, £1.74 **(L)**
Grab it. It gives more palate pleasure and is less bitter on the finish than the brand.

---

(9) **SOMERFIELD** Extra Virgin Oil, 500ml, £1.79
Put it in the trolley. Cheaper and much more flavoursome and pleasurable than the brand.

---

(8) **CO-OP** Extra Virgin Oil, 500ml, £2.39 **(L) (N/S) (V)**
An excellent buy for the Co-op shopper. Much cheaper and similar in taste quality.

---

(6) **MARKS & SPENCER** Italian Extra Virgin Oil, 500ml, £3.49 **(GF) (N/S)**
Next to the brand, it's a notch up in quality, and well worth the extra 14p.

---

(6) **WAITROSE** Italian Extra Virgin Oil, 500ml, £3.75 **(GF) (L) (N/S) (V)**
Buy it. More expensive, but it is much better tasting on all flavour fronts.

FILIPPO BERIO EXTRA VIRGIN OLIVE OIL, 500ml, £3.35
Olive oil is the healthy alternative to other oils and fats. Although it has a fat content of over 90%, most of this is unsaturated fat.

---

(3) **MORRISONS** Extra Virgin Olive Oil, 500ml, £1.59
Leave it on the shelf. This is at least two notches down from the brand in quality.

Crosse & Blackwell Branston Pickle

Colour, Maize, Salt, Sugar, Sulphur dioxide (E220)

---

(7) **TESCO** Original Pickle, 310g, 51p **(N/S) (V)**
Grab a jar. A little less salt, a comparable quality and cheaper than the brand.

---

(7) **SOMERFIELD** Sweet Pickle, 310g, 59p
This pickle looks the same and presents similar flavours to the brand at a cheaper price.

CROSS & BLACKWELL BRANSTON PICKLE, 310g, 64p
Branston Pickle is a popular accompaniment to sandwiches and salads. You'd never guess from the taste, but this jar contains 12.4g of salt and over 60g of sugar.

---

(5) **ASDA** Sandwich Pickle, 310g, 51p
Cheaper and a lot less salt, but the taste is not as good as the brand.

---

(4) **CO-OP** Sweet Pickle, 310g, 59p **(L) (V)**
Buy the brand. It's a few pence more, but it delivers another notch up in quality.

Haywards Pickled Onions

Mustard seeds, Salt, Sugar, Sulphites (E221–E228)

---

(9) **ASDA** Strong Onions, 440g, 77p (80p for 454g) **(V)**
Labelled "strong" but, side by side with the brand, there is little difference in taste.

---

(9) **TESCO** Traditional Pickled Onions, 440g, 77p (80p for 454g) **(V)**
Buy a jar. The taste is at least as good and they are lot cheaper.

---

(7) **CO-OP** Pickled Onions, 500g, £1.25 (£1.14 for 454g) **(GF) (L) (N/S) (V)**
Not the cheapest "own label", but it's less than the brand and it reveals a similar quality.

HAYWARDS PICKLED ONIONS, 454g, £1.27
Haywards are just sweet enough to be enjoyed on their own. Check the ingredient labels on the jars – most products contain a lot more than just onions and vinegar.

---

(5) **ALDI** Newland Sweet Pickled Onions, 440g, 39p (40p for 454g) **(L)**
Well worth a punt at this price. However, the onions are not quite as good.

---

(1) **SAINSBURY'S** Low Price Pickled Onions, 440g, 37p (38p for 454g) **(L)**
Don't – 10p would be too much. These would spoil rather than complement your food.

Sunpride Pickled Gherkins in Vinegar

Mustard, Salt

(8) ALDI Newland Pickled Gherkins in Vinegar, 680g, 49p (48p for 670g) **(L)**
The added dill looks a little messy in the jar, but the taste is as good.

(8) ASDA Gherkins in Vinegar, 680g, 51p (50p for 670g) **(GF) (N/S) (V)**
The gherkins are bigger and just as tasty, but the added dill does spoil the presentation.

(8) SAINSBURY'S Gherkins in Sweet Vinegar, 675g, 51p (50p for 670g) **(L)**
Buy Sainsbury's gherkins (in sweet or sour vinegar) – both versions deliver comparable quality, and they're cheaper.

(8) KWIK SAVE Gherkins in Vinegar, 670g, 56p
Put it in the trolley. Beats the brand on price and equals it on taste.

(8) MORRISONS Pickled Gherkins in Vinegar, 680g, 59p (58p for 670g)
It is cheaper and as good as the brand in both taste and appearance.

SUNPRIDE PICKLED GHERKINS IN VINEGAR, 670g, 75p
Pickled gherkins deliver a sweet and sour flavour. No salt content given on the label, but it's normally high, at around 0.5g a gherkin.

(5) SOMERFIELD Gherkins in Sweet & Sour Vinegar, 670g, 89p
Although labelled "pickled in sweet and sour vinegar", these taste very similar to the brand.

(5) CO-OP Pickled Gherkins in Vinegar, 680g, 97p (96p for 670g) **(GF) (L) (N/S) (V)**
This Co-op version costs more, but it's very similar to the brand on all other fronts.

(5) WAITROSE Gherkins Pickled in Sweet & Sour Vinegar, 680g, **(GF) (L) (N/S)**
99p (98p for 670g)
Buy the brand or try another shop. This costs more, but is no better in quality.

Crosse & Blackwell Branston Baby Beetroot in Sweet Vinegar

Salt, Sugar, Sulphites (E221–E228), Mustard seeds

---

(10) **ALDI** Newland Baby Beetroot in Sweet Vinegar, **(GF) (L) (V)**
445g, 45p (39p for 330g)
Buy it. Gram for gram it is half the brand's price and the taste is of similar quality.

---

(8) **TESCO** Whole Beetroot in Vinegar, 340g, 53p (51p for 330g)
Not pickled in sweet vinegar or as sweet tasting, but the quality is just as good.

---

(7) **SAINSBURY'S** Baby Beetroot in Sweet Vinegar, 340g, 69p (67p for 330g) **(L)**
This is a beat-the-brand buy for the Sainsbury's shopper – cheaper and just as good.

CROSSE & BLACKWELL BRANSTON BABY BEETROOT IN SWEET VINEGAR, 330g, 78p

Beetroot is an enjoyable cold accompaniment to salads. Although it's not labelled on this jar, the salt content is high, at around 7g. That's more than the RDA of 6g.

---

(5) **ASDA** Baby Beetroot in Sweet Vinegar, 440g, 67p (50p for 330g) **(N/S) (V)**
A cheaper alternative to the brand. However, the taste quality is not quite as good.

---

(4) **KWIK SAVE** Whole Beetroot in Water & Vinegar, 709g, 89p (42p for 330g)
This is a very cheap price, but the palate pleasure is a good notch down.

---

(3) **CO-OP** Pickled Baby Beetroot in Vinegar, 340g, 69p **(L) (N/S) (V)**
(67p for 330g)
Leave it. There is big step down in taste quality compared to the brand.

Crosse & Blackwell Sarson's Malt Vinegar

(10) **MORRISONS** Malt Vinegar, 568ml, 38p (17p for 250ml)
Under a third of the brand's price and it smells and tastes as good.

(10) **SAINSBURY'S** Malt Vinegar, 568ml, 38p (17p for 250ml)
Buy it. Put this into the brand's bottle and you would not know the difference.

(10) **ASDA** Malt Vinegar, 284ml, 21p (19p for 250ml) **(N/S) (V)**
Like for like, it's a third of the brand's price and it looks, smells and tastes the same.

(10) **TESCO** Malt Vinegar, 284ml, 21p (19p for 250ml) **(V)**
This beats the brand on price and equals it on taste – buy it.

(10) **SOMERFIELD** Malt Vinegar, 284ml, 25p (22p for 250ml)
Take this bottle. Well under half price and it delivers a similar quality to the brand.

(10) **CO-OP** Malt Vinegar, 284ml, 33p (30p for 250ml) **(N/S) (V)**
Not the cheapest "own label", but it's less than the brand and it tastes as good.

CROSS & BLACKWELL SARSON'S MALT VINEGAR, 250ml, 61p
Malt vinegar has many uses, but is best known is as an accompaniment for fish and chips.
Nothing is added to this brand: you get 100% malt vinegar.

(5) **ALDI** Colway Malt Vinegar, 568ml, 19p (9p for 250ml) **(L)**
This is a very good buy – and just a shake away from the brand in quality.

(4) **KWIK SAVE** Malt Vinegar, 1.14 litre, 83p (21p for 250ml) **(V)**
Acceptable quality, but next to the brand it does not smell or taste as good.

9
Savoury Biscuits, Snacks & Nuts

Most of us buy savoury snacks and bread substitutes at some time and unless you cannot tolerate gluten, milk, wheat or yeast, products like cream crackers, crispbreads, water biscuits and oatcakes present few problems for your health.

It's those delicious snacks that create the havoc – peanuts, cashews, crisps and cheddar biscuits, which have such a high saturated fat and salt content. If you give way to yourself and snack regularly during the day, you can soon be over the recommended upper limit for both saturated fat (20g for women, 30g for men) and salt (6g).

There's an upside, though. Peanuts and cashews are excellent sources of niacin (a B-complex vitamin without which there is a risk of the deficiency disease Pellagra), copper, zinc and protein, all essential for a healthy diet. It's all a matter of balance.

Jacobs Cream Crackers

Fibre, Yeast

---

(10)   **TESCO** Cream Crackers, 200g, 19p
Similar quality with a slightly different flavour, but with cheese, you won't notice the difference.

---

(9)   **ALDI** Snackrite Cream Crackers, 300g, 29p (20p for 200g)   **(L)**
A beat-the-brand buy. Gram for gram, they're nearly half the price and of similar quality.

---

(9)   **ASDA** Cream Crackers, 200g, 24p
Put it in the trolley. These crackers look and taste very similar to the brand.

---

(9)   **SAINSBURY'S** Cream Crackers, 200g, 24p   **(L) (V)**
A lighter colour, but otherwise a similar appearance. They're equal in taste quality and much cheaper.

---

(8)   **MORRISONS** Cream Crackers, 200g, 27p
Buy a packet. Morrisons beats the brand for price and equals it for taste.

---

(8)   **SOMERFIELD** Cream Crackers, 200g, 29p
Grab a couple of packets. This mirrors the brand on all fronts – except price.

---

(8)   **CO-OP** Cream Crackers, 200g, 32p   **(L) (V)**
A great buy for Co-op shoppers. A different taste from the brand, but just as good.

JACOBS CREAM CRACKERS, 200g, 39p
No fat, sugar or salt to worry about with Jacobs' plain crackers. However, most crackers are off limits to those allergic to wheat, gluten, yeast and nut and seed traces.

Jacobs High Bake Water Biscuits

Carbohydrate, Fibre, Soya, Yeast

(8) **ASDA** Water Biscuits, 200g, 62p **(V)**
Buy a pack. They look the same, taste similar and are cheaper than the brand.

(7) **SAINSBURY'S** High Bake Water Biscuits, 200g, 72p **(V)**
A beat-the-brand buy. A few pennies cheaper, with an almost identical taste to the brand.

(7) **TESCO** High Baked Water Biscuits, 200g, 72p **(V)**
Tesco beats the brand on price, and the bite, crunch and taste are as good.

(7) **SOMERFIELD** High Bake Water Biscuits, 200g, 75p
Grab a packet. Somerfield's water biscuits mirror the brand on all fronts – except price.

(7) **CO-OP** High Baked Water Biscuits, 200g, 76p **(N/S) (L) (V)**
Buy it. Every penny counts on a weekly shop – cheaper and hardly different in taste.

JACOBS HIGH BAKE WATER BISCUITS, 200g, 79p
These crisp circular biscuits are normally eaten with cheese. However, allergy sufferers should read the ingredient labels carefully.

Ryvita Dark Rye Crispbread

Emulsifier, Fibre, Yeast

(7) **MORRISONS** Original Crispbread, 200g, 32p
A different colour, a little longer and a little less healthy. But taste-wise these are the brand's equal.

RYVITA DARK RYE CRISPBREAD, 200g, 36p
Rich in fibre and a dieter's alternative to bread. However they do contain gluten and most versions of this product indicate that they may contain nut and/or seed traces.

(5) **ASDA** Good for You Rye Crispbread, 200g, 31p **(GF) (V)**
An alternative. However, the taste or health benefits are not as good as the brand.

(5) **SOMERFIELD** Brown Rye Crispbread, 200g, 36p
Buy the brand at this price! Similar to Morrisons' crispbread, but not as cheap.

Ferró Breadsticks

Emulsifier, Fibre, Salt, Yeast

---

(10) **ALDI** Grissotti Breadsticks with Black Olives, 200g, 79p (50p for 125g)   **(L)**
It's unfair to compare these with the brand, but if you like olives they're the business!

---

(8) **ASDA** Crisp Plain Breadsticks, 125g, 44p   **(V)**
Buy them. Asda beats the brand on price and equals it on the taste front.

---

(8) **SAINSBURY'S** Italian Grissini Breadsticks, 125g, 44p
Beat-the-brand breadsticks – put a packet in the trolley. Better price and a similar taste.

---

(8) **TESCO** Italian Original Breadsticks, 125g, 44p   **(V)**
Tesco beats the brand in breadsticks. Much cheaper and equal in taste pleasure.

---

(8) **MORRISONS** Italian Breadsticks, 125g, 49p
Great value compared to the brand. Similar in taste and more breadsticks for your money.

---

(7) **SOMERFIELD** Grissini Breadstick, 125g, 55p
A beat-the-brand buy for Somerfield shoppers. They're cheaper and comparable in quality.

---

(7) **CO-OP** Plain Breadsticks, 125g, 62p
Put a pack in the trolley. Co-op's thinner sticks deliver a similar flavour for less money.

FERRÓ BREADSTICKS, 125g, 69p
Popular with dips, the odd stick or two is nothing to worry about, but allergy sufferers should read the ingredient labels carefully.

---

(5) **ASDA** Good for You Breadsticks, 125g, 44p   **(V)**
They are healthier and cheaper than the brand, but they come second on the taste front.

Nairn's Fine Milled Oatcakes

Fibre, Salt

---

(7) **SAINSBURY'S** Rough Oatcakes, 300g, 64p (54p for 250g)　　**(L)**
These beat the brand for taste and price. They are wheat, but not gluten, free.

---

(7) **SAINSBURY'S** Highland Oatcakes, 300g, 65p (55p for 250g)　　**(L)**
Unlike the brand, these do contain wheat. However they taste better and are cheaper.

(?) **TESCO** Scottish Rough Oatcakes, 250g, 59p　　**(V)**
A beat-the-brand buy. A few pence less, but more flavoursome than the brand

---

NAIRN'S FINE MILLED OATCAKES, 250g, 63p
These named cakes certainly have more flavour, but in appearance and usage they are biscuits. These are wheat free, but not gluten free!

Cheddars Real Cheddar Cheese Biscuits

Egg, Fat, Fibre, Lactose, Salt, Soya

---

(8) **ASDA** Cheese Thins, 150g, 42p
Asda's Cheese Thins beat the brand on price. A tad more salt, but of similar quality.

---

(7) **CO-OP** Cheese Thins, 150g, 57p
Buy them. They look and taste so similar you could swap the packet with the brand and never know.

CHEDDARS REAL CHEDDAR CHEESE BISCUITS, 150g, 60p
A thin, moreish cheesy biscuit that has your hand reaching for the packet – again and again! They may look and taste innocent, but their saturated fat content is high.

---

(1) **ALDI** Snackrite Mini Cheese Thins, 210g, 65p (47p for 150g)
Don't! They taste so artificial that one small biscuit will be one too many.

Penn State Original Salted Pretzels

Fibre, Salt, Yeast

(7) **SAINSBURY'S** Salted Pretzels, 150g, 99p (£1.16 for 175g)
Put it in the trolley. Less cash and a little less salt but no difference in taste.

PENN STATE ORIGINAL SALTED PRETZELS, 175g, £1.29
A famous American snack, although these are made in the UK. Be warned, the salt content is fairly high – at 5.25g it's approaching the recommended daily limit.

(5) **TESCO** Jumbo Salted Pretzels, 150g, 87p (£1.02 for 175g)
Tesco's pretzels are a little too mouth-drying and, next to the brand, are not as inviting.

KP Original Salted Peanuts

Fat, Fibre, Salt

(10) **TESCO** Value Roasted Salted Peanuts, 200g, 21p   **(GF) (V)**
A great buy at a quarter of the brand's price, and you'd struggle to tell the difference.

(10) **TESCO** Roasted Salted Peanuts, 200g, 39p   **(GF) (V)**
A beat-the-brand buy for Tesco shoppers. Under half price and at least as good.

(9) **SAINSBURY'S** Salted Peanuts, 200g, 45p   **(V)**
Sainsbury's shoppers should grab a packet. Nearly half the price and they taste as good.

(8) **CO-OP** Roasted Salted Peanuts, 200g, 55p   **(GF) (L) (V)**
Put it in the trolley. Equals the brand on taste and beats it on price.

KP ORIGINAL SALTED PEANUTS, 300g, £1.29 (86p for 200g)
There are plenty of health benefits from nuts, but be aware that this 300g pack contains over 150g of fat (of which 28.5g is saturated) and 3.75g of salt.

(5) **ASDA** Smartprice Salted Peanuts, 200g, 21p   **(GF) (V)**
Well worth a punt at this price. However, side by side, the brand tastes better.

(5) **MARKS & SPENCER** Roasted Salted Peanuts, 200g, 99p   **(GF) (V)**
An alternative, but not a beat-the-brand buy, either on taste or price.

(1) **ALDI** Snackrite Salted Peanuts, 250g, 59p (47p for 200g)   **(L) (V)**
Don't waste your cash. Buy elsewhere – these nuts taste of poor-quality vegetable oil.

KP Salted Cashew Nuts

Fat, Fibre, Salt

(10) **ASDA** Salted Cashew Nuts, 100g, 88p **(GF) (V)**
Beat-the-brand cashew nuts. Under half the price and better tasting.

(10) **TESCO** Roasted Salted Cashew Nuts, 100g, 88p **(GF) (V)**
Don't bother with the brand at Tesco. Little taste difference and less than half the price.

(8) **SAINSBURY'S** Salted Cashews Nuts, 75g, 97p (£1.30 for 100g) **(GF) (L) (V)**
Buy a pack! Sainsbury's cashew nuts beat the brand on price and equal it on taste.

KP SALTED CASHEW NUTS, 100g, £1.84
Cashews, like most salted nuts, have high levels of saturated fat and salt. However, they're rich in vitamin C and are an excellent source of protein, niacin, iron and zinc.

(8) **MARKS & SPENCER** Roasted Salted Cashew Nuts, 100g, £1.39 **(GF) (V)**
It's rare that M&S makes the brand look expensive, but they do with cashews.

(8) **CO-OP** Roasted Salted Cashew Nuts, 100g, £1.45p **(GF) (L) (V)**
Not the cheapest "own label", but they're much cheaper than the brand and taste as good.

(4) **ALDI** Forresters Salted Cashew Nuts, 60g, 55p (92p for 100g) **(GF) (L)**
Nut for nut, they're half price, but the taste is only half as good as the brand.

Planters Unsalted Cashew Nuts

Fat, Fibre, Salt

PLANTERS UNSALTED CASHEW NUTS, 110g, 99p
Not as readily available as the salted version, but as an ingredient in cooking or for consumers watching their salt intake, they are perfect.

(5) **SAINSBURY'S** Unsalted Cashew Nuts, **(GF) (L) (V)**
150g, £1.64 (£1. 20 for 110g)
The taste quality is as good but, like for like, they cost more than the brand.

(5) **ASDA** Unsalted Cashew Nuts, 120g, 97p (89p for 110g) **(GF) (V)**
Worth a punt. However, side by side, they come second to the brand taste-wise.

(4) **CO-OP** Unsalted Cashew Nuts, 120g, 99p (91p for 110g) **(GF) (L)**
Cheaper, but the taste is a notch down from the brand. Buy the brand if it's available.

Walkers Ready Salted Crisps

Fat, Fibre, Salt

WALKERS READY SALTED CRISPS, 6 x 34.5g (207g), 98p (71p for 150g)

It's worth noting that you get a larger packet of crisps with Walkers than the "own labels". The odd packet of crisps should not be problem health-wise, but snackers should be aware that the fat (11.7g) and salt (0.5g) are very high for a 34.5g packet.

---

(5) **ASDA** Ready Salted Crisps, 6 x 25g (150g), 54p **(GF) (N/S) (V)**
Cheaper, but do not quite match the brand for taste, and contain a little more fat.

---

(5) **TESCO** Select Crisps Ready Salted Crisps, 6 x 25g (150g), 54p **(GF)**
Similar to Asda's Ready Salted and, likewise, they're a notch down when tasted next to the brand.

---

(5) **ALDI** Snackrite Ready Salted Crisps, 6 x 25g (150g), 55p **(L) (V)**
An alternative. Gram for gram, they are cheaper, but the taste is not as good as the brand.

---

(5) **SAINSBURY'S** Ready Salted Crisps, 6 x 25g (150g), 59p **(GF)**
A cheaper option. However, crisp for crisp, they don't taste as good as the brand.

---

(5) **MORRISONS** Ready Salted Crisps, 10 x 25g (250g), £1.39 (84p for 150g) **(GF)**
Morrisons' crisps taste as good as the brand but, gram for gram, they cost more money.

---

(4) **KWIK SAVE** Ready Salted Crisps, 6 x 25g (150g), 79p **(GF) (L) (N/S) (V)**
Not a beat-the-brand buy. Like for like, more expensive and less tasty.

---

(3) **CO-OP** Ready Salted Crisps, 6 x 25g (150g), 89p **(N/S) (L) (V)**
Leave them. Co-op crisps are no substitute for the brand – and they are more expensive.

Walkers Cheese & Onion Crisps

Fat, Fibre, Lactose, Salt, Yeast

(6) **MORRISONS** Cheese & Onion Crisps, 10 x 25g (250g), **(GF)**
£1.39, (84p for 150g)
Like for like, they are more expensive, but they taste much better than the brand.

WALKERS CHEESE & ONION CRISPS, 6 x 34.5g (207g), 98p (71p for 150g)
The fat and salt levels are similar to Walkers Ready Salted. Consumers should be aware that milk is listed amongst the ingredients.

(5) **TESCO** Select Crisps Cheese & Onion Crisps, 6 x 25g (150g), 54p **(GF)**
Worth a punt. Tesco beats the brand on price, but comes second on the flavour front.

(5) **ALDI** Snackrite Cheese & Onion Crisps, 6 x 25g (150g), 55p
A cheaper alternative to the brand but the taste is a small notch down.

(5) **SAINSBURY'S** Cheese & Onion Crisps, 6 x 25g (150g), 59p **(GF)**
Sainsbury's beats the brand for price, but it comes second on all the taste fronts.

(4) **CO-OP** Cheese & Onion Crisps, 6 x 25g (150g), 89p **(GF) (N/S)**
Like for like, these are more expensive and don't taste as good as the brand.

(3) **ASDA** Ready Cheese & Onion Crisps, 6 x 25g (150g), 54p **(GF)**
Cheaper, but the taste is spoilt by an unrewarding bitter flavour on the finish.

(2) **KWIK SAVE** Cheese & Onion Crisps, 6 x 25g (150g), 79p
Leave them on the shelf. Outside of the packet you'd struggle to identify these as cheese and onion crisps.

10
Sweet Biscuits
& Chocolate Bars

There is absolutely nothing wrong with the odd sweet biscuit or chocolate bar treat. However, when McVitie's includes the strap line: "can be enjoyed as part of a healthy diet and lifestyle" on its Penguin chocolate biscuit wrapper, it makes you wonder if their marketing department has actually read the ingredient and nutrition label! Crammed with emulsifiers, saturated fat, sugar and a host of other of "make-it-shelf-safe" ingredients, it does not add up to my idea of a healthy diet and lifestyle. But that's marketing for you!

Apart from that, and more dangerously, many of these biscuits and bars are sold as multi-packs and, for most, the nutrition and ingredient label is only required on the outside packaging and not on the individual item wrappers. Not good if you are at a party and you suffer from a nut, wheat, yeast, lactose or gluten allergy. Indeed, most of these multi-packs do not even contain a gram weight, so you have to guess how much saturated fat, salt and sugar you are consuming! This can't be right for consumers who want to buy and eat healthily.

McVitie's Ginger Nut Biscuits

Fat, Fibre, Salt, Soya

---

(10) **ASDA** Smartprice Ginger Nut Biscuits, 300g, 25p **(N/S) (V)**
A smart buy for the Asda shopper. They are cheap and taste as good the brand.

---

(10) **TESCO** Value Ginger Nut Biscuits, 300g, 25p
Tesco beats the brand with these. Very similar to Asda's and likewise, an excellent buy.

---

(10) **ALDI** Belmont Ginger Snaps, 400g, 35p (27p for 300g) **(L)**
Aldi also beats the brand. These are under half the price and of a similar quality.

---

(8) **ASDA** Ginger Nuts Biscuits, 400g, 60p (45p for 300g) **(N/S) (V)**
A lighter colour than the brand, but a match in taste quality – and for less cash.

---

(8) **TESCO** Ginger Nut Biscuits, 400g, 60p (45p for 300g) **(GF)**
Gram for gram, much better value. A slightly different style, but no less quality.

---

(5) **MARKS & SPENCER** Ginger Snaps, 250g, 69p (83p for 300g)
Like for like, these are more expensive and no better tasting than the brand.

MCVITIE'S GINGER NUT BISCUITS, 300g, 69p
Dieters should note that too many of these crunchy ginger biscuits will add on the pounds.
A single biscuit contains 3.8g of sugar, 0.9g of saturated fat and 0.25g of salt.

McVitie's Milk Chocolate Digestive Biscuits

Emulsifiers, Fat, Fibre, Lactose, Salt, Soya

(10) **ALDI** Belmont Milk Chocolate Digestive Biscuits, 400g, 46p
Aldi shoppers beat the brand with these. They look and taste the same as the brand.

(8) **SAINSBURY'S** Milk Chocolate Biscuits, 400g, 78p
Shoppers can buy these confidently. They beat the brand on price and equal it on taste.

(8) **MORRISONS** Milk Chocolate Digestive Biscuits, 400g, 79p
A much cheaper price than the brand, and both chocolate and biscuit are as good.

(7) **SOMERFIELD** Milk Chocolate Digestive Biscuits, 400g, 89p
The biscuit is a tad more crunchy than the brand. The quality is just as good.

(7) **ASDA** Milk Chocolate Digestive Biscuits, 300g, 68p (91p for 400g)   **(N/S)**
Put them in the trolley. You can't tell the difference between these and the brand.

(7) **TESCO** Milk Chocolate Digestive Biscuits, 300g, 68p (91p for 400g)
Tesco beats the brand on price and is very similar on the chocolate and biscuit front.

(7) **CO-OP** Milk Chocolate Digestive Biscuits, 300g, 72p (96p for 400g)
Buy it. Co-op beats the brand on price and is similar on all the taste fronts.

MCVITIE'S MILK CHOCOLATE DIGESTIVE BISCUITS, 400g, £1.04
If you eat six of these biscuits during a day (which can easily be done!), women will
have had half their recommeded upper limit of saturated fat and added sugar, as well
as 25% of their salt.

(5) **ASDA** Smartprice Milk Chocolate Digestive Biscuits, 300g, 34p (46p for 400g)
A cheaper alternative but the taste lacks the moreish quality of the brand.

(5) **MARKS & SPENCER** Milk Chocolate Digestive Biscuits,
300g, 89p (£1.19 for 400g)
An alternative but, like for like, they cost more than the brand and taste no better.

McVitie's Plain Chocolate Digestive Biscuits

Emulsifiers, Fat, Fibre, Lactose, Salt, Soya

(10) **ALDI** Belmont Plain Chocolate Digestive Biscuits, 400g, 46p
Grab a pack. Below half the brand's price, even though they mirror it in appearance and taste.

(8) **SAINSBURY'S** Plain Chocolate Biscuits, 400g, 78p
Grab a pack. They beat the brand on price and equal it on the taste front.

(8) **MORRISONS** Plain Chocolate Digestive Biscuits, 400g, 79p
Morrisons' cost less and equal both the chocolate and biscuit quality of the brand.

(7) **ASDA** Plain Chocolate Digestive Biscuits, 300g, 68p (91p for 400g)
Buy it. Like Asda's, you can't tell the difference between these and the brand.

(7) **CO-OP** Plain Chocolate Digestive Biscuits, 300g, 72p (96p for 400g)
Co-op beats the brand on price and is very comparable on all flavour fronts.

MCVITIE'S PLAIN CHOCOLATE DIGESTIVE BISCUITS, 400g, £1.04
Compared to the milk chocolate variety, plain or dark chocolate digestives deliver a cleaner and sharper taste. But don't be deceived: they're still high in sugar, saturated fat and salt.

(5) **TESCO** Plain Chocolate Digestive Biscuits, 300g, 83p (£1.11 for 400g)
At first glance they look cheaper than the brand but, gram for gram, they're not.

(5) **MARKS & SPENCER** Plain Digestive Biscuits, 300g, 89p (£1.19 for 400g)
An alternative but, gram for gram, they're more expensive than the brand and no better.

Maryland Chocolate Chip Cookies

Emulsifiers, Fat, Fibre, Lactose, Salt, Soya

(10) **ALDI** Temptations Luxury Choc Chunk and Hazelnut Cookies, 200g, 49p
A beat-the-brand buy! The perfect 10 score for outstanding quality; both chocolate and biscuit are delicious.

(8) **SAINSBURY'S** Chocolate Chip Cookies, 200g, 44p
Pick this pack. Sainsbury's cookies beat the brand for price and deliver a similar quality.

(8) **TESCO** Chocolate Chip Cookies, 250g, 55p (44p for 200g) **(GF)**
Grab it. Not so many chocolate chips on the surface, but plenty in the cookie.

(8) **MORRISONS** Chocolate Chip Cookies, 200g, 49p
Put it in your trolley. They taste as good and are cheaper than the brand.

(7) **SOMERFIELD** Chocolate Chip Cookies, 200g, 59p
Buy it. Little difference in taste quality and the price is lower than the brand.

(7) **SOMERFIELD** Double Chocolate Chip Cookies, 200g, 59p
Another option for the Somerfield shopper. More chocolate in the biscuit, but not more chips!

(7) **CO-OP** Choc Chip & Hazelnut Cookies, 200g, 66p
It may say "hazelnut" on the label, but these look and taste just like the brand.

MARYLAND CHOCOLATE CHIP COOKIES, 150g, 58p (78p for 200g)
A munchy, crunchy biscuit diced with chocolate chips. These cookies, like most biscuits, have a high sugar and saturated fat content.

(5) **ASDA** Smartprice Chocolate Chip Cookies, 200g, 25p
Almost as good as the brand and worth a punt at this seriously low price. Fewer chocolate chips though.

(5) **ASDA** Chocolate Chip Cookies, 250g, 40p (32p for 200g)
Cheaper, but like Asda's Smartprice, these cookies have fewer choc chips than the brand.

(3) **CO-OP** Mini Choc Chip Cookies, 100g, 59p (£1.18 for 200g)
Expensive and second rate! Try another shop if you're seeking an alternative to the brand.

McVitie's Penguin Chocolate Sandwich Biscuit Bar

Emulsifiers, Fat, Fibre, Lactose, Salt, Soya, Yeast

(8) **TESCO** Milk Chocolate Sandwich Biscuit Bar, 14 pack,
360g, £1.04 (64p for 220g)
A crunchier biscuit than the brand. The bite and taste quality is just as rewarding.

(8) **ASDA** Puffin Milk Chocolate Sandwich Biscuit Bar, 8 pack,
200g, 60p (66p for 220g)
A crunchier biscuit, of equal quality and, gram for gram, cheaper than the brand.

(8) **MORRISONS** Skipper Milk Chocolate Sandwich Biscuit Bar, 12 pack,
300g, 95p (70p for 220g)
Buy a Skipper. A similar crunchy style to Tesco and Asda, and comparable in taste.

MCVITIE'S PENGUIN CHOCOLATE SANDWICH BISCUIT BAR, 9 PACK, 220g, 89p
"Penguin can be enjoyed as part of a healthy diet and lifestyle" is what the packet says.
But it contains emulsifiers, flavourings, sugar, soya and saturated fat!

(5) **CO-OP** Break Bars Milk Chocolate Sandwich Biscuit Bar, 7 pack,
180g, 76p (93p for 220g)
Not a beat-the-brand buy. Very similar in taste but, gram for gram, more expensive.

Kit Kat Milk Chocolate Wafer Biscuits

Emulsifiers, Fat, Fibre, Gluten, Lactose, Salt, Soya, Yeast

(10) **CO-OP** Double Break Milk Chocolate Wafer Biscuits,
12 pack x 2 fingers, 280g, 76p (49p for 180g)
A beat-the-brand buy. A crunchier wafer, but no less in quality and under half the price.

(9) **TESCO** Milk Chocolate Break Wafer Bars, 8 pack x 2 fingers, 180g, 63p
Buy it. Cheaper, and the chocolate and wafer are of a similar quality to the brand.

(8) **SOMERFIELD** Milk Chocolate Wafer Break, 8 pack x 2 fingers, 180g, 74p
A good buy. Much cheaper, and it equals the brand for taste.

KIT KAT MILK CHOCOLATE WAFER BISCUITS, 9 PACK x 2 FINGERS, 180g, 99p
You have no idea if you are getting a bargain with these multi-packs as there is no gram weight on the packet. Moreover, the sugar and saturated fat content is high.

(5) **ASDA** Take A Break Milk Chocolate Wafer Biscuits,
8 pack x 2 fingers, 180g, 60p
Cheaper than the brand, but the chocolate coating is thicker and not as palate pleasing.

(5) **MORRISONS** Break Milk Chocolate Wafer Biscuits,
8 pack x 2 fingers, 180g, 69p
Much cheaper, but the milk-chocolate coating is a notch down from the brand.

(5) **SAINSBURY'S** Double Take Milk Chocolate Wafer Biscuits,
8 pack x 2 fingers, 160g, 63p (71p for 180g)
A cheaper alternative and worth a punt. But in taste terms the brand wins.

(4) **ALDI** Tandem Milk Chocolate Crispy Wafer Bars,
8 pack x 2 fingers, 200g, 55p (50p for 180g)
Still worth a punt, although the chocolate coating is a big step down from the brand in quality.

11
Tea, Coffee & Hot Chocolate

The consumer's reluctance to pay more than 3p a tea bag (and often a lot less), coupled with our desire for a quicker-than-instant "cuppa" has resulted in bags filled with tea dust rather than tea leaves! Our only buying criterion, apparently, is that it colours quickly with milk. The taste or quality of the tea hardly seems to matter. Try some good loose-leaf tea, allow it to brew and taste that difference.

Both tea and coffee contain caffeine, unless of course they are decaffeinated. Coffee contains about 60mg of caffeine per 100ml and tea just a little less. As yet there is no official dietary reference value for caffeine, but there is a recommended upper limit of 160mg for children and 300mg for pregnant women. So take caffeine care.

Meanwhile the humble cocoa can have far more taste than drinking chocolate and it's healthier, since it's not loaded with sugar.

PG Tips Tea Bags

Caffeine

(10) **ALDI** Diplomat Red Label 240 Round Tea Bags,   **(GF) (L) (V)**
750g, £1.39 (47p for 250g)
Put it in the trolley. Seriously cheap and the cup quality is as good as the brand.

(8) **WAITROSE** Original Blend 80 Round Tea Bags, 250g, 99p   **(GF) (L) (N/S) (V)**
A beat-the-brand buy. These bags deliver better quality and are cheaper than PG.

(6) **CO-OP** Organic 80 Round Tea Bags, 250g, £1.89   **(GF) (L) (N/S) (V)**
Co-op costs more than the brand, but offers a big step up in taste quality.

(6) **SOMERFIELD** Gold Label 40 Round Tea Bags, 125g,   **(GF) (V)**
99p (£1.98 for 250g)
Much better quality than the brand. Yes, they cost more, but only just over 2p per bag.

PG TIPS 80 PYRAMID TEA BAGS, 250g, £1.38

PG Tips is a strong tea with plenty of tannin. The type and shape of the tea bag does make a difference to the taste of the tea, but the main factor is the quality of the tea inside the bag.

(5) **ASDA** 80 Round Tea Bags, 250g, 81p   **(GF) (N/S) (V)**
A fair price for the quality but, in the cup, the tea is not as gutsy as the brand.

(5) **MORRISONS** Red Label 80 Round Tea Bags, 250g, 82p   **(GF) (N/S) (V)**
This delivers acceptable quality for the money, but next to the brand it comes second on the taste front.

(4) **SOMERFIELD** Red Label 80 Round Tea Bags, 250g, 69p   **(GF) (V)**
Not as good as the brand. But if you it colour well with milk, then it will do.

(4) **KWIK SAVE** Red Label 40 Round Tea Bags, 125g,   **(GF) (N/S) (V)**
59p (£1.18 for 250g)
Buy the brand. Bag for bag, there's only few pence difference, and there is a big step down in quality.

(1) **ASDA** Smartprice 80 Rectangle Tea Bags, 250g, 31p
Asda's tea buyer should be made to drink this. Cabbage water would taste better.

(1) **TESCO** Value 80 Rectangle Tea Bags, 250g, 31p   **(GF) (V)**
Don't! 31p for these tea bags is outrageous – 1p would be too much.

PG Tips Loose Leaf Tea

Caffeine

---

(8) **KWIK SAVE** Red Label Loose Leaf Tea, 250g, 99p   **(GF) (N/S) (V)**
Put it in the trolley. This is of similar quality to the brand, at a much cheaper price.

---

(7) **SOMERFIELD** Red Label Loose Leaf Tea, 250g, £1.15
A beat-the-brand buy. Similar in quality to PG – and you'll get more cups for your money.

---

(6) **MARKS & SPENCER** Extra Strong Loose Leaf Tea, 250g, £1.29   **(GF) (N/S) (V)**
Well worth the extra 2p. M&S delivers a more harmonious taste than the brand.

PG TIPS LOOSE LEAF TEA, 250g, £1.27
PG Tips loose leaf is a strong tea with plenty of tannin and although the tea quality is very similar to that in its bags, it does taste a little better when loose.

---

(5) **ASDA** Loose Leaf Tea, 250g, 98p   **(GF) (N/S) (V)**
A cheaper alternative to the brand. However, if you want tannic strength, then buy PG.

---

(5) **TESCO** Premium Loose Leaf Tea, 250g, 98p   **(GF) (V)**
Very similar to Asda's on all fronts. Lacks the tannic grip of the brand.

---

(5) **CO-OP** 99 Loose Leaf Tea, 250g, £1.29   **(GF) (L) (N/S) (V)**
Buy whichever is the cheapest. There is little difference in taste between this and the brand.

---

(5) **SOMERFIELD** Gold Label Loose Leaf Tea, 250g, £1.69   **(GF) (V)**
Not worth the extra! Slightly better in quality than the brand, but a big step up in price.

---

(4) **CO-OP** Premium Indian Prince Loose Leaf Tea, 125g,   **(GF) (L) (N/S) (V)**
97p (£1.94 for 250g)
Leave it. The tiny tea leaves look no different, and the taste is no better than the brand.

Twinings Earl Grey Tea

Bergamot, Caffeine

---

(9) **MORRISONS** Speciality Tea Earl Grey Tea, 50 Tea Bags,   **(GF) (N/S) (V)**
125g, 69p
Put it in the trolley. Beats the brand for price and equals it for taste.

---

(8) **CO-OP** Earl Grey Tea, 100 Tea Bags, 250g, £2.09   **(GF) (L) (N/S) (V)**
(£1.05 for 125g)
Buy it. Gram for gram, it's cheaper and equals the brand for aroma and taste.

---

(8) **WAITROSE** Earl Grey Tea, 50 Tea Bags, 125g, £1.19   **(GF) (L) (N/S) (V)**
A beat-the-brand buy. Delivers a similar quality and the same pungency of bergamot
at a cheaper price.

---

(8) **MARKS & SPENCER** Earl Grey Tea, 50 Tea Bags, £1.29   **(GF) (N/S) (V)**
M&S beats the brand: it's cheaper and of a comparable quality.

TWININGS EARL GREY TEA, 50 TEA BAGS, 125g, £1.58

Earl Grey is a tea flavoured with bergamot-peel oil and is usually drunk with a dash of milk
or a slice of lemon. Bergamot's perfumed citrus oil dominates the smell and taste of this tea.

---

(5) **SAINSBURY'S** Earl Grey Tea, 50 Tea Bags, 125g, £1.29   **(GF) (L) (N/S) (V)**
A cheaper alternative, but it comes second to the brand in aroma and taste.

---

(3) **ASDA** Earl Grey Tea, 50 Tea Bags, 125g, 97p   **(GF) (N/S) (V)**
Leave it on the shelf. Much cheaper, but the aroma and taste do not approach those of
the brand.

---

(2) **TESCO** Finest Earl Grey Tea, 50 Tea Bag, 125g, £1.29   **(GF) (V)**
Let somebody else be disappointed. Buy the brand and you'll have something drinkable.

Twinings English Breakfast Tea Bags

Caffeine

---

(8) **WAITROSE** English Breakfast Tea, 50 Tea Bags, 125g, £1.19 **(GF) (L) (N/S) (V)**
Put it in the trolley. This equals the brand for quality, and at a much cheaper price.

---

(8) **Marks & Spencer** English Breakfast Tea, 50 Tea Bags, 125g, £1.29 **(GF) (N/S) (V)**
A beat-the-brand buy. M&S tastes much better than Twinings and is better value.

TWININGS ENGLISH BREAKFAST TEA, 50 TEA BAGS, 125G, £1.44

This was originally blended to be drunk with a hearty breakfast. Although breakfasts have changed over time, this full-bodied style of tea remains popular. As with PG Tips, if it's available, loose tea will be better and cheaper.

---

(5) **SAINSBURY'S** English Breakfast Tea, 80 Tea Bags, **(GF) (L) (N/S) (V)**
250g, £1.99 (£1.00 for 125g)
Worth a punt! Better than most "own labels", but not as good as the brand.

---

(5) **SAINSBURY'S** Taste the Difference English Breakfast Tea, **(GF) (L) (N/S) (V)**
40 Tea Bags, 125g, 85p
Fewer bags, but more tea! Sainsbury's needs to improve the quality to beat the brand.

---

(5) **SOMERFIELD** English Breakfast Tea, 50 Tea Bags, 125g, £1.39 **(GF) (V)**
Beats the brand for price and colours well with milk, but comes second on taste quality.

---

(4) **MORRISONS** English Breakfast Tea, 50 Tea Bags, 125g, 69p **(GF) (N/S) (V)**
If you want colour, this delivers it in tea dust. Cheaper, but a big step down from the brand.

---

(4) **ASDA** English Breakfast Tea, 50 Tea Bags, 125g, 97p **(GF) (N/S) (V)**
With milk, this is a cheaper alternative. But without it is a good notch down in taste.

---

(3) **CO-OP** English Breakfast Tea, 50 Tea Bags, 125g, £1.27 **(GF) (L) (N/S) (V)**
Buy the brand. This tastes too woody to be drunk without milk, but is little better with it.

---

(3) **TESCO** Finest English Breakfast Tea, 50 Tea Bags, 125g, £1.29 **(GF) (V)**
Pay the extra few pence and buy the brand; you'll get a cuppa that tastes twice as good.

Nescafé Gold Blend Freeze Dried Coffee

Caffeine

---

(7) **MARKS & SPENCER** Café Gold Freeze Dried Coffee, 100g, £1.99   **(GF) (N/S) (V)**
Put it in your trolley. M&S Café Gold is better tasting and cheaper than the brand.

NESCAFÉ GOLD BLEND FREEZE DRIED COFFEE, 100g, £2.14
Most regular freeze dried coffees have a gold lid and are more expensive. But they are better tasting than both regular instant coffee and decaffeinated freeze dried coffee.

---

(5) **ALDI** Alcafe Rich & Smooth Freeze Dried (Gluten Free) Coffee, 100g, £1.39 **(GF)**
This beats the brand for price, but the aroma and taste come second.

---

(5) **WAITROSE** Gold Rich & Smooth, Freeze Dried Coffee,   **(GF) (L) (N/S) (V)**
100g, £1.89
A cheaper alternative to the brand. But, side by side, Waitrose is edged into second place.

---

(5) **ASDA** Colombian Freeze Dried Coffee, 100g, £1.78   **(GF) (N/S)**
A cheaper alternative! Better than Asda Gold, but not as good as the brand.

---

(5) **CO-OP** Fair Trade Gold Roast Freeze Dried Coffee,   **(GF) (L) (N/S) (V)**
100g, £2.05
A few pence less than the brand, and just a couple of granules off in quality.

---

(5) **SAINSBURY'S** Taste the Difference Colombian   **(GF) (N/S) (V)**
Freeze Dried Coffee, 100g, £2.69
This equals the brand on aroma and flavour, but doesn't beat it on price.

---

(4) **SAINSBURY'S** Gold Roast Freeze Dried Coffee, 100g, £1.40   **(GF) (N/S) (V)**
Acceptable quality and worth the money, though there's a noticeable difference in taste.

---

(3) **MORRISONS** Gold Rich & Smooth Freeze Dried Coffee,   **(GF) (N/S) (V)**
100g, £1.40
Not so smooth! Tastes bitter with and without milk, so not an alternative to the brand.

---

(3) **KWIK SAVE** Gold Roast Freeze Dried Coffee, 100g, £ 1.69   **(GF) (N/S) (V)**
This requires milk to get it past your lips. Compared to the brand it is a big step down.

---

(3) **SOMERFIELD** Gold Roast Freeze Dried Coffee, 100g, £2.05   **(GF) (V)**
Too bitter. Somerfield shoppers should pay the extra and buy the brand.

---

(1) **ASDA** Smartprice Freeze Dried Coffee, 100g, 36p   **(GF) (N/S) (V)**
Undrinkable -1p would be too much! A coffee bean may just have passed over the jar.

Nescafé Original Instant Coffee

Caffeine

---

(10) **MARKS & SPENCER** Café Smooth Rich Roast Instant Coffee, **(GF) (N/S)**
100g, £1.39
A perfect 10 for taste – buy it. This is very much better than Nescafé and it's cheaper.

NESCAFÉ ORIGINAL INSTANT COFFEE, 100g, £1.63

Instant coffee is cheaper to produce than freeze drid coffee, but it retains less of that desirable coffee aroma. However, the caffeine levels (60mg per cup) are similar.

---

(5) **ASDA** Rich Roast Instant Coffee, 100g, 88p **(GF) (N/S) (V)**
This beats the brand for price, but is a notch down in aroma and flavour.

---

(5) **SAINSBURY'S** Full Roast Instant Coffee, 100g, 88p **(GF) (N/S) (V)**
Acceptable quality with milk, but without, it is not as good as the brand.

---

(5) **COOP** Fair Trade Medium Roast Instant Coffee, 100g, 99p **(GF) (N/S) (V)**
A lot more coffee for your money, but it comes second to the brand in aroma and taste.

---

(5) **MORRISONS** Full Roast Instant Coffee, 100g, £1.15 **(GF) (N/S) (V)**
A cheaper alternative, especially if you drink your coffee with milk and sugar.
The brand's better, though.

---

(5) **WAITROSE** Rich Roast Coffee, 100g, £1.24 **(GF) (L) (N/S) (V)**
Cheaper by a good few cups, but a few grains behind the brand in aroma and taste.

---

(4) **SOMERFIELD** Rich Roast Instant Coffee, 100g, £1.24 **(GF) (V)**
The brand beats this for taste, but it's a cheaper alternative for those who drink their coffee with milk and sugar.

---

(4) **KWIK SAVE** Rich Roast Instant Coffee, 100g, £1.25 **(GF) (N/S) (V)**
Without milk, this is a big step down in aroma and flavour. But it does go up a notch with milk.

---

(3) **ALDI** Alcafe Rich Roast Instant Coffee, 100g, 85p **(L)**
Almost half the price, but tasting this against the brand reveals about half the taste pleasure too.

Nescafé Original Decaffeinated Instant Coffee

NESCAFÉ ORIGINAL DECAFFEINATED INSTANT COFFEE, 100g, £2.14

The decaffeinated instant has a red lid, but the coffee granules are a darker brown. Like for like, the price is cheaper but the aroma and flavour are not as good as freeze dried.

(5) **ASDA** Rich Roast Decaffeinated Instant Coffee, 100g, 88p **(GF) (N/S) (V)**
Taste-wise this is a few granules down from the brand, but it is very good value.

(5) **MORRISONS** Full Roast Decaffeinated Instant Coffee, **(GF) (N/S) (V)**
100g, £1.39
People who drink their coffee with milk and sugar won't be able to tell the difference between this and the brand.

(5) **CO-OP** Fair Trade Rich Roast Decaffeinated Instant Coffee, **(GF) (L) (N/S) (V)**
100g, £2.05
Take your pick. Almost as good as the brand, but not that much cheaper.

(4) **WAITROSE** Decaffeinated Rich Roast Instant Coffee, **(GF) (L) (N/S) (V)**
100g, £1.49
A cheaper alternative to the brand for the Waitrose shopper, but not worth a special trip.

(3) **SOMERFIELD** Decaffeinated Rich Roast Instant Coffee, 100g, £1.57 **(GF) (V)**
Leave it on the shelf. This is a big step down in quality, with or without milk.

Taylors of Harrogate Colombian High Andes Ground Coffee

Caffeine, Niacin

(10) **ASDA** Colombian Ground Coffee, 227g, £1.26   **(GF) (N/S) (V)**
Under half price, and without or with milk it is difficult to distinguish this from the brand.

(10) **MORRISONS** Colombian Ground Coffee, 227g, £1.29   **(GF) (N/S) (V)**
Put it in the trolley. Under half price and of similar quality to the brand.

(8) **TESCO** Colombian Ground Coffee, 227g, £1.89
Grab a pack. Much cheaper and it delivers a similar aroma and taste quality to the brand.

(8) **WAITROSE** Colombian Filter Coffee, 227g, £1.99   **(GF) (L) (N/S) (V)**
A beat-the-brand buy for Waitrose shoppers. A similar quality and much cheaper.

(8) **WAITROSE** Colombian Cafétière Coffee, 227g, £1.99   **(GF) (L) (N/S) (V)**
This is the same quality as Waitrose's filter coffee and, likewise, an excellent buy.

(8) **SAINSBURY'S** Colombian Ground Coffee, 227g, £2.08   **(GF) (N/S) (V)**
Sainsbury's beans just edge this one for flavour, but it's quite a bit cheaper than the brand.

(8) **ASDA** Extra Special Colombian Supremo Ground Coffee, 227g, £2.18 **(GF) (N/S) (V)**
An "Extra Special" coffee that's worth the money. This is cheaper than the brand and of similar quality.

(8) **MARKS & SPENCER** Colombian Medium Roast,   **(GF) (N/S) (V)**
Ground Coffee, 227g, £2.49
Buy it. It tastes better than the brand, and it's a good few coffee cups cheaper.

(7) **TESCO** Finest Colombian Supremo Ground Coffee, 227g, £2.79   **(GF) (V)**
Buy it. A few pence cheaper than the brand, and the aroma and flavour are better.

TAYLORS OF HARROGATE COLOMBIAN HIGH ANDES GROUND COFFEE, 227g, £2.89

Ground coffee from a freshly opened packet is just as good as beans. Once opened, though, ground coffee starts to lose aroma and flavour.

(5) **COOP** Fair Trade Colombian Ground Coffee, 227g, £2.89   **(GF) (N/S) (V)**
Buy whatever is cheaper, for this is the same quality as the brand.

Horlicks Malted Drink

Milk, Niacin. Not suitable for babies under 12 months.

(8) **SAINSBURY'S** Malted Drink, 400g, 98p
Put it in the trolley. Much cheaper and it reveals similar flavours to the brand.

(7) **KWIK SAVE** Malted Drink, 400g, £1.38
You'll sleep better with this one. Beats the brand for price and equals it for taste.

(7) **SOMERFIELD** Malted Drink, 400g, £1.49
Buy it. This delivers similar taste quality to the brand, and it's a few cups cheaper.

HORLICKS MALTED DRINK, 400g, £1.64
A malted powder with added hot milk (or water and milk) delivers a soothing drink. It's caffeine-free and rich in vitamins. Remember, it is not suitable for babies under 12 months.

(4) **CO-OP** Malted Drink, 400g, £1.69 **(N/S)**
Better than Asda's, but a big notch down when tasted next to the brand.

(3) **ASDA** Malted Drink, 400g, 91p
Don't waste your money. Much cheaper than the brand, but the taste does not compare.

Cadbury Drinking Chocolate

Fat, Milk, Salt, Sugar

---

(9) **MORRISONS** Drinking Chocolate, 250g, 79p
A beat-the-brand buy. This is much cheaper and it equals the brand for taste.

---

(9) **SOMERFIELD** Drinking Chocolate, 250g, 79p
Grab it. This delivers similar chocolate flavours and sweetness at a cheaper price.

---

(8) **ASDA** Good for You Instant Hot Chocolate Drink, **(GF) (N/S)**
350g, £1.17 (£1.67 for 500g)
Similar quality to the brand and, gram for gram, it's 10p cheaper and has less sugar.

---

(8) **CO-OP** Drinking Chocolate, 250g, 95p **(GF) (V)**
Put it in the trolley. A similar taste to the brand at a cheaper price.

---

(8) **WAITROSE** Drinking Chocolate, 500g, £1.49 **(GF) (L) (N/S) (V)**
Similar quality and, when compared to price of the brand, it's an excellent buy.

---

(6) **SAINSBURY'S** Cocoa, 250g, £1.39 **(GF) (V)**
More expensive, but a much better option: very low in sugar with a real blast of cocoa.

---

(6) **TESCO** Finest Chocolate Drink, 220g, £2.49 (£2.83 for 250g)
This is very much better in quality and healthier too. It's well worth the extra hike in price.

CADBURY DRINKING CHOCOLATE, 250g, £1.25 (£1.79 for 500g)
A chocolate powder recommended with milk – semi-skimmed is the healthier option.
Be aware that this powder is high in sugar.

---

(5) **ASDA** Smartprice Hot Chocolate, 400g, 59p (74p for 500g)
Acceptable quality for the price, but it does not beat the brand for flavour.

---

(5) **ALDI** Camelot Instant Hot Chocolate Drink, 400g, 79p (99p for 250g) **(GF)**
Beats the brand for price, but the milky chocolate taste is not as good.

---

(5) **KWIK SAVE** Instant Hot Chocolate Drink, 400g, £1.58 (£1.97 for 500g)
Buy the brand unless the price has dropped. Gram for gram, this costs more for no better quality.

12
Mixers, Fizzy Drinks & Water

OK, we've seen by now that food labelling is far from perfect. In addition, however, the soft drinks industry has gone to new lengths to prove that nutritional information is not important. The vague labelling on so many of these highly sugared and acidic drinks is probably best exemplified by Coca Cola, the leading player in this field. Labels give little away, simply stating: "Further information can be found on www.coca-cola.co.uk/nutrition". This lack of easily accessible nutritional information is hardly helpful for the customer with a loaded trolley, shopping against the clock in a busy supermarket!

As with the fruit juices and cordials in the next chapter, much of the ingredient and nutritional labelling is poor. Manufacturers shouldn't be permitted to label just with E numbers, but they are and they do. It's very likely that you don't know that E211 is Sodium benzoate and E223 is Sodium metabisulphite. And yet both have been associated with food intolerance. To help you, I've listed the additives (and their E numbers) that should be avoided by those with food intolerances.

Schweppes Indian Tonic Water

Citric acid, Quinine, Sodium benzoate (E211), Sugar, Sweetener

(10) **ASDA** Indian Tonic Water, 1l, 32p **(GF) (V) (N/S)**
Great value! Not as dry-tasting as Schweppes, veering more towards a Britvic tonic.

SCHWEPPES INDIAN TONIC WATER, 1l, 82p
The drier tasting Schweppes tonic is more popular than the sweeter Britvic on our supermarket shelves. Sugar, at 50g per litre, is very high.

(5) **TESCO** Indian Tonic Water, 1l, 30p **(GF) (V)**
Much better than Tesco's low calorie version, but the brand still beats it for overall quality.

(5) **SAINSBURY'S** Indian Tonic Water, 1l, 35p **(N/S)**
More the style of Britvic than Schweppes, and sits just below the brand in quality.

(5) **SOMERFIELD** Indian Tonic Water, 1l, 39p
Worth a punt but, although dry and tingling, the taste quality is not as good.

(5) **WAITROSE** Indian Tonic Water Free from Artificial Sweetners, **(GF) (N/S) (V)**
1l, 45p
A much cheaper alternative, but the brand beats this on quinine aroma and flavour.

(5) **MARKS & SPENCER** Tonic Water, 500ml, 50p (£1.00 for 1l) **(GF)**
An alternative for the M&S shopper, though it lacks the quinine bite of the brand.

(4) **CO-OP** Indian Tonic Water, 1l, 39p **(GF) (N/S) (V)**
Under half price, but a good step down in taste quality compared to the brand.

(4) **TESCO** Finest Tonic Water, 6 x 150ml, £1.39 (£1.54 for 1l) **(GF) (V)**
Although a few pence cheaper per can, it won't convince the Schweppes drinker.

Schweppes Slimline Indian Tonic Water

Citric acid, Quinine, Sodium benzoate (E211), Sugar, Sweetener

SCHWEPPES SLIMLINE INDIAN TONIC WATER, 1l, 82p
The sugar has been replaced with sweeteners in this slimline tonic water. So there are fewer calories, but it tastes sweeter and leaves a metallic edge to the palate after the swallow.

(5) **ASDA** Low Calorie Indian Tonic Water, 1l, 32p **(GF) (N/S) (V)**
More acidic and drier tasting tonic than the brand, but it lacks its quinine punch.

(5) **KWIK SAVE** Low Calorie Indian Tonic Water, 1l, 33p **(GF) (V)**
A cheaper alternative, but if you want that piercing quinine and acidic bite – forget it!

(5) **SAINSBURY'S** Diet Indian Tonic Water, 1l, 35p **(N/S)**
Great value! However, the quinine is not as pungent on the palate as the brand.

(5) **CO-OP** Low Calorie Indian Tonic Water, 1l, 39p **(GF) (N/S) (V)**
Worth a punt, but it will lack sufficient quinine flavour for the regular Schweppes drinker.

(5) **SOMERFIELD** Low Calorie Indian Tonic Water, 1l, 39p **(V)**
Just edged into second place by the brand, but at below half price it's worth a punt.

(5) **WAITROSE** Indian Low Calorie Tonic Water, 1l, 45p **(GF) (N/S) (V)**
An excellent alternative for the Waitrose shopper, but it still comes second to the brand.

(3) **TESCO** Indian Low Calorie Tonic Water, 1l, 30p **(GF) (V)**
The cheapest "own label" tonic water, but it is a big step down in quality.

Schweppes Bitter Lemon

Citric acid, Quinine, Sodium benzoate (E211), Sugar, Sweetener, Wheat.
Some of the colouring can stain fabrics.

(10) **CO-OP** Bitter Lemon, 1l, 39p   **(GF) (N/S) (V)**
Buy it. This matches the brand for zingy lemon and it's less than half the price.

(10) **SOMERFIELD** Bitter Lemon, 1l, 39p   **(V)**
Put it in the trolley. Beats the brand on price and sugar and equals it on taste.

(9) **WAITROSE** Bitter Lemon Free from Artificial Sweeteners,   **(GF) (N/S) (V)**
1l, 45p
This beats the brand for taste and price, but it does contain more sugar and wheat.

SCHWEPPES BITTER LEMON, 1l, 82p

Bitter lemon is mouth-wateringly dry but, like most mixers, it's laced with sugar. This litre
bottle has over 80g of it – well over the recommended upper limit of 60g.

(5) **ASDA** Bitter Lemon, 1l, 32p   **(GF) (N/S) (V)**
Does not have the zingy pungency of the brand, but at 32p it's an alternative.

(5) **SAINSBURY'S** Bitter Lemon, 1l, 35p   **(N/S)**
Worth a punt! Contains almost half the sugar of the brand and runs very close taste-wise.

(5) **MARKS & SPENCER** Bitter Lemon, 500ml, 50p (£1.00 for 1l)
Millilitre for millilitre this costs more, but the taste is as good and it has less sugar.

(4) **TESCO** Bitter Lemon, 1l, 32p   **(GF)**
This contains more sugar and taste-wise it's a good notch down from the brand.

Schweppes Slimline Bitter Lemon

Citric acid, Quinine, Sodium benzoate (E211), Sugar, Sweetener, Wheat.
Some of the colouring can stain fabrics.

(10) **SOMERFIELD** Low Calorie Bitter Lemon, 1l, 39p
Buy it. Under half the price and delivers a similar zippy lemon flavour to the brand.

(9) **WAITROSE** Bitter Low Calorie Lemon, 1l, 45p   **(GF) (N/S) (V)**
This is much cheaper than the brand, and it has plenty of mouthwatering lemon flavours.

SCHWEPPES SLIMLINE BITTER LEMON, 1l, 82p
If you are weight watching or sugar counting, then slimline or low calorie bitter lemon is the one to buy. The sweetness is achieved with sweeteners rather than bags of sugar.

(5) **ASDA** Low Calorie Bitter Lemon, 1l, 32p   **(GF) (N/S) (V)**
Next to the brand this tastes watery, but it still has that zippy lemon bite.

(5) **SAINSBURY'S** Diet Bitter Lemon, 1l, 35p   **(N/S)**
Good value. Better than Sainsbury's regular, but taste-wise it's still second to the brand

(4) **TESCO** Low Calorie Bitter Lemon, 1l, 32p   **(GF)**
Like Tesco's regular Bitter Lemon, taste-wise this is a big step down from the brand.

Canada Dry Ginger Ale

Citric acid, Quinine, Sodium benzoate (E211), Sugar, Sweetener, Wheat

---

(10) **ASDA** Dry Ginger Ale, 1l, 32p **(GF) (N/S) (V)**
Grab a couple of bottles. It's cheaper, better tasting and has less sugar than the brand.

---

(10) **CO-OP** Ginger Ale, 1l, 39p **(GF) (N/S) (V)**
Buy it. Delivers a similar quality to the brand, bu with a bigger ginger hit – and it's under half the price.

---

(10) **SAINSBURY'S** Dry Ginger Ale, 1l, 35p **(N/S)**
The fiery ginger flavours may swamp some whiskies, but taste-wise it's better and cheaper than the brand.

---

(10) **SAINSBURY'S** American Dry Ginger Ale, 1l, 35p **(N/S)**
Taste-wise not as fiery as Sainsbury's regular, but there's fractionally more ginger spice than in the brand.

---

(10) **SAINSBURY'S** Dry Ginger Ale with Sparkling Spring Water, 1l, 35p **(N/S)**
Under half the price and it delivers comparable quality with a similar ginger hit to the brand.

---

(10) **SOMERFIELD** American Dry Ginger Ale, 1l, 39p **(V)**
A tad more fiery than the brand, but with less sugar and at under half the price.

---

(9) **WAITROSE** Dry Ginger Ale Free from Artificial Sweeteners, 1l, 45p **(GF) (N/S) (V)**
Cheaper and better tasting than the brand, but it contains wheat and has more sugar.

---

(7) **TESCO** Finest American Dry Ginger Ale, 6 x 150ml, £1.39 (£1.54 for 1l) **(GF)**
If you are happy with a small can, then this will suit: cheaper and comparable to the brand in taste.

---

(6) **MARKS & SPENCER** American Dry Ginger Ale, 500ml, 50p **(GF)**
Millilitre for millilitre this costs more, but you get a lot less sugar and a better taste.

CANADA DRY GINGER ALE, 1l, 82p

Carbonated water, ginger extract, citric acid, caramel and bags of sugar are the ingredients for this subtle ginger-favoured mixer. One can contains a quarter of your RDA of sugar.

---

(5) **TESCO** American Dry Ginger Ale, 1l, 32p **(GF)**
Worth a punt! Although this is much cheaper and contains less sugar, the brand beats it on taste.

Canada Dry Low Calorie Ginger Ale

Citric acid, Quinine, Sodium benzoate (E211), Sugar, Sweetener

(10) **ASDA** Low Calorie Dry Ginger Ale, 1l, 32p **(GF) (N/S) (V)**
If you want low calorie and a fiery ginger flavour, then this will hit the spot.

(10) **SAINSBURY'S** Diet American Dry Ginger Ale, 1l, 35p **(N/S)**
A tad more ginger aroma and flavour, but it delivers a similar quality to the brand.

(10) **CO-OP** Low Calorie Dry Ginger Ale, 1l, 39p **(GF) (N/S) (V)**
An excellent price! Slightly more spicy than the brand, but it's of no lesser quality.

CANADA DRY LOW CALORIE GINGER ALE, 1l, 82p
As a mixer to whisky this has to be the better alternative to the regular Canada Dry – it delivers its subtle ginger kick without the hefty sugar intake.

Schweppes Soda Water

Sodium bicarbonate

(10) **TESCO** Soda Water, 1l, 30p **(GF)**
Tesco beats the brand here. Nearly a third of the price for similar quality.

(10) **SAINSBURY'S** Soda Water, 1l, 35p **(N/S)**
Buy it. Under half the brand's price and there is little or no difference in taste quality.

(10) **SOMERFIELD** Soda Water, 1l, 39p **(V)**
Put it in the trolley. Matches the brand for taste and beats it on price.

(9) **WAITROSE** Soda Water, 1l, 45p **(GF) (N/S) (V)**
Pick it from the shelf. Beats the brand on price and delivers a comparable taste.

SCHWEPPES SODA WATER, 1l, 89p
There is nothing to worry about health-wise here; the ingredients are simply water and sodium bicarbonate. Soda water tends to taste better from cans and glass bottles.

(5) **ASDA** Soda Water, 1l, 32p **(GF) (N/S) (V)**
At this price it's worth a punt. However, taste-wise it comes second to the brand.

Coca Cola

Caffeine, Citric acid, Phosphoric acid, Sodium benzoate (E211), Sugar

(9) **SAINSBURY'S** Classic Cola, 2l, 69p   **(N/S)**
Many will prefer this drier tasting cola. As a mixer, you won't notice a difference.

(9) **WAITROSE** Cola, 2l, 69p   **(GF) (N/S) (V)**
Similar tasting to Sainsbury's. This too beats the brand for price and equals it for quality.

(8) **MARKS & SPENCER** Cola, 2l, 79p   **(GF)**
Slightly different taste, but the quality is comparable and it's as enjoyable as the brand.

COCA COLA, 2l, £1.32
Loved by kids and adults alike, but the combination of high sugar and tonnes of teeth-disolving acidity means that the world's dentists will never be short of work...

(5) **ALDI** Ameristar Cola, 2l, 39p   **(GF) (V)**
At this price it has to be worth a punt, but it comes second to the brand on taste.

(5) **ASDA** Cola, 2l, 44p   **(GF) (N/S)**
An alternative and well worth the money, but the brand still has the better taste.

(5) **MORRISONS** Select Cola, 2l, 45p   **(GF) (N/S)**
Worth the money. The flavours are close to the brand, but it still comes second.

(5) **KWIK SAVE** Cola, 2l, 55p   **(GF) (V)**
Well worth a punt. Not as satisfying as the brand, but comes close.

(5) **SOMERFIELD** Cola, 2l, 69p   **(V)**
More lemony and not as soft on the palate, but it's still a good buy.

(5) **CO-OP** Cola, 2l, 75p   **(GF) (N/S) (V)**
A cheaper alternative for the thirsty, but you're going a step down in quality.

(3) **TESCO** Cola, 2l, 44p   **(GF) (V)**
Not an alternative. Too lemony and, tasted blind, you'd struggle to identify this as cola.

Diet Coca Cola

Caffeine, Phenylalanine (high concentrations can cause disruption of brain development in the unborn foetus and children under 12), Phosphoric acid, Sodium benzoate (E211), Sugar

(10) **ASDA** Diet Cola, 2l, 44p **(GF) (N/S)**
Buy it. It tastes as good as the brand and it's well under half the price.

(9) **SAINSBURY'S** Diet Classic Cola, 2l, 69p **(N/S)**
A beat-the-brand buy. Harmonised flavours and plenty of sparkle at almost half the price!

(9) **SOMERFIELD** Diet Cola, 2l, 69p **(V)**
Put it in the trolley. A similar quality to the brand and lots cheaper.

(9) **WAITROSE** Diet Cola, 2l, 69p **(GF) (N/S) (V)**
Grab a bottle. Much cheaper, and it competes with the brand on taste quality.

DIET COCA COLA, 2l, £1.32

A healthier alternative to the regular cola, with sweeteners substituted for the usual high amount of sugar. However there's still plenty of acidity and caffeine to worry about.

(5) **MORRISONS** Diet Select Cola, 2l, 45p **(GF) (N/S)**
Used as a mixer this is fine. However, the acidity bites a bit too hard when it is drunk on its own.

(5) **CO-OP** Diet Cola, 2l, 75p **(GF) (N/S) (V)**
Cheaper, but the lemon flavours are a little too aggressive to beat the brand for taste.

(3) **SAINSBURY'S** Basic Cola, 2l, 23p **(N/S)**
This is drinkable, just. Surprisingly, the label does not say it's low calorie, when it is.

(2) **ASDA** SmartPrice Low Calorie Cola, 2l, 18p **(GF) (N/S)**
The Coca Cola drinker will find this difficult to swallow. Buy the brand or Asda's regular.

(2) **ALDI** Diet Ameristar Cola, 2l, 25p **(GF) (V)**
Leave it on the shelf. It's the same colour as cola, but that's where the similarity ends.

(2) **TESCO** Diet Cola, 2l, 44p **(GF) (V)**
This won't impress the Cola or Pepsi drinkers. It really requires a recipe revamp.

(1) **TESCO** Valu Cola, 2l, 26p **(GF) (V)**
Don't. This is undrinkable. Perhaps better poured down the sink?

(1) **CO-OP** No Added Sugar & Caffeine Free Diet Cola, 2l, 54p **(GF) (N/S) (V)**
Don't touch this, even if you have a caffeine intolerance. Good idea, but it tastes awful!

Fanta Icy Lemon

Phenylalanine (high concentrations can cause disruption of brain development in the unborn foetus and children under 12), Sodium benzoate (E211), Sugar, Sulhpur dioxide, Wheat

(10) **TESCO** Cloudy Lemonade, 2l, 44p **(GF)**
This beats the brand on price, contains less sugar, and delivers a comparable taste.

(6) **MARKS & SPENCER** Traditional Style Lemonade, 1l, 79p (£1.58 for 2l) **(GF)**
This cloudy lemonade is very much better than the brand, and well worth the extra.

FANTA ICY LEMON, 2l, £1.32
This "Icy Lemon" is what's known as cloudy lemonade: carbonated, cloudy, lemon-scented and tasting, with bags of sugar – this bottle has 240g of it which is quadruple your upper limit of 60g!

(5) **SAINSBURY'S** Cloudy Lemonade, 2l, 45p **(N/S)**
Worth a punt! The brand beats it for taste, but this still has that lemonade bite.

(5) **CO-OP** Cloudy Lemonade, 2l, 69p **(GF) (N/S) (V)**
A cheaper alternative, but with more sugar. It doesn't taste as good as the brand.

(5) **SOMERFIELD** Cloudy Lemonade, 2l, 69p **(V)**
This tastes much sweeter than the brand, although it has 150g less sugar in it.

(5) **WAITROSE** Cloudy Lemonade, 2l, 95p **(GF) (N/S) (V)**
Drier than the brand and not as lemony. It also contains wheat and more sugar.

Tango Orange

Phenylalanine (high concentrations can cause disruption of brain development in the unborn foetus and children under 12), Sodium benzoate (E211), Sugar

(10) **TESCO** Sparkling Orange, 2l, 44p **(GF)**
A beat-the-brand buy. A third of the price of the brand and of comparable quality.

(8) **MARKS & SPENCER** Sparkling Florida Orange, 2l, 79p **(GF)**
Put it in the trolley. It's cheaper, and the orange is better tasting than the brand.

TANGO ORANGE, 2l, £1.32
There are around 140g of teeth-rotting sugar in this bottle! (It is recommended that you consume no more than 60g of added sugar each day.) Don't bother looking on the label though – you only find that info on the Tango website.

Fanta Icy Lemon Zero Added Sugar

...henylalanine (high concentrations can cause disruption of brain development in the unborn foetus and in children under 12), Sodium benzoate (E211), Sugar, Sulphur dioxide

(10) **TESCO** Diet Cloudy Lemonade, 2l, 44p **(GF)**
A real thirst quencher that delivers a harmonious mouthful with a sweet-and-sour twist.

(9) **CO-OP** Diet Cloudy Lemonade, 2l, 69p **(GF) (N/S) (V)**
Buy it. This delivers plenty of lemony bite, and is of comparable quality to the brand.

...ANTA ICY LEMON ZERO ADDED SUGAR, 2l, £1.32
...nly 8g of sugar give this more lemony bite than Fanta's regular, which has 240g of sugar.

(5) **ALDI** Westdales Diet Cloudy Lemonade, 2l, 45p **(GF)**
Worth a punt at this price. However, compared to the brand it is not as flavoursome.

(5) **SAINSBURY'S** Diet Cloudy Lemonade, 2l, 48p **(N/S)**
A cheaper alternative to the brand, but the spiky acidity overpowers the lemon taste.

(3) **ASDA** Diet Cloudy Lemonade, 2l, 39p **(N/S)**
Leave it. The lemon tastes are not as assertive or as pleasurable as the brand's.

(3) **KWIK SAVE** Diet Cloudy Lemonade, 2l, 55p
Not a beat-the-brand buy. This has an artificial lemon twang that spoils your enjoyment.

Tango Diet Orange

...henylalanine (high concentrations can cause disruption of brain development in the unborn foetus and in children under 12), Sodium benzoate (E211), Sugar

(10) **ASDA** Sugar Free Orangeade, 2l, 33p **(GF) (N/S) (V)**
Similar quality, and at this price you'll get four bottles for the cost of one branded bottle.

(10) **TESCO** Diet Orange, 2l, 44p **(GF)**
If it's fizzy orange you want, then this is much cheaper than, and as good as, the brand.

...ANGO DIET ORANGE, 2l, £1.32
...ot as good as the regular Tango, but with just 14g of sugar.

(5) **CO-OP** No Added Sugar Orangeade, 2l, 55p **(GF) (N/S) (V)**
Healthier, with just 2g of sugar. But the taste is not as good as the brand.

R Whites Lemonade

Sodium benzoate (E211)

(10) **MARKS & SPENCER** Sparkling Lemonade, 2l, 79p   **(GF)**
Put it in the trolley. Cheaper and very much better than the brand on all fronts!

(9) **TESCO** Lemonade, 2l, 44p   **(GF) (V)**
A beat-the-brand buy. It's better than the brand on price and equals it on taste.

R WHITES LEMONADE, 2l, 82p

In my view clear lemonade is not as good, nor as tasty, as cloudy lemonade, but it has around half the sugar content (although it still contains 120g, which is twice the recommended upper limit.)

(5) **ALDI** Ameristar Lemonade, 2l, 39p   **(GF) (V)**
Just a whisper away in quality from the brand; but good value at this price.

(5) **CO-OP** Lemonade, 2l, 45p   **(GF) (N/S) (V)**
A cheaper alternative, but the brand has an extra layer of lemon flavour in the mouth.

(4) **SAINSBURY'S** Lemonade, 2l, 38p   **(N/S)**
Not an alternative to the brand, but it could work as mixer for a shandy.

(4) **ASDA** Lemonade, 2l, 39p   **(GF) (N/S) (V)**
As a mixer, maybe, but it's a good step down in taste quality compared to the brand.

(3) **SOMERFIELD** Lemonade, 1l, 35p   **(V)**
Lacks the lemon hit of the brand and tastes more like sugary water than lemonade!

R Whites Diet Lemonade

Phenylalanine (high concentrations can cause disruption of brain development in the unborn foetus and in children under 12), Sodium benzoate (E211), Sugar

(10)   **ASDA** Diet Lemonade, 2l, 39p   **(GF) (N/S) (V)**
Not that great, but it's under half the price and tastes as good as the brand.

(9)   **TESCO** Diet Lemonade, 2l, 44p   **(GF) (V)**
Grab a couple of bottles. This beats the brand for price and matches it on taste.

(9)   **CO-OP** Diet Lemonade, 2l, 45p   **(GF) (N/S) (V)**
Put it in the trolley. Co-op delivers everything the brand does, only much cheaper.

R WHITES DIET LEMONADE, 2l, 82p

Although a healthier option, this reduced-sugar version does not taste as good as the regular R Whites Lemonade. For most lemonade drinkers this would not be an alternative.

(5)   **KWIK SAVE** Diet Lemonade, 2l, 35p
Taste-wise the brand just edges it. However, it tastes better as a mixer than alone.

(5)   **SAINSBURY'S** Diet Lemonade, 2l, 48p
Straight from the bottle it comes second, but as a mixer or in a spritzer it will do fine.

(1)   **ASDA** Smartprice Low Calorie Lemonade, 2l, 18p   **(GF) (N/S)**
There's more taste in a bottle of soda water. Pay the extra and buy Asda's regular.

(1)   **SAINSBURY'S** Basics No Less Fizz Lemonade, 2l, 23p
Don't waste your money. It seems you can't make lemonade for this price – so why try.

(1)   **TESCO** Value Sugar Free Lemonade, 2l, 23p   **(GF)**
Not lemonade as we know it. A glass of tap water would please the palate more.

Evian Still Natural Mineral Water

(9) **ASDA** Eden Falls Still Water, 2l, 43p   **(GF) (N/S) (V)**
A brand beater. This delivers as much taste pleasure and is very much cheaper.

(9) **TESCO** Ashbrook Mountain Still Spring Water, 2l, 43p   **(GF) (N/S) (V)**
Put it in the trolley. Great saving, and it presents taste quality comparable to the brand's.

EVIAN STILL NATURAL MINERAL WATER, 2l, 72p
Tap water with pronounced chlorine can ruin the taste of a drink and home-filtered water tastes bland. For coffee and tea aficionados, it must be bottled.

(5) **ASDA** Smartprice Fountain Head Still Spring Water, 2l, 18p   **(GF) (N/S) (V)**
As a thirst quencher this will take some beating, but the brand beats it for flavour.

(5) **ALDI** Moreton Hills Elmhurst Spring Still Natural Mineral Water, 2l, 25p   **(GF) (V)**
Although the brand beats this for taste, it's excellent value for money.

(5) **MORRISONS** Still Spring Water, 2l, 42p   **(GF) (N/S) (V)**
A good water. Much cheaper, but next to the brand the taste comes second.

(5) **SAINSBURY'S** Caledonian Still Natural Mineral Water, 2l, 47p
A cheaper alternative, but the brand has an extra layer of flavour.

(5) **CO-OP** Fairbourne Spring Still Natural Mineral Water, 2l, 51p   **(GF) (N/S) (V)**
Not as flavoursome as the brand, but it's still a good drinker at a cheaper price.

(5) **MARKS & SPENCER** Still Water, 1.5l, 48p (64p for 2l)   **(GF)**
A cheaper alternative, but the brand beats the M&S water on pure taste pleasure.

(4) **SOMERFIELD** Strathglen Spring Still Natural Mineral Water, 2l, 49p   **(GF) (V)**
If you want cheap water, try another shop. This beats the brand on price, but not on taste.

(3) **SAINSBURY'S** Basics Still Table Water, 2l, 21p
No better than home-filtered water, and a big step down taste-wise from the brand.

(3) **CO-OP** Everyday Still Table Water, 2l, 31p   **(GF) (N/S) (V)**
For tea-making, it's worth a punt. However, alone it tastes bland next to the brand.

Highland Spring Mineral Sparkling Water

(10) **ALDI** Moreton Hills Brook Spring Sparkling Water, **(V) (GF)**
Plastic Bottle, 2l, 18p
A beat-the-brand buy. Amazingly cheap, and still delivers comparable quality to the brand.

(10) **MORRISONS** Sparkling Spring Water, Plastic Bottle, 2l, 42p **(GF) (N/S) (V)**
Ignore the brand and buy this. It's well under half the price and tastes just as good.

(10) **TESCO** Ashbrook Mountain Spring Sparkling Water, **(GF) (N/S) (V)**
Plastic Bottle, 2l, 43p
A beat-the-brand buy. Similar in quality to the brand, and perfect for drinking and diluting.

(10) **SAINSBURY'S** Caledonian Sparkling Mineral Water, Plastic Bottle, 2l, 55p
Put it in the trolley. Beats the brand on price and delivers comparable quality.

(10) **MARKS & SPENCER** Sparkling Water, Plastic Bottle, 1.5l, 48p (64p for 2l) **(GF)**
Beats the brand. Similar in quality to the brand and a lot more water for your money.

HIGHLAND SPRING SPARKLING MINERAL WATER, GLASS BOTTLE, 1l, 72p (£1.44 for 2l)
Like for like, water in glass bottles is more expensive than in plastic, but often tastes better.

(5) **SAINSBURY'S** Basics Sparkling Table Water, Plastic Bottle, 2l, 21p
This does not match the brand for taste, but it is great value.

(5) **TESCO** Value Sparkling Water, Plastic Bottle, 2l, 21p **(GF) (V)**
Similar tasting to Sainsbury's and, likewise, an excellent purchase for adding to cordials.

(5) **CO-OP** Everyday Sparkling Table Water, Plastic Bottle, 2l, 31p **(GF) (N/S) (V)**
Worth a punt. Not the quality of the brand, but suitable for diluting drinks.

(5) **ASDA** Eden Falls Sparkling Water, Plastic Bottle, 2l, 43p **(GF) (N/S) (V)**
A sound buy! Very much cheaper, and just a bubble away from the brand's quality.

(5) **SOMERFIELD** Strathglen Sparkling Mineral Water, **(GF) (V)**
Plastic Bottle, 2l, 55p
Compared to the brand this is good value, but it comes second on the bubble front.

13
Fruit Juice
& Cordials

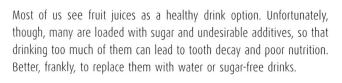

Most of us see fruit juices as a healthy drink option. Unfortunately, though, many are loaded with sugar and undesirable additives, so that drinking too much of them can lead to tooth decay and poor nutrition. Better, frankly, to replace them with water or sugar-free drinks.

As with the fizzy drinks in the previous chapter, much of the ingredient and nutritional labelling is poor. Many of the drinks in this and the previous section contain a source of Phenylalanine (amino acid). They should be labelled with the warning that too high a concentration of Phenylalanine can disrupt brain development in children under 12 and in a woman's unborn foetus. Drink in moderation!

Robinsons High Juice Pink Grapefruit

Citric acid, Colouring, Phenylalanine (high concentrations can cause disruption of brain development in the unborn foetus and in children under 12), Sodium benzoate (E211), Sugar, Sulphites (E221–E228), Sweeteners

---

(10) **ASDA** No Added Sugar High Juice Pink Grapefruit, 1l, £1.12 **(GF) (N/S)**
Put it in the trolley. Much cheaper, fewer calories and better tasting than the brand.

---

(10) **SAINSBURY'S** No Added Sugar High Juice Pink Grapefruit, 1l, £1.23
A beat-the-brand buy. This is cheaper, healthier and better tasting than Robinsons.

---

(10) **SAINSBURY'S** High Juice Pink Grapefruit, 1l, £1.23
Not as healthy as Sainsbury's No Added Sugar High Juice, but better in quality and tastier than the brand.

---

(8) **TESCO** High Juice Pink Grapefruit, 1l, £1.12 **(GF)**
Buy it. Not as pink as the brand, but it's cheaper and tastes just as good.

---

(7) **SOMERFIELD** High Juice Pink Grapefruit, 1l, £1.29 **(V)**
Grab it. This costs less money and tastes at least as good as the brand.

ROBINSONS HIGH JUICE PINK GRAPEFRUIT, 1l, £1.43
When diluted, this pink grapefruit delivers a sharp and refreshing mouthful of squash. However, don't let high acidity fool you; this bottle contains 446g of sugar (remember that the recommended daily intake of added sugar is 60g).

---

(5) **MARKS & SPENCER** High Juice Florida Pink Grapefruit, 1l, £1.11 **(GF) (N/S) (V)**
Cheaper than the brand. This makes a refreshing squash, although it comes second taste-wise when compared to the brand.

---

(4) **ALDI** Hyberry High Juice Pink Grapefruit, 1l, 89p **(V)**
Very much cheaper, but it is a big step down from the brand's taste quality.

Robinsons No Added Sugar High Juice Orange

Citric acid, Phenylalanine (high concentrations can cause disruption of brain development in the unborn foetus and in children under 12), Sodium benzoate (E211), Sugar, Sulphites (E221–228)

(10) **TESCO** High Juice Orange, 1l, £1.12 (GF)
A beat-the-brand buy. Cheaper and a much better balance of fruit, sugar and acidity.

(10) **TESCO** No Added Sugar High Juice Orange, 1l, £1.12 (GF)
Put it in the trolley. Healthier than the brand and with a more rewarding orange taste.

(10) **SAINSBURY'S** High Juice Orange, 1l, £1.23
Another brand beater. Cheaper, and it smells and tastes much better than the brand.

(7) **SAINSBURY'S** No Added Sugar High Juice Orange, 1l, £1.23
Beats the brand on price and health, and equals it on taste. But Sainsbury's regular is better.

(7) **SOMERFIELD** High Juice Orange, 1l, £1.29 (V)
Cheaper, and tastes at least as good as the brand.

(7) **CO-OP** High Juice Orange, 1l, £1.42 (GF) (N/S) (V)
Comparable taste and you'll find that this is a lot cheaper than the brand at the Co-op.

ROBINSONS NO ADDED SUGAR HIGH JUICE ORANGE, 1l, £1.43
This contains 50% juice and is better tasting than regular squashes. However, there is still a bucket load of sugar in this branded bottle; 440g to be precise.

(5) **MARKS & SPENCER** High Juice Florida Orange, 1l, £1.11 (GF) (N/S) (V)
Still worth a punt. Competitively priced, but the orange tastes watery compared to the brand.

(4) **WAITROSE** High Juice Orange, 1l, £1.32 (GF) (N/S) (V)
Cheaper, but it contains 60g more sugar than the brand, and the taste is not as good.

(3) **ASDA** High Juice Orange, 1l, £1.12 (GF) (N/S) (V)
A big drop in quality. Although much cheaper, it's not an alternative to the brand.

(3) **ASDA** No Added Sugar High Juice Orange, 1l, £1.12 (GF) (N/S) (V)
Healthier, but no better tasting than Asda's regular, and not an alternative to the brand.

Ribena Blackcurrant

Citric acid, Phenylalanine (high concentrations can cause disruption of brain development in the unborn foetus and in children under 12), Sodium benzoate (E211), Sugar, Sulphites (E221–E228), Vitamin C. Not suitable for children under three years.

---

(9) **ALDI** Hyberry High Juice Blackcurrant, 1l, £1.49   **(GF) (V)**
Grab it. This is very much cheaper and tastes as good as the brand.

---

(8) **MARKS & SPENCER** High Juice Blackcurrant, 1l, £1.59   **(GF) (V)**
Buy it. This is cheaper and matches the brand in aroma and taste.

---

(6) **WAITROSE** High Blackcurrant, 1l, £2.49   **(GF) (N/S) (V)**
Buy it. It's worth it. This delivers a great whoosh of blackcurrants to the nose and palate.

RIBENA BLACKCURRANT, 2L, £4.68 (£2.34 for 1l)
Ribena is rich in blackcurrant flavours. After dilution, a 100ml serving will deliver your RDA of vitamin C, but it does contain 10.6g of sugar. Not suitable for children under 3 years.

---

(5) **ASDA** High Juice Blackcurrant, 1l, £1.48   **(GF) (N/S) (V)**
A cheaper alternative, but it is beaten by the brand for blackcurrant aroma and flavour.

---

(5) **CO-OP** High Juice Blackcurrant, 1l, £1.78   **(GF) (N/S) (V)**
Much cheaper, and only a blackcurrant away from the brand in aroma and flavour quality.

---

(4) **KWIK SAVE** High Juice Blackcurrant, 1l, £1.55   **(GF)**
Not as good as the brand. The flavours taste more like wine gums than blackcurrants.

---

(4) **SOMERFIELD** High Juice Blackcurrant, 1l, £1.85   **(V)**
Less expensive than the brand, but there is a big step down in taste quality.

---

(3) **TESCO** High Juice Blackcurrant, 1l, £1.48
Leave it. Although it contains 35% fruit juice, you struggle to tell that it is blackcurrant.

Ribena No Added Sugar Light Blackcurrant

Citric acid, Phenylalanine (high concentrations can cause disruption of brain development in the unborn foetus and in children under 12), Sodium benzoate (E211), Sugar, Sulphites (E221–E228)

RIBENA NO ADDED SUGAR LIGHT BLACKCURRANT, 2l, £4.68 (£2.34 for 1l)

This Ribena Light contains 13% more fruit than the regular version, and has much less sugar. Why even bother to make the regular when this is healthier, better for your teeth and better tasting?

(4) **ASDA** No Added Sugar High Juice Blackcurrant, 1l, £1.48 **(GF) (N/S) (V)**
This does not taste as good as Asda's regular, or come close to the brand.

(4) **TESCO** No Added Sugar High Juice Blackcurrant, 1l, £1.78 **(V)**
Better tasting than Tesco's regular, but it's still a big step down from the brand.

Ocean Spray Cranberry Classic

Colouring, Malic acid, Phenylalanine (high concentrations can cause disruption of brain development in the unborn foetus and in children under 12), Sugar, Sweeteners

(9) **TESCO** Cranberry Juice, 1l, 57p
Put it in the trolley. This offers a similar taste quality and is almost half price.

(6) **MARKS & SPENCER** Cranberry Juice, 1l, £1.79 **(GF) (V)**
Almost double the price of the brand, but it delivers at least double the taste quality.

OCEAN SPRAY CRANBERRY CLASSIC, 1l, 94p
A juice that's rich in vitamin C; indeed, 200ml will deliver your RDA of 60mg. Unfortunately, the same quantity contains 24g of sugar and that's over one-third of your recommended daily intake of added sugar.

(5) **SAINSBURY'S** Cranberry Juice, 1l, 75p
Worth a punt. However, next to the brand, the flavour is a small step down in quality.

(4) **ALDI** Del Rivo Cranberry Juice, 1l, 69p **(GF) (V)**
Much cheaper than the brand, but it tastes more like wine gums than cranberries.

Ocean Spray Cranberry Classic Light

Colouring, Malic acid, Phenylalanine (high concentrations can cause disruption of brain development in the unborn foetus and in children under 12), Sugar, Sweeteners

(9) **ASDA** No Added Sugar Cranberry Juice, 1l, 57p **(GF) (N/S) (V)**
Grab a couple. Much cheaper, less sugar, and a better taste than the brand.

(7) **SOMERFIELD** No Added Sugar Cranberry Juice, 1l, 85p
Put it in the trolley. A similar taste, much less sugar and cheaper than the brand.

(7) **CO-OP** No Added Sugar Cranberry Juice, 1l, 89p **(N/S) (V)**
Buy it. A few pence cheaper than the brand and it presents similar flavours and quality.

OCEAN SPRAY CRANBERRY CLASSIC LIGHT, 1l, 94p
Half the sugar and a similar Vitamin C content, but the taste is so poor that health watchers and cystitis sufferers may find cranberry capsules/tablets a more palatable alternative.

(5) **SAINSBURY'S** Be Good To Yourself No Added Sugar Cranberry Juice, 1l, 79p
A healthier and cheaper alternative than the brand, but taste-wise it comes in second.

Ocean Spray
Cranberry & Raspberry Juice

Colouring, Malic acid, Phenylalanine (high concentrations can cause disruption of brain development in the unborn foetus and in children under 12), Sugar, Sweeteners

OCEAN SPRAY CRANBERRY & RASPBERRY JUICE, 1l, £1.14

This offers the same health benefits as unblended cranberry juice; however, it contains a little more sugar, and the flavour is altered by the addition of 5% raspberries and 4% apples.

(5) **ASDA** Cranberry & Raspberry Juice, 1l, 57p **(GF) (V)**
Excellent value! But the brand edges it into second place on all taste fronts.

(5) **SAINSBURY'S** Be Good to Yourself Cranberry & Raspberry Juice, 1l, 79p
A cheaper alternative, but neither the fruit blend nor the concentration is as good as the brand.

(5) **MARKS & SPENCER** Cranberry & Raspberry Juice, 1l, £1.99 **(GF) (V)**
Not worth the extra premium. Buy M&S Cranberry Juice (*see* opposite), which is cheaper and tastes better.

(3) **TESCO** Healthy Living Cranberry & Raspberry Juice, 1l, 57p
Although cheaper and healthier, this tastes watery and does not compete with the brand.

Del Monte Tomato Juice from Concentrate

Citric acid, Salt, Vitamin E

---

(10) **ASDA** Smartprice Tomato Juice, 1l, 38p   **(GF) (N/S) (V)**
A Smartprice that beats the brand! Poorer packaging, but you can't dispute the quality.

---

(10) **TESCO** Value Tomato Juice, 1l, 38p   **(N/S)**
A beat-the-brand buy. A cheap tomato juice that delivers super value on all fronts.

---

(7) **SAINSBURY'S** Tomato Juice, 1l, 75p
Put it in the trolley. This is of similar quality to the brand, costs less and the label gives you all the nutritional data.

---

(7) **TESCO** Tomato Juice, 1l, 75p   **(N/S) (V)**
Grab a carton. Cheaper, with a customer-friendly nutrition label, and it delivers a similar taste to the brand.

DEL MONTE TOMATO JUICE FROM CONCENTRATE, 1l, 83p
Tomato juice is rich in vitamin E, and a 200ml serving will deliver 22% of your RDA. However, that same quantity does contain around 7g of sugar (it is recommended that you consume no more than 60g of added sugar per day).

Del Monte Clear Apple Juice from Concentrate

Sugar

(9) **ASDA** Pure Apple Juice, 1l, 57p   **(GF) (N/S) (V)**
Beats the brand. Much cheaper, similar packaging and it delivers a similar flavour quality.

(9) **TESCO** Pure Apple Clear Juice, 1l, 57p   **(GF)**
This mirrors the taste of the brand, and you get more juice for your money.

(8) **SOMERFIELD** Pure Unsweetened Apple Juice, 1l, 63p
Beats the brand for price, equals it for taste and contains similar sugar levels.

(7) **CO-OP** Pure Apple Juice, 1l, 82p   **(GF) (N/S) (V)**
This is a beat-the-brand buy for Co-op shoppers. Less sugar and it tastes as good.

DEL MONTE CLEAR APPLE JUICE FROM CONCENTRATE, 1l, 83p
Clear/pure is not as tasty as cloudy apple juice. Healthwise, a 200ml drink will deliver one of your recommended five daily portions of fruit and vegetables; the downside is that it contains 22g of sugar.

(5) **ASDA** Smartprice Pure Apple Juice, 1l, 35p   **(GF) (N/S) (V)**
A very good alternative to the brand, under half the price, and just a pip away from the brand taste-wise.

(5) **SAINSBURY'S** Basics Apple Juice, 1l, 35p
Buy it. This tastes as good as Sainsbury's regular apple juice (*see* below) and is under half its price.

(5) **ALDI** Del Rivo Pure Apple Juice, 1l, 43p
Much cheaper, less sugar than the brand, but taste-wise it is a small step away.

(5) **SAINSBURY'S** Pure Apple Juice, 1l, 76p
Cheaper than the brand by a few pennies, but it comes second on the taste front.

Del Monte Pure Pineapple Juice from Concentrate

Citric acid, Sugar

DEL MONTE PURE PINEAPPLE JUICE FROM CONCENTRATE, 1l, 99p

You'll have had one of your recommended daily five portions of fruit and vegetables if you drink 200ml of this juice. But in doing so you will also have consumed over a third of your recommended upper limit of added sugar.

---

(5) **ASDA** Pure Pineapple Juice, 1l, 57p   **(GF) (N/S) (V)**
An excellent "own label" that's cheaper and just a squeeze below the brand in taste.

---

(5) **TESCO** Pure Pineapple Juice, 1l, 57p   **(GF)**
Tastes almost as good as the brand and, at this price, it's a seriously good buy.

---

(3) **CO-OP** Pure Pineapple Juice, 1l, 85p   **(GF) (N/S) (V)**
Pay the extra few pence and buy the brand, for this is not a palate pleaser.

---

(2) **KWIK SAVE** Pure Unsweetened Pineapple Juice, 1l, 59p   **(GF)**
Don't. This tastes metallic. It's labelled unsweetened – but it actually contains more sugar than the brand.

---

(2) **SAINSBURY'S** Pure Pineapple Juice, 1l, 63p
Leave it and buy the brand instead. It is cheaper, but the taste is at least four steps below Del Monte.

---

(2) **SOMERFIELD** Unsweetened Pineapple Juice, 1l, 63p
Like Kwik Save's, this does not compete with the brand taste-wise. Buy the brand.

Del Monte Smooth Orange Juice from Concentrate

Folic acid, Vitamin C

(9) **ASDA** Pure Smooth Orange Juice, 1l, 57p   **(GF) (N/S) (V)**
Put it in the trolley. This beats the brand on price and delivers comparable taste quality.

(9) **ASDA** Pure Orange Juice with Fruity Bits, 1l, 57p   **(GF) (N/S) (V)**
If you don't mind the bits, this has more flavour than Asda's smooth juice and the brand.

(9) **SOMERFIELD** Unsweetened Orange Juice, 1l, 57p
Buy it. Cheaper, smooth and of similar quality to the brand. Contains a bit more sugar.

(9) **TESCO** Smooth Pure Orange Juice, 1l, 57p   **(GF)**
Grab a carton. Next to the brand this delivers a similar taste quality at a cheaper price.

(9) **TESCO** Pure Orange Juice with Bits, 1l, 57p   **(GF) (N/S) (V)**
Great buy. The bits do add an extra flavour twist, though some people don't like them.

(9) **SAINSBURY'S** Pure Orange Juice, 1l, 57p
Grab it. It's cheaper and tastes as good as both the juice with bits and the brand.

(8) **CO-OP** Pure Orange Juice, 1l, 62p   **(GF) (N/S) (V)**
A smooth juice that's cheaper, has less sugar and delivers a similar quality to the brand.

(8) **SAINSBURY'S** Pure Orange Juice with Juicy Bits, 1l, 63p
Buy it if you like orange bits. Cheaper and delivers comparable taste quality to the brand.

DEL MONTE SMOOTH ORANGE JUICE FROM CONCENTRATE, 1l, 83p
Vitamin C and folic acid are both important to retain a healthy and balanced diet. However, the downside here is the high level of acidity and sugar, which can cause teeth decay.

(5) **TESCO** Value Pure Orange Juice, 1l, 35p   **(GF)**
Worth a punt! It's smooth, under half price and just a squeeze below the brand taste-wise.

(5) **CO-OP** Everyday Pure Orange Juice, 1l, 51p
Most drinkers would be happy with this Everyday juice, but it does not beat the brand.

(4) **SAINSBURY'S** Basics Orange Juice, 1l, 33p
Better than most hotel breakfast orange juice, but it's a notch down from this brand.

(4) **ALDI** Del Rivo Pure Orange Juice, 1l, 59p   **(GF) (V)**
A good buy for the Aldi shopper, but next to the brand it comes second.

14
Beer, Lager, Cider & Shandy

The take-home beer and lager market is a huge one, and the brands are constantly fighting for a bigger share. Nearly every week one of the prominent players announces a "not to be missed" special offer in the big retailers. Watch your step, though; often the savings are not as attractive as they sound. For instance, the bottles or cans in that discounted 24-pack may be smaller than in the regular 4 pack and/or the alcohol level may be lower. The marketeers are well aware that most shoppers don't stop to check. And even if you did, you'd need the latest duty rates and a calculator to work out the discount!

Sometimes, though, the brand is trying to claw back its market share, and then you can get the genuine good buys. But check carefully: the best before date may be about to expire. It's not often the shopper gets "ought for nought". The real bargains in this chapter are the best "own labels". Check them out!

John Smiths Original Bitter

Sulphites (E221–E228), Yeast *Number indicates units of alcohol per can/bottle*

---

(9) **ASDA** Best Bitter, 4 x 440ml cans, Alc. 3%, £1.69 **(N/S) 1.32**
A great buy for Asda shoppers. Cheaper and with less alcohol, but a comparable flavour to the brand.

---

(8) **MORRISONS** Best Bitter, 4 x 440ml cans, Alc. 3.5%, £1.79 **1.54**
A tad less alcohol, but it's cheaper and has better quality than the brand.

---

(8) **ALDI** Shipstones Bitter, 4 x 440ml cans, Alc. 4%, £1.99 **1.8**
Put a pack in the trolley! Much cheaper, and it delivers a similar quality to the brand.

---

(7) **SAINSBURY'S** Parkin's Special Bitter, 4 x 500ml cans, Alc. 4%, £3.05 **(N/S) 2**
At least as good as the brand and millilitre for millilitre it's a few pence cheaper.

---

(6) **TESCO** Strong Bitter, 4 x 440ml cans, Alc. 5%, £3.65 **(N/S) 2.2**
The best bitter of the tasting and well worth the extra premium over the brand.

JOHN SMITHS ORIGINAL BITTER, 4 x 440ml CANS, 1.8
ALC. 4%, £2.78

John Smiths Original does not have a draught widget, and is therefore cheaper than its Extra Smooth. Taste-wise though it does not have the Extra Smooth's pub-like quality.

---

(5) **TESCO** Best Bitter, 4 x 440ml cans, Alc. 3%, £1.69 **1.32**
Less alcohol and a cheaper alternative, but taste-wise it just comes second to the brand.

---

(2) **TESCO** Value Bitter, 4 x 440ml cans, Alc. 2.1%, 90p **(N/S) 0.92**
Cheap as hops, but most bitter drinkers will struggle to get a sip past their lips.

Stella Artois Belgian Lager

Sulphites (E221–E228), Yeast   *Number indicates units of alcohol per can/bottle*

(9) **ALDI** Sainte-Etienne Belgian Lager, 4 x 500ml cans, Alc. 5%, £2.69   **(V) 2.5**
Grab a 4-pack. Very much cheaper and it delivers comparable quality to the brand.

(8) **ASDA** Bière de Belgigue Belgian Lager, 4 x 500ml cans,   **(N/S) (V) 2.5**
Alc. 5%, £3.04
A beat-the-brand buy. This delivers a similar taste quality at a much reduced price.

(7) **MARKS & SPENCER** Etoile d'Or Belgian Lager,   **(N/S) (V) 2.5**
4 x 500ml cans, Alc. 5%, £4.49
Buy it. Like for like, it's a few pence cheaper, but it reveals comparable taste quality.

(6) **CO-OP** Belgian Premium Lager, 4 x 330ml bottles   **(N/S) (V) 1.7**
Alc. 5.2%, £3.05 (£4.06 for 4 x 440ml)
A few pence more when you compare millilitre for millilitre, but it tastes better
than the brand.

STELLA ARTOIS BELGIAN LAGER, brewed in the UK, 4 x 440ml CANS, ALC. 5.2%, £3.98 (£4.52 for 4 x 500ml)   2.29

Stella Artois, like most beers and lagers, tastes better when brewed in its home town.
Hopefully, soon there'll be a Stella from Belgium on our shelves.

(5) **SAINSBURY'S** Première Gold Continental Lager Brewed in Belgium,   **(N/S) 2.5**
4 x 500ml cans, Alc. 5%, £3.29
Cheaper and worth a punt for the Sainsbury's shopper, but the brand beats it on taste.

(4) **SAINSBURY'S** Bière des Moulins Belgian Lager, 4 x 500ml cans,   **(N/S) 2**
Alc. 4%, £2.49
If you're a lager and lime drinker, this will suit. However, on its own it's second best.

(4) **SOMERFIELD** Bière de Belgigue, 10 x 250 bottles,   **(N/S) 1.25**
Alc. 5%, £5.68 (£4.55 for 2l)
Buy the brand or try another shop, unless of course you want small bottles.

Heineken Dutch Lager

Sulphites (E221–E228), Yeast *Number indicates units of alcohol per can/bottle*

HEINEKEN DUTCH LAGER, 4 x 500ml CANS, ALC. 5%, £3.94 2.5
Heineken now brews this lager back in Holland rather than in the UK. The result is that both alcohol and quality have risen big time.

(5) **CO-OP** Imported Dutch Lager, 4 x 500ml cans, Alc. 3%, £2.19 **(N/S) (V) 1.5**
Well worth a punt! It's nearly half price and not that far off the brand's quality.

(5) **TESCO** Imported Premium Lager, 4 x 440ml cans, **(N/S) 2.2**
Alc. 5%, £3.11 (£3,47 for 4 x 500ml)
A cheaper alternative to the brand, but the Co-op's lager delivers better value and taste.

(4) **TESCO** Imported Highest Quality Lager, 4 x 500ml cans, **(N/S) 2**
Alc. 4%, £2.40
Not an alternative if you're a Heineken drinker, but it will be fine mixed with lemonade.

(3) **TESCO** Imported Light & Refreshing Lager, 4 x 500ml cans, **(N/S) 1.5**
Alc. 3%, £1.74
Less alcohol and under half price, but the taste quality is a massive step down.

(2) **TESCO** Imported Strong Lager, 4 x 440ml cans, Alc. 8.6%, £4.04 **(N/S) 3.7**
Buy the brand. Whatever the alcohol content, it should always be harmonious – this isn't.

San Miguel Spanish Lager

Sulphites (E221–E228), Yeast *Number indicates units of alcohol per can/bottle*

(10) **SAINSBURY'S** Cerveza de España Spanish Lager, 10 x 250ml bottles, **(N/S) 1.3**
Alc. 5%, £4.99
A 10-pack that's a real brand beater. Cheaper, more alcohol, and much better tasting.

SAN MIGUEL SPANISH LAGER, 4 x 330ml BOTTLES, ALC. 4.5%, £3.38 (£6.40 for 2.5l) 1.5
Ice cold on a hot Spanish beach, San Miguel is the perfect thirst quencher, but it lacks the depth and flavour of the Belgian and the Dutch lagers back at home.

Kronenbourg
1664 French Lager

Sulphites (E221–E228), Yeast *Number indicates units of alcohol per can/bottle*

KRONENBOURG 1664 FRENCH LAGER, 10 x 250ml BOTTLES, **1.25**
ALC. 5%, £5.58
Uses hops from Alsace, but is brewed in the UK. Bottles from France are also available here.

---

(5) **ASDA** Bière Continentale French Lager, 24 x 250ml bottles, **(N/S) (V) 1**
Alc. 4%, £6.68 (£2.78 for 10 x 250ml)
Not as good as the brand, but it'll hit the lager spot as a cheap thirst quencher.

---

(5) **ALDI** Brasserie French Lager, 10 x 250ml bottles, Alc. 5%, £3.29 **1.25**
Worth a punt! However, the brand has an extra layer of aroma and flavour.

---

(5) **ASDA** Bière de Deluxe French Lager, 10 x 250ml bottles, **(N/S) (V) 1.25**
Alc. 5%, £3.68
The same alcohol strength as – and a lot cheaper than – the brand, but not as tasty.

---

(5) **MORRISONS** Bière d'Alsace, 24 x 250ml bottles, Alc. 4.9%, **1.23**
£8.99 (£3.75 for 10 x 250ml)
This 24-bottle pack is much cheaper, but the quality is not as good as the brand.

---

(5) **SAINSBURY'S** Saint Cervois Brewed in France, 10 x 250ml bottles, **(N/S) 1.25**
Alc. 5%, £3.99
A cheaper alternative but, compared to the brand, it comes second on all taste fronts.

---

(4) **TESCO** Bière d'Or Brewed in France, 20 x 250ml bottles, **(N/S) 1**
Alc. 4%, £5.54 (£2.77 for 10 x 250ml)
Best value of the Tesco French lagers, but still a long way behind the brand taste-wise.

---

(4) **TESCO** Bière Spéciale French Lager, 8 x 250ml bottles, **(N/S) 1.25**
Alc. 5%, £2.94 (£3.67 for 10 x 250ml)
Not as good as Sainsbury's, and it won't please the palate of the Kronenbourg drinker.

---

(3) **TESCO** Bière Blonde Brewed in France, 8 x 250ml bottles **(N/S) 0.7**
Alc. 2.8%, £2.18 (£2.73 for 10 x 250ml)
Better Asda's (*see* below), but taste-wise, this is a very long way behind the brand.

---

(2) **ASDA** French Lager, 10 x 250 bottles, Alc. 2.8%, £1.99 **(GF) (N/S) (V) 0.7**
Cheap and low alcohol, but tasteless! Forget it. This is a poor example of French lager.

Carling British Lager

Sulphites (E221–E228), Yeast   *Number indicates units of alcohol per can/bottle*

---

(8)   **MORRISONS** Full Flavour Lager, 4 x 440ml cans, Alc. 3.5%,   **1.54**
£1.79 (£2.03 for 4 x 500ml)
Grab a four pack for the trolley. Much cheaper and it delivers comparable taste quality.

CARLING BRITISH LAGER, 4 x 500ml CANS, ALC. 4.1%, £2.97   **2**
At this quality level it's become difficult to tell British and Continental lagers apart.
This is an easy-drinking British lager with a hoppy twist on the swallow.

---

(3)   **TESCO** Value Lager, 4 x 440ml cans, Alc. 2%, 88p (£1 for 4 x 500ml)   **(N/S) 0.8**
Very cheap, and perhaps with lemonade? But you'll not get a Carling drinker to touch it.

---

(3)   **CO-OP** Premium Lager, Made in the UK, 4 x 440ml cans,   **(N/S) (V) 1.9**
Alc. 4.3%, £2.89 (£3.28 for 4 x 500ml)
Like for like, this is more expensive than the brand, and it does not compete taste-wise.

---

(2)   **ASDA** Lager Made in Great Britain, 4 x 500ml cans, Alc. 3%, £1.74   **1.5**
Don't! The smells delivers, but the swallow leaves an unpleasant, lingering, metallic twang.

Saint Omer Shandy

Sugar, Sulphites (E221–E228), Yeast   *Number indicates units of alcohol per can/bottle*

SAINT OMER SHANDY, 10 x 250ml BOTTLES, ALC. 1%, £1.59   **0.25**
This shandy is a mix of French lager and lemonade. Although the alcohol is just 1%, the
addition of lemonade means the sugar content has increased.

---

(5)   **ASDA** Traditional Lager Shandy, 10 x 250ml bottles,   **(V) 0.125**
Alc. 0.5%, £1.58
An alternative to the brand, but the lower alcohol means that the lemonade dominates.

Strongbow Dry Cider

Sugar, Sulphites (E221–E228)   *Number indicates units of alcohol per can/bottle*

(9) **ALDI** Taurus Strong Dry Cider, 2l, plastic bottle, 5.3%, £1.49   **(GF) 10.6**
Need cider? Grab this from the shelf. A couple of apples off half-price and better tasting.

(9) **ASDA** Premium Strong Dry Cider, 3l, plastic bottle, Alc. 5.3%,   **(GF) 15.9**
£2.48 (£1.65 for 2l)
Buy it. A big plastic bottle that delivers comparable quality and great value for money.

(9) **MORRISONS** Strong Dry Cider, 3l plastic bottle, Alc. 6.0%,   **18**
£2.59 (£1.73 for 2l)
Put it in the trolley. This is cheaper, has more alcohol and is better tasting than the brand.

(8) **TESCO** Strong Dry Cider, 4 x 440ml cans, Alc. 5.3%, £2.48   **2.3**
Pick this four pack from the shelf. It tastes better than the brand and it's cheaper.

(6) **CO-OP** Strong Dry Cider, 4 x 440ml cans, Alc. 5.3%, £2.99   **(N/S) (V) 2.3**
This costs a little more than the brand, but it smells and tastes better.

(6) **CO-OP** Strong White Cider, 4 x 440ml cans, Alc. 7.5%, £3.39   **(N/S) (V) 3.3**
Better tasting than the brand, and if you require the extra alcoholic kick, buy it.

(6) **ODDBINS** Westons Strong Extra Dry Oak Conditioned Cider, 500ml bottle,   **3**
Alc. 6%, £1.49 (£5.96 for 2l)
This is an exclusive cider to Oddbins and is well worth the extra premium taste-wise.

STRONGBOW DRY CIDER, 4 x 440ml CANS, ALC. 5.3%, £2.86 (£3.25 FOR 2L)   2.3
There are many ciders on our shelves that taste drier than this, but, in big-brand terms, this is dry. The apple flavours are sharp and thirst quenching.

(5) **TESCO** Value Cider, 2l, plastic bottle, Alc 4.2%, £1.38   **(GF) 8.4**
A real thirst quencher. It does not beat the brand for taste, but it's a great buy.

(4) **TESCO** Strong Dry Premium Cider, 4 x 440ml cans, Alc. 6%, £2.99   **(GF) 2.6**
You're paying the extra for the increased alcohol and the taste is not as good.

15
Wine (Red, Rosé, White & Sparkling)

Two thirds of all wine drunk in the UK is red, perhaps a result of publicity about the health benefits of red wine over white. However we still buy white wine in huge quantities and drinkers who are allergic to the colour pigments (anthocyanins) in red wine, could well find that those morning-after headaches would be cured if they drank the less healthy white!

Many will be surprised to learn that we in the UK are the second biggest consumers of Champagne – no prizes for guessing who comes first! Big discounts by the supermarkets, and competitively priced "own label" Champagne have been the main reasons for us quaffing nearly 35 million bottles yearly. But that's still around 150 million bottles less than France!

Unlike beer and lager, all wine is gluten free and suitable for coeliacs. Vegans, however, will find that some producers use egg whites or isinglass in their fining process. All alcohol can be enjoyed in moderation as part of a healthy lifestyle. It is recommended that men drink no more than 4 units a day and 3 for women. Unfortunately most bottles provide little or no information about units of alcohol. To make it easy for you, all the wines in this section are marked as units of alcohol per bottle. Enjoy!

Blason de Bourgogne (Red Burgundy)

Sulphites (E221–E228)   *Number indicates units of alcohol per bottle*

---

(7) **SAINSBURY'S** 2003 Red Burgundy, France, Alc. 13%, £5.49   **(GF) (N/S) 9.75**
This won't impress the burgundy aficionado, but it's cheaper, and as good as the brand.

---

(7) **TESCO** 2003 Finest Oak Aged Burgundy, France,   **(GF) (N/S) 9.75**
Alc. 13%, £5.49
Similar quality to Sainsbury's and, likewise, cheaper and of comparable quality to
the brand.

---

(6) **MARKS & SPENCER** 2003 Bourgogne Pinot Noir, Burgundy,   **(GF) (N/S) 9.75**
France, 13%, £6.99
A good buy! Not as good as Oddbins, but in a different league from the brand.

---

(6) **ODDBINS** 2002 Emotion de Terroirs Vincent Girardin,   **(GF) (N/S) 9.75**
Burgundy, France, 13%, £12.49
Worth it! Over double the price of the brand, but four times the quality.

BLASON DE BOURGOGNE 2002 PINOT NOIR, BURGUNDY, FRANCE
ALC. 13%, £5.96   9.75
Not the greatest red burgundy in the world. However, it would challenge any of the region's
very best winemakers to produce a palate-pleasing wine at this shelf price.

---

(2) **SOMERFIELD** 2002 Red Burgundy, France, Alc. 13%, £4.49   **(GF) (N/S) 9.75**
This wine makes the brand seem good value. Buy the brand or try another shop.

Calvet Reserve Red Bordeaux (Claret)

Sulphites (E221–E228)   *Number indicates units of alcohol per bottle*

CALVET RESERVE 2002, BORDEAUX, FRANCE, ALC. 12%, £6.99   9
Although this smells and tastes like Bordeaux, it's at the bottom rung of what is expected from this region. As with burgundy, you need to pay lot more than this to get good claret.

---

(4) **ASDA** Claret, Bordeaux, France, 12.5%, £2.62   **(GF) (N/S) 9.36**
Worth the money! It has the same aroma as claret, but lacks the power, depth and complexity of the brand.

---

(4) **TESCO** Claret, Bordeaux, France, Alc. 12.5%, £2.62   **(GF) (N/S) 9.36**
Quaffable, but it's very difficult to produce drinkable wine at this price – let alone one from Bordeaux.

---

(4) **SAINSBURY'S** Claret Special Reserve, Bordeaux, France,   **(GF) (N/S) 9.36**
Alc. 12.5%, £4.39
Less cash, but it is a step down on the brand's aroma, flavour and finish.

---

(4) **MORRISONS** Sichel Claret, Bordeaux, France,   **(GF) (N/S) 9.36**
Alc. 12.5%, £4.99
A cheaper alternative, but compared to the brand it comes second in sniffing and tasting pleasure.

---

(4) **ODDBINS** 2004 Château Daulibey, Bordeaux, France,   **(GF) (N/S) 9**
Alc.12%, £5.19
Cheaper, but the acidity out-bites the fruit. This comes a poor second to the brand.

---

(4) **MAJESTIC** 2001 Château Méaume, Bordeaux, France,   **(GF) (N/S) 10.13**
Alc. 13.5%, £6.99
The same price, but the brand still beats this for aroma, flavour and overall pleasure.

---

(2) **ALDI** 2003 Claret Château Selection, Bordeaux, France, Alc. 12%, £3.29   **(GF) 9**
This is poor plonk with "claret" on the label; it certainly makes the brand taste good.

---

(2) **SOMERFIELD** Claret, Bordeaux, France, Alc. 12%, £3.29   **(GF) (N/S) 9**
Don't! If it must be claret, buy the brand. Or at this price, try southern Italy.

---

(2) **CO-OP** 2003 Claret Reserve, Bordeaux, France,   **(GF) (N/S) 9.36**
Alc. 12.5%, £4.79
Leave it. This is a poor example of claret and it's not worth half this price.

Jacobs Creek (Australian Shiraz)

Sulphites (E221–E228)   *Number indicates units of alcohol per bottle*

---

(8) **ODDBINS** 2003 Snake Creek Shiraz, SE Australia, Alc. 14%, £4.99 **(GF) (N/S) 10.5**
Grab a bottle from the shelf. This tastes better than the brand and is cheaper.

---

(8) **MAJESTIC** 2003 Griffin Vineyard's Shiraz, SE Australia, **(GF) (N/S) 10.13**
Alc. 13.5%, £4.99
Buy it. This is of comparable quality to the brand and it costs a glass of wine less.

JACOB'S CREEK SHIRAZ 2002 SE AUSTRALIA, ALC. 14%, £5.99   10.5
A big fruit-driven wine that can be drunk on its own or trade tastes with the spiciest of foods.

---

(5) **ASDA** Australia Shiraz, SE Australia, Alc. 13.5%, £3.48 **(GF) (N/S) 10.13**
This will keep shoppers' wallets and palates happy. But the brand just beats it taste-wise.

---

(5) **ASDA** 2003 Reserve Shiraz, SE Australia, Alc. 14%, £3.98 **(GF) (N/S) 10.5**
A cheaper alternative, but it comes second on aroma power and palate concentration.

---

(5) **ALDI** Ransome's Vale Shiraz/Petit Verdot, SE Australia, **(GF) 10.88**
Alc. 14.5%, £3.99
Shiraz with a dash of the Petit Verdot grape, but it still comes second to the brand.

---

(5) **THRESHERS** 2002 Flinders Realm Shiraz, SE Australia, **(GF) (N/S) 10.88**
Screwcap, Alc. 14.5%, £6.99
Similar in quality to the brand, but at this bottle price it's too expensive.

---

(4) **SAINSBURY'S** Australian Shiraz, SE Australia, **(GF) (N/S) 10.13**
Alc. 13.5%, £3.49
A cheap slurper! The brand is more expensive but it's two leagues above this taste-wise.

---

(4) **ALDI** 2003 Evolution Old Vines Shiraz, SE Australia, Alc. 13%, £3.99 **(GF) 9.75**
Only beats the brand on price. The best "old vines" will generally produce much better wine. These don't.

---

(4) **CO-OP** 2004 Jacaranda Hill Shiraz, SE Australia, **(GF) (N/S) (V) 9.75**
Alc. 13%, £3.99
A £4 quaffer! Although it beats the brand on price, it certainly doesn't on taste.

---

(4) **SOMERFIELD** 2003 Australian Reserve Shiraz, SE Australia, **(GF) (N/S) 10.5**
Alc. 14%, £4.99
An easy-drinking Aussie wine! But taste-wise it's a good notch down on the brand.

---

(4) **CO-OP** 2001 Underworld Shiraz & Viognier, **(GF) (N/S) (V) 10.5**
New South Wales, Australia, Alc. 14%, £6.99
An unusual blend of Shiraz and the white grape Viognier, but the brand still beats it on taste and price.

(3) **TESCO** Australian Shiraz, SE Australia, Screwcap, **(GF) (N/S) 10.13**
Alc. 13.5%, £3.48
Although this is an easier drinker than Tesco's Finest (*see* below), the acidity still beats too hard.

(3) **TESCO** Finest 2003 Australian Reserve Shiraz, SE Australia, **(GF) (N/S) 10.13**
Screwcap, Alc. 13.5%, £4.99
Pay the extra and buy the brand. From lips to swallow the acidity is just too sharp.

Jacobs Creek (Australian Cabernet Sauvignon)

Sulphites (E221–E228)   *Number indicates units of alcohol per bottle*

(8) **CO-OP** 2004 Lime Tree Cabernet Sauvignon, **(GF) (N/S) (V) 10.5**
SE Australia, Alc. 14%, £4.49
Pick this bottle. The taste is different, but it's of similar quality and much cheaper.

JACOB'S CREEK 2003 CABERNET SAUVIGNON, SE AUSTRALIA, ALC. 14%, £5.99   **10.5**

Jacob's Creek Cabernet Sauvignon is a solid £6 worth of rich black fruits and vanillin oak notes, threaded with ripe tannins and backed by firm acidity.

(5) **THRESHERS** 2004 Flinders Realm Cabernet Sauvignon, **(GF) (N/S) 10.13**
SE Australia, Screwcap, Alc. 13.5%, £4.99
A cheaper alternative to the brand, which taste-wise more than delivers the extra cost.

(3) **ALDI** Mayrah Estates Cabernet Sauvignon, SE Australia, **(GF) 10.5**
Alc. 14%, £3.49
This is just plonk. You'd struggle to identify it as wine made from Cabernet Sauvignon.

Cono Sur (Chilean Merlot)

Sulphites (E221–E228) *Number indicates units of alcohol per bottle*

(8) **MORRISONS** 2004 Antu Mapu Merlot, Central Valley, Chile, **(GF) (N/S) 10.13**
Alc. 13.5%, £3.99
A beat-the-brand buy. Much cheaper and it delivers a similar aroma and taste quality.

(8) **ODDBINS** 2004 Carta Vieja Merlot, Loncomilla Valley, Chile, **(GF) (N/S) 9.75**
Alc. 13%, £4.49
Pick it from the shelf. This wine reveals comparable smells and taste quality to the brand.

CONO SUR 2004 MERLOT, CENTRAL VALLEY, CHILE, ALC. 14%, £4.99 10.5

If you are looking for value for money at below a fiver, then Merlot from Chile takes some beating. Here, ripe black fruits give pleasure from sniff to swallow.

(5) **ASDA** 2004 Chilean Merlot, Central Valley, Chile, **(GF) (N/S) 9.75**
Alc. 13%, £2.98
Great value for money! But it's a step down from the brand in aroma and taste.

(5) **TESCO** 2004 Chilean Merlot, Central Valley, Chile, Alc. 13.5%, £2.98 **10.13**
Comparable to Asda's. Likewise, the aroma and flavour are a step down from the brand.

(5) **SAINSBURY'S** 2004 Chilean Merlot, Central Valley, Chile, **(GF) (N/S) 10.13**
Alc. 13.5%, £3.25
Sip for sip, the brand wins. However, at this price this is good quality and value.

(5) **CO-OP** 2004 Chilean Merlot, Central Valley, Chile, **(GF) (N/S) (V) 10.5**
Alc. 14%, £3.99
A cheaper alternative! But It's a notch down on aroma and taste compared to the brand.

(5) **MARKS & SPENCER** 2004 Casa Leona Merlot, Rapel Valley, **(GF) (N/S) 10.13**
Chile, Alc. 13.5%, £4.99
Take your pick. Same price and it delivers a similar taste quality to the brand.

(4) **SOMERFIELD** 2003 Viña Morandé Merlot, Central Valley, Chile, **(GF) (N/S) 10.13**
Alc. 13.5%, £4.03
Buy the brand or try another shop. Although drinkable, it's not good value from Chile.

Antinori Peppoli (Chianti Classico)

Sulphites (E221–E228)   *Number indicates units of alcohol per bottle*

---

(10) **TESCO** 2000 Chianti Classico Reserva, Tuscany, Italy, **(GF) (N/S) 9.38**
Alc. 12.5%, £6.99
Stunning value. Delivers better tastes than the brand and is very much cheaper. Buy it.

---

(8) **ODDBINS** 2001 Il Tarocco Chianti Classico, Tuscany, Italy, **(GF) (N/S) 9.75**
Alc. 13%, £9.49
This is a beat-the-brand buy. Much cheaper and it delivers more palate pleasure.

---

(8) **MARKS & SPENCER** Basilica Cafaggio Chianti Classico, **(GF) (N/S) 9.75**
Tuscany, Italy, Alc. 13%, £9.99
One bottle won't be enough! This is cheaper and much better tasting than the brand.

ANTINORI 2002 PEPPOLI CHIANTI CLASSICO, TUSCANY, ITALY, ALC. 13%, £10.99   9.75

The price of good quality, drinkable Chianti has soared in the last few years. This is a pleasant drinking experience – and so it should be at £11!

---

(5) **ASDA** 2003 Chianti Classico, Tuscany, Italy, Alc.13%, £5.49 **(GF) (N/S) 9.75**
Passable as a cheaper alternative to the brand. Indeed, it smells and tastes like a Chianti.

---

(5) **ASDA** 2001 Chianti Classico Reserva, Tuscany, Italy, **(GF) (N/S) 9.75**
Alc.13%, £6.99
Mature fruit and old oak reveal a taste that most wine drinkers would associate with Rioja.

---

(5) **SAINSBURY'S** Classic Selection Chianti Classico, Tuscany, **(GF) (N/S) 9.75**
Italy, Alc. 13%, £7.59
Worth a punt! Cheaper, and not that far off the aroma and taste quality of the brand.

---

(4) **TESCO** 2002 Chianti Classico, Tuscany, Italy, **(GF) (N/S) 9.38**
Alc. 12.5%, £4.99
Trade up to Tesco's Reserva (*see* above)! Even at a fiver this is two big steps down from the brand in quality.

---

(3) **CO-OP** 2002 Chianti Classico, Tuscany, Italy, Alc. 12.5%, £6.79 **9.38**
This is another price level up from Co-op's Chianti, but it's still only just drinkable.

Melini (Chianti)

Sulphites (E221–E228)

Number indicates units of alcohol per bottle

(6) **SAINSBURY'S** 2003 Chianti, Tuscany, Italy,   **(GF) (N/S) 9.38**
Alc. 12.5%, £4.99
Buy it. This is another notch up in quality from the brand and it's well worth the extra.

(6) **MORRISONS** 2002 Chianti dei Colli Fiorentini, Tuscany,   **(GF) (N/S) 9.38**
Italy, Alc. 12.5%, £5.29
Put this in the trolley. It costs more, but you get a much better wine.

(6) **THRESHERS** Radcliffe's 2003 Chianti Colli Senesi,   **(GF) (N/S) 9.38**
Tuscany, Italy, Alc. 12.5%, £7.49
Much better quality than the brand! If you buy three, it reduces to £4.99 a bottle.

MELINI CHIANTI 2003, TUSCANY, ITALY, 12.5% £4.49   9.38
Chianti is a classification down from Chianti Classico, hence the price reduction.
However from the best producers, you'll pay at least double this.

(4) **ASDA** 2003 Chianti, Tuscany, Italy, Alc.12%, £2.99   **(GF) (N/S) (V) 9**
Worth three quid. But tasted blind, you would never guess that this was Chianti.

(3) **CO-OP** 2003 Chianti, Tuscany, Italy, Alc. 12.5%, £3.99   **(GF) (N/S) 9.38**
Only just! Indeed, it's almost impossible to source drinkable Chianti at this price.

(2) **ALDI** Chianti 2003, Casalaora, Tuscany, Italy, Alc. 12%, £3.49   **(GF) 9**
This is just plonk. At this price level, leave Chianti alone and try something from Chile.

Mateus Rosé

Sulphites (E221–E228)   *Number indicates units of alcohol per bottle*

(8) **TESCO** Portuguese Rosé, Screwcap, Alc. 11%, £2.52   **(GF) (N/S) 8.25**
Pick it from the shelf. Cheaper and comparable to the brand on all its flavour fronts.

(8) **SAINSBURY'S** Portuguese Rosé, Screwcap, Alc. 10%, £2.69   **(GF) (N/S) 7.5**
Buy it. Similar style and quality to the brand, but it's cheaper and has less alcohol.

(8) **MORRISONS** Portuguese Rosé, Screwcap, Alc. 10%, £2.99   **(GF) (N/S) 7.5**
Put it in the trolley. Much cheaper and it reveals a similar taste to the brand.

(7) **SOMERFIELD** Portuguese Rosé, Screwcap, Alc.11%, £3.49   **(GF) (N/S) 8.25**
A beat-the-brand buy. Cheaper, and delivers comparable quality to the brand.

MATEUS ROSÉ, PORTUGAL, ALC. 11%, £3.98   8.25
A clean, crisp and refreshing rosé in the famous flat, oval bottle. Unfortunately, many people in the wine trade get rather sniffy about this wine – and they shouldn't.

(5) **ASDA** Portuguese Rosé, Screwcap, Alc.10%, £2.52   **(GF) (N/S) 7.5**
Cheaper, but a small step down in quality. Taste-wise, this is slightly sweeter than the brand.

Michel Laroche (Chablis)

Sulphites (E221–E228)   *Number indicates units of alcohol per bottle*

(7)   **MORRISONS** 2002 Chablis/Chardonnay, Burgundy, France,   **(GF) (N/S) 9.38**
Alc. 12.5%, £7.49
Buy it. This reveals a similar quality to the brand, and it's cheaper.

(6)   **ODDBINS** 2004 Chablis, Bichat Frères, Burgundy, France,   **(GF) (N/S) 9.38**
Screwcap, Alc.12.5%, £8.49
Well worth the extra money – and it delivers another layer of flavour over the brand.

(6)   **MARKS & SPENCER** 2002 Chablis, Burgundy, France,   **(GF) (N/S) 9.38**
Alc. 12.5%, £8.99
This is as good as some *premier crus,* and it's much better than the brand.

(6)   **MAJESTIC** 2003 Chablis La Maladière, William Fèvre, Burgundy,   **(GF) (N/S) 9.38**
France, Alc. 12.5%, £9.99
Class act. This was the best Chablis of the tasting – and that includes the *premier crus.*

MICHEL LAROCHE 2003, CHABLIS, BURGUNDY, FRANCE, ALC. 12.5%, £7.99   9.38

This is one classification up from Petit Chablis – and one down from *premier cru.* It delivers the flinty and chalky dryness of the Labouré-Roi but lacks its concentration.

(5)   **ASDA** 2003 Chablis, Burgundy, France, Alc. 13%, £6.16   **(GF) (N/S) 9.38**
Better than Asda's Petit Chablis, but it still comes second to the brand taste-wise.

(5)   **SOMERFIELD** 2003 Chablis, Burgundy, France,   **(GF) (N/S) (V) 9.75**
Alc. 13%, £6.99
A cheaper alternative! However, taste-wise, the brand edges this into second place.

(5)   **SAINSBURY'S** 2004 Chablis, Domaine Sainte Céline,   **(GF) (N/S) 9.38**
Burgundy, France, Alc. 12.5%, £7.99
Take your pick, the same price and of similar taste quality to the brand.

(5)   **WAITROSE** 2004 Chablis, Cave Vignerons de Chablis,   **(GF) (N/S) 9.38**
Burgundy, France, Alc. 12.5%, £8.99
An alternative, but it's more expensive and no better in quality than the brand.

(5)   **THRESHERS** 2003 Radcliffe's Chablis, Burgundy, France,   **(GF) (N/S) 9.38**
Alc. 12.5%, £10.99
Too expensive! This is no better than the brand and it's four quid more.

(4) **CO-OP** 2002 Chablis, Burgundy, France, Alc. 12.5%, £8.99   **(GF) (N/S) 9.38**
Brand not available? Then try another shop. This is not as good as the brand and costs more.

(3) **ALDI** 2003 Chablis La Larme d'Oc, Burgundy, France,   **(GF) 9.38**
Alc. 12.5%, £5.99
Leave it. Drinkable, but it's a massive drop in quality when compared to the brand.

Blason de Bourgogne (White Burgundy)

Sulphites (E221–E228)   *Number indicates units of alcohol per bottle*

(6) **MARKS & SPENCER** 2004 Chardonnay, Burgundy, France,   **(GF) (N/S) 9.75**
Alc. 13%, £5.99
This costs half a glass more, but will double the palate pleasure of the brand.

(6) **TESCO** Finest 2003 Oak Aged White Burgundy, Burgundy,   **(GF) (N/S) 9.75**
France, Screwcap, Alc. 13%, £6.99
Buy it. The oak is harmonious and many drinkers will hardly notice its intrusion.

(6) **THRESHERS** 2004 Radcliffe's White Burgundy, Burgundy,   **(GF) (N & S) 9.75**
France, Alc.13%, £6.99
Even at this price (reduces to £4.66 when you buy three) it's a better buy than the brand.

BLASON DE BOURGOGNE CHARDONNAY, BURGUNDY, FRANCE
ALC. 13%, £5.61   9.75
If you compare this with Chardonnay from Australia at a similar price point, it competes well.
Unfortunately, you have to pay a lot more than this to get the true burgundian taste.

(3) **SAINSBURY'S** White Burgundy, Burgundy, France,   **(GF) (N/S) 9.38**
Alc. 12.5%, £5.19
Try another shop or buy the brand. This is a poor example of white Burgundy.

(1) **MORRISONS** 2003 Jean-Pierre Teissèdre, Macon Villages,   **9.75**
Burgundy, France, Alc.13%, £4.99
Don't waste your money. The label sends the right signals, but the wine is a disgrace.

Jacob's Creek (Australian Chardonnay)

Sulphites (E221–E228)   *Number indicates units of alcohol per bottle*

(9) **ASDA** Australian Chardonnay, SE Australia, Alc. 13%, £3.32   **(GF) (N/S) 9.75**
Grab a bottle. This fruit-driven Chardonnay is just as drinkable as the brand, and cheaper.

(9) **SAINSBURY'S** Australian Chardonnay, SE Australia,   **(GF) (N/S) 9.75**
13%, £3.49
A beat-the-brand buy. An easier drink compared to the brand and very much cheaper.

(8) **TESCO** Finest 2004 Australian Chardonnay Reserve,   **(GF) (N/S) 9.75**
SE Australia, Screwcap, Alc. 13%, £4.99
Pick it from the shelf. Cheaper and there's little difference in taste from the brand.

(6) **ODDBINS** 2003 The Olive Grove, Chardonnay,   **(GF) (N/S) 10.5**
McLaren Vale, South Australia, Screwcap, Alc. 14%, £7.99
More money, but it's worth it! This has an extra layer of flavour when compared to
the brand.

JACOB'S CREEK 2004 CHARDONNAY, SE AUSTRALIA, ALC. 12.5%, £5.99   9.38

Chardonnay is the same grape that is used to make Chablis. But unlike the flinty dryness
that is associated with Chablis, in Australia the grape gives ripe melon flavours threaded
with sharp acidity and finished with toasty oak.

(5) **MORRISONS** 2003 Woolpunda Chardonnay, South Australia,   **(GF) (N/S) 9.75**
Screwcap, Alc. 13%, £3.69
A cheaper alternative for the Morrisons shopper, but the brand just edges it taste-wise.

(5) **MAJESTIC** 2003 Coldridge Estate Chardonnay, SE Australia,   **(GF) (N/S) 9.38**
Alc. 12.5%, £3.69
Worth a punt! It's close in quality, but the brand just beats it on the complete palate
experience.

(5) **SOMERFIELD** 2003, First Flight, Reserve Chardonnay,   **(GF) (N/S) 10.13**
SE Australia, Alc. 13.5%, £4.99
Worth a punt for the Somerfield shopper, but taste-wise the brand just beats it.

Ernest & Julio Gallo Turning Leaf (Californian Chardonnay)

Sulphites (E221–E228)   *Number indicates units of alcohol per bottle*

---

(9) **ASDA** 2003 Californian Chardonnay, California,   **(GF) (N/S) (V) 9.75**
Alc. 13%, £3.52
Pick a couple from the shelf. Much cheaper and you'll get as much palate pleasure.

---

(8) **ASDA** 2002 Californian Reserve Chardonnay, California,   **(GF) (N/S) (V) 10.13**
Alc. 13.5%, £4.52
Buy it. However, this fruity wine does include oak notes that beat from sip to swallow.

ERNEST & JULIO GALLO TURNING LEAF CHARDONNAY, CALIFORNIA, SCREWCAP, ALC.13.5%, £4.99   10.13

It's rare for a wine to actually present the flavours it says on the back label: apples and pears flavoured with vanilla on the finish. I would add ripe acidity and a touch of oak to that description.

---

(5) **SAINSBURY'S** 2003 Californian Chardonnay, California,   **(GF) (N/S) 10.13**
Alc. 13.5%, £3.99
A cheaper alternative to the brand, but taste-wise it is a step down in quality.

---

(4) **ALDI** 2002 Gold Coast Chardonnay, California, Alc. 14%, £2.99   **(GF) 10.5**
Worth three quid, but it does not compete with the brand on any taste front.

---

(4) **MAJESTIC** 2003 Leaping Horse Chardonnay, California,   **(GF) (N/S) 10.13**
Alc. 13.5%, £4.99
Cheaper, but taste-wise this is a couple of notches down in quality from the brand.

---

(3) **CO-OP** 2002 Starlight Coast, California, Screwcap,   **(GF) (N/S) (V) 10.13**
Alc. 13.5%, £5.49
More expensive, and the oak beats out of tune, leaving an unpleasant sour taste.

Montana Sauvignon Blanc

Sulphites (E221–E228)   *Number indicates units of alcohol per bottle*

---

(6)   **MAJESTIC** 2004 Fairleigh Estate Sauvignon Blanc,   **(GF) (N/S) 10.13**
Marlborough, New Zealand, Screwcap, Alc. 13.5%, £6.99
As pungent as the brand, but this has more palate pleasure and is worth the extra cash.

(6)   **MORRISONS** 2004 Sancerre Le Haugeard, Loire, France,   **(GF) (N/S) 9.38**
Alc. 12.5%, £7.99
Worth the extra! This French wine has an extra of layer of flavour over the brand.

MONTANA 2004 SAUVIGNON BLANC, MARLBOROUGH, NEW ZEALAND, SCREWCAP, ALC. 12.5%, £6.49   9.38

Sauvignon Blanc from New Zealand is the benchmark here. Indeed, if you want pungent and mouth-watering, grassy, gooseberry aromas and flavours then this brand delivers.

---

(5)   **CO-OP** 2004 Explorers Vineyard Sauvignon Blanc,   **(GF) (N/S) 9.38**
Marlborough, New Zealand, Screwcap, Alc. 12.5%, £6.49
Buy whichever is the cheapest! The price and quality is similar to the brand.

(5)   **SAINSBURY'S** Reserve Selection 2004, Sauvignon Blanc,   **(GF) (N/S) 9.38**
Marlborough, New Zealand, Screwcap, Alc. 12.5%, £6.49
Take your pick. Same price and similar in aroma and taste quality to the brand.

(5)   **ASDA** Extra Special 2004 Sauvignon Blanc, Marlborough,   **(GF) (N/S) 9.75**
New Zealand, Screwcap, Alc. 13%, £6.98
An alternative if the brand's not around, for it delivers similar quality on all fronts.

(5)   **ODDBINS** 2004 Matahiwi Sauvignon Blanc, Wairarapa,   **(GF) (N/S) 9**
New Zealand, Screwcap, Alc. 12%, £7.49
As good as the brand, but it does nothing to suggest it's worth the extra quid.

(5)   **TESCO** Finest 2004 Sauvignon Blanc, Marlborough,   **(GF) (N/S) 9.38**
New Zealand, Screwcap, Alc. 12.5%, £7.49
Buy the brand – unless it has rocketed up in price – for this is no better quality.

(5)   **ASDA** 2004 Sancerre Vieilles Vignes, Loire, France, Alc. 13%, £9.98 **(GF) (N/S) 9.75**
Made from grapes from old vines. Different, but of similar quality to the brand.

(5)   **THRESHERS** Radcliffe's 2004 Pouilly Fumé, Loire, France,   **(GF) (N/S) 9.38**
Alc. 12.5%, £12.99
Very expensive! No better quality – you'll get two bottles of the brand for the this price.

Hugel Gewürztraminer

Number indicates units of alcohol per bottle

(9) **SAINSBURY'S** 2003 Alsace Gewürztraminer, Alsace, France, **(GF) (N/S) 10.13**
Alc. 13.5%, £6.99
"Own labels" like this make it worthwhile. Much cheaper and comparable in palate pleasure.

HUGEL 2003, GEWÜRZTRAMINER, ALSACE, FRANCE, ALC. 14%, £11.50   10.5

Hugel is one of Alsace's top producers. This wine is made from the Gewürztraminer grape and it presents a harmonised mix of spice, sultanas and acidity.

(5) **MORRISONS** 2003 Preiss-Zimmer Gewürztraminer, Alsace, France,   **10.13**
Alc. 13.5%, £6.49
Good value and worth a punt but, as you might expect, it's a step down from the brand.

(5) **SOMERFIELD'S** 2003 Gewürztraminer, Alsace, France,   **(GF) (N/S) (V) 10.13**
Alc. 13.5%, £6.99
You'll be more than happy with this wine – nearly the brand's quality, but much cheaper.

(5) **MARKS & SPENCER** 2003 Gewürztraminer, Alsace, France,   **(GF) (N/S) 9.75**
Alc. 13%, £6.99
If you can't get the brand then this will hit the spot.

(5) **WAITROSE** 2004 Gewürztraminer, Alsace, France, Screwcap,   **(GF) (N/S) 10.5**
Alc. 14%, £6.99
This is an alternative. The brand is quality wine, but this is certainly a cheaper option.

(5) **TESCO** Finest Gewürztraminer, Alsace, France, Alc. 13.5%, £6.99 **(GF) (N/S) 10.13**
Does not have the concentration of the brand, but it is well worth seven quid.

(5) **THRESHERS** Radcliffe's 2003 Gewürztraminer, Alsace, France,   **(GF) (N/S) 10.13**
Alc. 13.5%, £9.99
Try another shop. This is no better than the M&S bottle and it's £3 more.

(4) **CO-OP** 2004 Chilean Gewürztraminer, Central Valley, Chile,   **(GF) (N/S) 9.75**
Alc. 13%, £4.79
Couple of notches down from the brand taste-wise, but it's still worth a punt.

(3) **ODDBINS** 2004 Hare Label Lingenfelder Gewürztraminer,   **(GF) (N/S) 9.75**
Germany, Screwcap, Alc. 13%, £6.49
Leave it. This is poor value – Co-op's Chilean delivers better value and taste.

Blue Nun (Medium-Dry German White Wine)

Sugar, Sulphites (E221–E228)

Number indicates units of alcohol per bottle

(9) **MORRISONS** Franz Reh Kabinett, Rheinhessen, Germany, **(GF) (N/S) 6.75**
Alc. 9%, £2.79
This won't work for the sweet toothed, but it matches the brand for taste quality.

(9) **ALDI** 2003 Gisbertus Riesling, Mosel, Germany, Screwcap, **(GF) 9**
Alc. 12%, £2.99
Very good value. Medium dry palates may find this a little too dry, though.

(8) **ASDA** Piesporter Riesling, Mosel-Saar-Ruwer, Germany, **(GF) (N/S) 6.75**
Screwcap, Alc. 9%, £3.52
A beat-the-brand buy. A tad drier than the brand, but the taste is better and it's cheaper.

(8) **CO-OP** Piesporter Michelsberg, Mosel-Saar-Ruwer, Germany, **(GF) (N/S) 6.75**
Screwcap, Alc. 9%, £3.35
Buy it. Cheaper, cleaner fruit flavours and more palate pleasure than the brand.

(8) **MARKS & SPENCER** 2004 Liebfraumilch, Rheinhessen, **(GF) (N/S) 8.25**
Germany, Screwcap, Alc. 11%, £3.79
Buy it. This tastes a little drier than the brand, but the quality is as good.

BLUE NUN 2003, RHEINHESSEN, GERMANY, ALC. 10.5%, £4.49   7.88
A German wine that has been on our shelves for years! Although this medium-dry style is
losing its market share, this and the supermarket equivalents still command shelf space.

(5) **COOP** Liebfraumilch, Rheinhessen, Germany, Screwcap, **(GF) (N/S) 7.5**
Alc. 10%, £2.45
Worth a punt! The quality here does not quite match up to the brand taste-wise.

(1) **SAINSBURY'S** Liebfraumilch, Nahe, Germany, Screwcap, **(GF) (N/S) 6.75**
Alc. 9%, £2.05
Leave it. This tastes rubbish. Sainsbury's shoppers deserve much better than this.

La Grille Muscadet

Number indicates units of alcohol per bottle

(8) **ASDA** 2004 Muscadet de Sèvre-et-Maine, Loire, France,   **(GF) (N/S) 9**
Alc. 12%, £3.61
Buy it. Cheaper, and its mouth-watering dryness competes with the brand taste-wise.

(8) **SAINSBURY'S** Muscadet de Sèvre-et-Maine, Loire, France,   **(GF) (N/S) 9**
Alc. 12%, £3.99
Pick it from the shelf. This wine will hit the spot taste-wise and it's cheaper than the brand.

(6) **ODDBINS** 2004 Dom Vieux Chais, Muscadet de Sèvre-et-Maine,   **(GF) (N/S) 9**
Loire, France, Alc. 12%, £5.49
It costs more, but it's worth it. An extra layer of flavour from sip to swallow.

LA GRILLE 2004 MUSCADET, LOIRE, FRANCE, ALC. 12%, £4.99   9

Muscadet is a bone-dry white wine made from Melon de Bourgogne grapes. Its subtle
nuances have the ability to complement, rather than overpower, delicate dishes.

(5) **MORRISONS** 2003 Remy Pannier Muscadet de Sèvre-et-Maine,   **(GF) (N/S) 9**
Loire, France, Alc. 12%, £3.99
A cheaper alternative, but next to the brand it comes second on all taste fronts.

(4) **COOP** Muscadet, Loire, France, Alc. 12%, £2.99   **(GF) (N/S) 9**
A much cheaper option, but next to the brand it delivers a mean, pippy dryness.

(4) **THRESHERS** Radcliffe's Muscadet de Sèvre-et-Maine, Loire,   **(GF) (N/S) 9**
France, Alc. 12%, £5.49
Too expensive, and it's a big step down from the brand taste-wise.

Freixenet Non-Vintage Cava

Number indicates units of alcohol per bottle

(9) **SAINSBURY'S** Brut NV Traditional Method Cava, Spain, **(GF) (N/S) 8.63**
Alc. 11.5%, £3.79
Put it in the trolley. Very much cheaper and it reveals comparable quality to the brand.

(8) **CO-OP** Brut NV Traditional Method, Cava, Spain, **(GF) (N/S) 8.63**
Alc. 11.5%, £4.99
Grab a bottle from the shelf. Cheaper and of similar quality to the brand.

(8) **WAITROSE** Brut NV Traditional Method Cava, Spain, **(GF) (N/S) 8.63**
Alc. 11.5%, £4.99
A beat-the-brand buy for the Waitrose shopper. Cheaper and tastes as good as the brand.

(8) **SOMERFIELD** Blanc de Blancs Brut NV Medium-Dry Cava, **(GF) (N/S) (V) 8.63**
Spain, Alc. 11.5%, £4.99
Produced from the juice of white grapes this delivers a fizz of comparable quality.

(8) **SOMERFIELD** Blanc de Blancs NV Cava, Spain, **(GF) (N/S) (V) 8.63**
Alc. 11.5%, £4.99
Similar quality to Somerfield's brut, but with a sweet and sour swirl on the swallow.

(7) **MARKS & SPENCER** Brut NV Traditional Method Cava, **(GF) (N/S) 8.63**
Spain, Alc. 11.5%, £6.25
Not as cheap as other "own labels, but it beats the brand and delivers similar quality.

(7) **MARKS & SPENCER** Traditional Method NV Cava **(GF) (N/S) (V) 8.63**
Medium-Dry, Spain, Alc. 11.5%, £6.25
This sweeter version is of no lesser quality and will be preferred by many drinkers.

FREIXENET NON-VINTAGE BRUT TRADITIONAL METHOD CAVA, SPAIN, ALC. 11.5%, £6.47–£7.49 8.63

Cava is Spain's most well known fizz. "Brut" on the label indicates that it will taste dry, and "traditional method" means it has been made in a similar way to Champagne.

(5) **ASDA** Mas Miralda NV Brut Cava, Spain, Alc. 11.5%, £3.72 **(GF) (N/S) (V) 8.63**
At this price it's well worth a punt. However, the brand has that extra flavour twist.

Freixenet Vintage Cava

Sulphites (E221–E228)

Number indicates units of alcohol per bottle

FREIXENET 2001 BRUT NATURE TRADITIONAL METHOD CAVA, SPAIN, ALC. 11.5%, £8.99
8.63

This is a seriously dry cava! Almost all sparkling wines (including Champagne) undergo *dosage* – a process by which sugar is added before corking. This process determines if the fizz will be bone dry (brut), dry (sec) or medium-dry (demi-sec). This has none!

(5) **ASDA** 2002 Mas Miralda Brut Cava, Spain, Alc. 11.5%, £5.93 **(GF) (N/S) (V) 8.63**
Cheaper alternative to the brand, but a step down on the aroma and flavour fronts.

(5) **MORRISONS** 2001 Roca I Amat Brut Cava, Spain, **(GF) (N/S) 8.63**
Alc. 11.5%, £5.99
This bubbles well and tastes good, but it's still edged into second place by the brand.

(5) **SOMERFIELD** 2000 Brut Cava, Spain, Alc. 11.5%, £6.99 **(GF) (N/S) (V) 8.63**
A cheaper option! However, next to the brand, it's a step down in palate pleasure.

(5) **THRESHERS** Radcliffe's 2003 Vintage Reserva Brut Cava, **(GF) (N/S) 8.63**
Spain, Alc. 11.5%, £7.49
A cheaper option. Although the brand is drier, it's a notch up in taste quality.

(5) **THRESHERS** Radcliffe's 2003 Vintage Reserva Demi-Sec Cava, **(GF) (N/S) 8.63**
Spain, Alc. 11.5%, £7.49
Not as good, but this medium-dry cava will complement cake better than the brand does.

Codorniu Rosé Cava (Spanish Sparkling Wine)

Sulphites (E221–E228)   *Number indicates units of alcohol per bottle*

CODORNIU PINOT NOIR ROSÉ BRUT TRADITIONAL METHOD CAVA, SPAIN, ALC.12%, £7.99

9

An elegant, clear bottle holding a rosé wine made from the Pinot Noir grape.
The quality is such that it's a cheaper alternative to rosé Champagne.

(5) **ASDA** Rosado Mas Miralda Brut Cava, Spain,   **(GF) (N/S) (V) 8.63**
Alc. 11.5%, £3.82
Comes second to the brand, but the biscuit nuances make this an interesting rosé.

(5) **SAINSBURY'S** Rosé Brut Traditional Method Cava, Spain,   **(GF) (N/S) 8.63**
Alc. 11.5%, £3.99
This is a good value fizz. Very drinkable, but without the fineness of the brand.

(5) **MARKS & SPENCER** Rosado Brut Traditional Method Cava,   **(GF) (N/S) (V) 9**
Spain, Alc. 12%, £6.99
Not as elegant as the brand, but it's cheaper and a good alternative for pink bubbles.

(4) **CO-OP** Rosado Brut Traditional Method Cava, Spain,   **(GF) (N/S) 9**
Alc. 12%, £4.99
Still worth a punt at this price, but the quality is a big step down from the brand.

(3) **MORRISONS** Pink Pink Fizz Traditional Method Rosé   **(GF) (N/S) 8.63**
Brut Cava, Spain, Alc.11.5%, £4.99
The bright pink foil catches the eye. But the quality does not compare to the brand!

Jacob's Creek Non-Vintage (Australian Sparkling Wine)

Sulphites (E221–E228)

Number indicates units of alcohol per bottle

---

(8) **MAJESTIC** Griffin Vineyards Brut NV Reserve, Australia, **(GF) (N/S) 9**
Alc.12%, £5.99
Grab a bottle or two. Cheaper, with more fruit flavour and of a similar quality to the brand.

---

(7) **MARKS & SPENCER** Bluff Hill Brut NV Traditional Method, **(GF) (N/S) 9**
New Zealand, Alc.12%, £7.99
The same price, but this reveals more Champagne-like notes and it tastes better than the brand.

JACOB'S CREEK NV BRUT TRADITIONAL METHOD CHARDONNAY/PINOT NOIR, AUSTRALIA, ALC.11.5%, £7.99   8.63

The grape varieties (Chardonnay and Pinot Noir) are the same as those used to make Champagne and the production method is similar. However this dry sparkling wine is not an alternative for the true Champagne aficionado.

---

(5) **CO-OP** Australian Brut Sparkling Wine, Australia, **(GF) (N/S) 9.38**
Alc. 12.5%, £5.49
An alternative. This fruit-driven sparkler will be relished by some, but scorned by others.

---

(5) **MARKS & SPENCER** Honey Tree Sparkling Chardonnay **(GF) (N/S) 9.38**
Brut NV, Australia, Alc. 12.5%, £7.99
Has fine bubbles. However, the pronounced, honeyed grassy flavours might not be to the taste of all drinkers.

Martini Asti (Sweet Italian Sparkling Wine)

Sugar, Sulphites (E221–E228) *Number indicates units of alcohol per bottle*

MARTINI ASTI, MARTINI ROSSI, ITALY, ALC. 7%, £5.48 **5.25**

Asti, at its best, reveals floral notes and ripe apples threaded with refreshing acidity and topped with a creamy sweetness. At its worst, it's just cheap, sweet fizz.

---

(5) **SAINSBURY'S** Asti Sweet Sparkling Wine, Italy, Alc.7%, £3.49 **(GF) (N/S) 5.25**
At this price it's a cheaper option, but the brand beats it on smell and taste.

---

(5) **ASDA** Asti Sweet Sparkling Wine, Italy, Alc. 7.5%, £3.49 **(GF) (N/S) 5.63**
Very good value! Although the aroma and taste are good, the swallow has a metallic edge.

---

(5) **MORRISONS** Asti Capetta Sweet Sparkling Wine, Italy, **(GF) (N/S) 5.25**
Alc. 7%, £ 3.69
Similar in style to Asda's, but likewise the brand beats this for all round taste quality.

---

(5) **SOMERFIELD** Asti Sweet Sparkling Wine, Italy, Alc. 7%, £3.99 **(GF) (N/S) 5.25**
Drinks well! However, next to the brand, it's a few bubbles below in taste quality.

---

(5) **MAJESTIC** Castelvero Asti Sweet Sparkling Wine, Italy, **(GF) (N/S) 5.25**
Alc. 7%, £5.99
This is more expensive, yet it smells and tastes no better than the brand.

---

(5) **MARKS & SPENCER** Gibo Asti Sweet Sparkling Wine, Italy, **(GF) (N/S) 5.63**
Alc. 7.5%, £5.99
This costs more than the brand, and it presents no better taste quality.

---

(4) **WAITROSE** Arione Moscato Sweet Sparkling Wine, Italy, **(GF) 4.88**
Alc. 6.5%, £3.99
A cheap price, but not an alternative! The brand beats this by some margin on taste.

---

(2) **CO-OP** Moscato Sweet Sparkling Wine, Italy, **(GF) (N/S) (V) 4.13**
Alc. 5.5%, £1.99
Don't waste your money. It's cheap, sweet and sparkling, but it's not very good.

Moët & Chandon Vintage Champagne

Sugar, Sulphites (E221–E228)   *Number indicates units of alcohol per bottle*

(10) **MARKS & SPENCER** 2000 De Saint Gall Brut Champagne, France, **(GF) (N/S) 9**
Alc. 12%, £19.99
A classy glass of bubbles and a beat-the-brand buy! Congratulations the Champagne buyer at M&S.

(10) **WAITROSE** 1996 Brut Champagne, France, Alc.12%, £20.99   **(GF) (N/S) 9**
Buy it if you like biscuity Champagnes. Older, cheaper, and much better quality than the brand.

(9) **TESCO** 2000 Brut Champagne, France, Alc. 12%, £16.94   **(GF) (N/S) 9**
Grab a bottle. A better vintage, a cheaper price and it tastes as good as the brand.

(6) **ODDBINS** 1996 Billecart-Salmon Brut Champagne, France,   **(GF) (N/S) 9**
Alc. 12%, £50.49
Special occasion Champagne! It costs a lot more, but you'll get triple the palate pleasure.

MOËT & CHANDON BRUT CHAMPAGNE 1999, FRANCE, ALC. 12.5%, £31.99   9.38

Vintage Champagne is produced from grapes harvested in the year shown on the label (in this case 1999). So, unlike Non-Vintage (NV), this means the style will change from year to year. This vintage is softer and better tasting than the NV.

(5) **MORRISONS** 1999 Albert Etienne Brut Champagne, France,   **(GF) (N/S) 9.38**
Alc. 12.5%, £17.49
Tesco does it cheaper and better, but for Morrisons' shoppers this is a cheaper alternative to the brand and much better-tasting than the Albert Etienne NV (*see* page 230).

(5) **MAJESTIC** 2000 De Telmont Brut Champagne, France,   **(GF) (N/S) 9**
Alc. 12%, £22.49
An option, but it comes second to the brand on all fronts except for the price.

(5) **ODDBINS** 1999 Pierre Gimonnet & Fils Brut Champagne, France,   **(GF) (N/S) 9**
Alc.12%, £22.99
A cheaper alternative, but the brand beats it on all the taste fronts.

Moët & Chandon
Non-Vintage Champagne

Sulphites (E221–E228)   *Number indicates units of alcohol per bottle*

(10) **WAITROSE** Brut NV Champagne, France, Alc. 12%, £14.99   **(GF) (N/S)** 9
Although Waitrose is on the label, this Champagne is a few bubbles up from the brand.

(10) **MARKS & SPENCER** De Saint Gall Brut NV Champagne, France   **(GF) (N/S)** 9
Alc.12%, £15.99
A beat-the-brand buy for the M&S shopper. Cheaper and much better quality.

(9) **SAINSBURY'S** N V Blanc de Noirs, Brut, Champagne, France,   **(GF) (N/S)** 9
Alc. 12%, £13.69
Buy it. This Blanc de Noirs Champagne is made only from black grapes (Pinot Noir and
Pinot Meunier), which give a similar quality to the brand – and for less money.

(9) **SOMERFIELD** Blanc de Noirs Brut NV Champagne, France,   **(GF) (N/S)** 9
Alc. 12%, £13.99
The black grapes deliver a little more roundness on the palate compared to the brand.

(9) **MORRISONS** Albert Etienne Brut NV Champagne, France,   **(GF) (N/S)** 9.38
Alc. 12.5%, £13.99
Grab a bottle from the shelf and celebrate with just as much style, only more cheaply.

(9) **SAINSBURY'S** Duval-Leroy Extra Dry NV Champagne, France,   **(GF) (N/S)** 9
Alc. 12%, £14.79
Sainsbury's "own label" may offend the posh drinker. But it's cheaper, and as good as
the brand.

(9) **TESCO** Premier Cru NV Champagne, France Alc. 12%, £14.79   **(GF) (N/S)** 9
Beats the brand! Wrap a napkin round the bottle and guests will think you've paid double.

(9) **SOMERFIELD** Prince William Brut NV Champagne, France,   **(GF) (N/S)** 9
Alc. 12%, £14.99
Buy it. This presents a similar style to the brand at a much cheaper price.

(8) **WAITROSE** Blanc de Noirs Brut NV Champagne, France,   **(GF) (N/S)** 9
Alc. 12%, £15.99
As good as the brand! Although this wine is white, it tastes more like a sparkling,
delicate red burgundy.

(7) **WAITROSE** Blanc de Blancs Brut NV Champagne, France, **(GF) (N/S)** 9
Alc. 12%, £17.99
Blanc de Blancs Champagne is produced from just white grapes (Chardonnay.) This one
is cheaper than the brand and it delivers a better taste.

(7) **MARKS & SPENCER** De Saint Gall Blanc de Blancs Brut NV **(GF) (N/S)** 9
Champagne, France, Alc. 12%, £18.99
No juice from black grapes added here – only white. But the taste will impress any
Champagne aficionado!

(7) **ODDBINS** Pierre Gimonnet & Fils Brut NV Champagne, France, **(GF) (N/S)** 9
Alc. 12%, £19.99
Pick it from the shelf. Cheaper, not as acidic, and more flavoursome than the brand.

(7) **ODDBINS** F Bonnet Brut NV Champagne, France, **(GF) (N/S)** 9
Alc. 12%, £18.49
Oddbins' Pierre Gimonnet is the better buy. But this is as good, and cheaper than the brand.

MOËT & CHANDON BRUT NV CHAMPAGNE, FRANCE,
ALC. 12%, £22.99 9
To keep the quality and style consistent, Non-Vintage (NV) is a blend of Champagnes
from several different years. This is mouth-wateringly dry so it won't be appreciated by
the medium-dry palates.

(5) **CO-OP** Les Pionniers Brut NV Champagne, France, **(GF) (N/S) (V)** 9
Alc. 12%, £13.99
A cheaper option than the brand. A similar dryness, but just a bubble away in quality.

(4) **MAJESTIC** L. Jaunay Brut NV Champagne, France, **(GF) (N/S)** 9
Alc. 12%, £15.99
Costs less than the brand, but the lemony flavour starts to annoy after the second sip.

(2) **THRESHERS** Dubois Caron Brut NV Champagne, France, **(GF) (N/S)** 9
Alc. 12%, £19.99
Buy the brand or try another retailer. Worse than the poorest cava in this section.

Piper Heidsieck
Demi-Sec Champagne

Sugar, Sulphites (E221–E228)   *Number indicates units of alcohol per bottle*

(6)   **ODDBINS** N V Billecart-Salmon, Demi-Sec, Champagne,   **(GF) (N/S) 9**
France, Alc.12%, £24.99
This is a more harmonious Champagne and well worth the extra premium.

PIPER-HEIDSIECK DEMI-SEC NV CHAMPAGNE, FRANCE,
ALC. 12%, £20.99   9
Demi-Sec will complement your strawberries or wedding cake far better than Brut (dry)
Champagne. There is sweetness, but the biscuity notes and acidic bite are still there.

(5)   **SAINSBURY'S** Demi-Sec NV Champagne, France,   **(GF) (N/S) 9**
Alc. 12%, £14.99
A cheaper alternative to the brand, but it's a step down on all taste fronts.

(5)   **TESCO** Jacquart Demi-Sec NV Champagne, France,   **(GF) (N/S) 9.38**
Alc. 12.5%, £14.99
This does not have the depth of flavour of the Piper-Heidsieck, but it's worth a punt.

Moët & Chandon
Rosé Champagne

Sulphites (E221–E228)   *Number indicates units of alcohol per bottle*

---

(8)   **WAITROSE** Alexandre Bonnet NV Rosé Champagne, France,   **(GF) 9**
Alc.12%, £17.99
Grab a bottle! Similar colour and quality to the brand at a much cheaper price.

---

(6)   **ODDBINS** Billecart-Salmon Brut NV Rosé Champagne, France,   **(GF) (N/S) 9**
Alc. 12%, £35.99
This is better quality than the brand. But it's only worth the extra premium for the
Champagne aficionado.

MOËT & CHANDON BRUT NV ROSÉ CHAMPAGNE, FRANCE,
ALC.12%, £29.99   9
Rosé Champagne's pinkness comes from skin contact with black grapes or the addition
of red wine. It not only looks pretty, but this colour addition also helps to soften and
reduce the acidic bite.

---

(5)   **MORRISONS** Albert Etienne Brut NV Rosé Champagne,   **(GF) (N/S) 9**
France, Alc.12%, £16.99
Cheaper and it drinks well. But its light golden colour is not rosé in my book.

---

(4)   **ASDA** Brut NV Rosé Champagne, France, Alc. 12%, £14.97   **(GF) (N/S) (V) 9**
A cheaper alternative to the brand, but it's a good step down in both bubble and
taste quality.

16
Spirits, Vermouth, Port & Sherry

Vodka, gin and white rum are the big players in the white spirits category and we consume them with enthusiasm both neat and mixed! All brown spirits start off white and their colour is achieved through ageing in oak barrels. To ensure consistency of appearance many brands add food colouring before bottling.

Fortified wines, popular for hundreds of years, are currently out of fashion. This downturn in popularity has meant that there are plenty of great tasting vermouths, ports and sherries readily available on our shelves, with the retailers' "own labels" offering some of the best value you'll find. Fortified wines contain high alcohol (15-20%) and sweet ones have high sugar levels - sometimes over 70g a bottle. Drink in moderation.

There are constant complaints about the high alcohol duty in this country. Spirit duty on 70cl bottle at 40% is £5.48 (around 14p per 1% of alcohol) and that does not include VAT. Obviously when a blended whisky sells for £6.99, there are only pennies for the producer and the retailer. When they can, many producers water down their spirits to 37.5% to save about 35p in duty. (But this extra water does dilute the spirit's flavour.)

Smirnoff Triple Distilled Vodka

Number indicates units of alcohol per bottle

---

(9) **ASDA** Export Strength Vodka, UK, Alc. 43%, £8.38   **(GF) (N/S) (V) 30.10**
A beat-the-brand buy for the Asda shopper. Cheaper, better tasting and more alcohol.

---

(8) **MORRISONS** Morrinov Triple Distilled Premium Vodka, UK   **(GF) (N/S) 28**
Alc. 40%, £8.99
Grab a bottle from the shelf. Cheaper, more alcohol and it tastes better than the brand.

---

(6) **MAJESTIC** Classic Vodka, Russia, Alc. 40%, £10.99   **(GF) (N/S) 28**
This costs a sip more, but the alcohol and the taste is another notch up.

---

(6) **ODDBINS** Sputnik Pure Grain Vodka, Russia, Alc. 40%, £10.99   **(GF) (N/S) 28**
Buy it. Much better tasting than the brand, and well worth the extra few pence.

SMIRNOFF TRIPLE DISTILLED VODKA, RUSSIA, ALC. 37.5%, £10.88 26.25
A smooth liquid with a grainy twist, but without the alcoholic kick of vodkas over 40% ABV.

---

(5) **SAINSBURY'S** Triple Distilled Vodka, UK,   **(GF) (N/S) (V) 26.25**
Alc. 37.5%, £7.29
A cheaper option! Although similar to the brand, the swallow is a little more aggressive.

---

(5) **ASDA** Tripled Distilled Vodka, UK, Alc. 37.5%, £7.24   **(GF) (N/S) (V) 26.25**
Distilled from molasses, this delivers a vodka that's not as clean or crisp as the brand.

---

(5) **CO-OP** Imperial Vodka, UK, Alc. 37.5%, £7.89   **(GF) (N/S) (V) 26.25**
A cheaper option for drinkers who mix their vodka, but lacks the brand's clean and crisp taste.

---

(5) **CO-OP** Premium Triple Distilled Vodka, Scotland,   **(GF) (N/S) (V) 28**
Alc. 40%, £9.49
Better than the Co-op's regular vodka, but it's still a grain or two down from the brand!

---

(5) **THRESHERS** Triple Distilled Imperial Vodka, UK,   **(GF) (N/S) 26.25**
Alc. 37.5%, £9.49
With a mixer you'd never know but, on its own the brand just edges this taste-wise.

---

(4) **ASDA** Vodka, UK, Alc. 37.5%, £6.42   **(GF) (N/S) (V) 26.25**
Distilled from molasses rather than grain and a big step down from the brand taste-wise.

---

(4) **MORRISONS** Moskova Imperial Vodka, UK, Alc. 37.5%, £6.49   **(GF) (N/S) 26.25**
Sounds Russian, but it's made in the UK. Cheaper, but a big drop down in quality.

---

(4) **ALDI** Tamova Vodka, UK, Alc. 37.5%, £6.99   **(GF) 26.25**
Couple of notches below the brand, but it may still work for the vodka and Red Bull drinker.

Gordon's Dry London Gin

Botanicals   *Number indicates units of alcohol per bottle*

---

(10) **MORRISONS** Mountain Light Premium London Dry Gin, UK, **(GF) (N/S) 30.1**
Alc. 43%, £9.99
Beat-the-brand buy for Morrisons shoppers. Cheaper, better quality and more alcohol.

---

(9) **SAINSBURY'S** Dry London Gin Double Distilled, UK, **(GF) (N/S) (V) 26.25**
Alc. 37.5%, £7.08
Put it in the trolley. Cheaper, and it presents comparable tastes to the brand.

---

(9) **ASDA** London Dry Gin, Triple Distilled, UK, Alc. 37.5%, £7.08 **(GF) (N/S) (V) 26.25**
Pick from the shelf. Less money and it offers a similar quality from sniff to swallow.

---

(9) **MORRISONS** London Dry Gin, UK, Alc. 40%, £7.59 **(GF) (N/S) 28**
Great buy for the G-and-T drinker! More alcohol, comparable flavour and a cheaper price.

---

(8) **CO-OP** Special Dry London Gin, UK, Alc. 37.5%, £8.59 **(GF) (N/S) (V) 26.25**
Grab it from the shelf. Delivers similar pungency to the brand and it's cheaper.

---

(8) **THRESHERS** Victory Dry London Gin, UK, Alc. 37.5%, £9.49 **(GF) (N/S) 26.25**
Not the cheapest "own label" around. But it's cheaper than, and as good as the brand.

---

(8) **WAITROSE** Original Dry London Gin, UK, Alc. 40%, £9.69 **(GF) (N/S) 28**
If you want purity of flavour, buy this. It's cheaper and better tasting than the brand.

---

(7) **MAJESTIC** Dry London Gin, UK, Alc. 40%, £11.49 **(GF) (N/S) 28**
The same price as the brand, but it has more alcohol and a great depth of flavour.

---

(6) **ODDBINS** Pavilion Dry London Dry Gin, UK, Alc. 40%, £11.99 **(GF) (N/S) 28**
More expensive, but a big step up in quality and well worth the extra premium.

GORDON'S SPECIAL DRY LONDON GIN, UK, ALC. 37.5%, £11.49 26.25
Gordon's is not made in London. It delivers a perfumed botanical hit from sniff to swallow.

---

(5) **MARKS & SPENCER** London Dry Gin, UK, Alc. 37.5%, £12.99 **(GF) (N/S) (V) 26.25**
This is no better quality than the brand, has the same ABV and is more expensive.

---

(4) **KWIK SAVE** Special Dry London Gin, UK, Alc. 37.5%, £7.24 **(GF) (N/S) (V) 26.25**
A big notch down from the brand, so it's not a buy for neat gin drinkers.

---

(4) **SOMERFIELD** Special Dry London Gin, UK, Alc. 37.5%, £7.47 **(GF) (N/S) (V) 26.25**
With plenty of tonic, ice and lemon, this is fine. But it's a big step down from the brand.

---

(3) **ALDI** Oliver Cromwell Special Dry London Gin, UK, Alc. 37.5%, £6.99 **(GF) 26.25**
Certainly cheap! But the hard, mean flavours prevent it being an alternative to the brand.

Martell VS Cognac (French Brandy)

Number indicates units of alcohol per bottle

MARTELL VS COGNAC, FRANCE, ALC. 40%, £15.53   28

VS stands for Very Special/Superior and indicates that a Cognac has been aged for a minimum of two-and-a-half years. Martell is smooth and rounded with a gentle glow on the swallow.

(5)   **ASDA** VS Fine Cognac, France, Alc. 40%, £11.47   **(GF) (N/S) 28**
Side by side the brand beats this "own label" on aroma and flavour – just!

(5)   **MORRISONS** VS Cognac, France, Alc.40%, £11.99   **(GF) (N/S) 28**
The smell and palate pleasure come close to the brand. It's certainly a cheaper option.

(5)   **SAINSBURY'S** VS Cognac, France, Alc. 40%, £11.99   **(GF) (N/S) (V) 28**
A cheaper alternative, but it comes second to the brand on the aroma and taste fronts.

(5)   **WAITROSE** VS Fine Cognac, France, Alc. 40%, £16.49   **(GF) (N/S) 28**
This tastes as good as the brand, but it's not worth spending the extra.

(5)   **ODDBINS** Fine Cognac Reserve, France, Alc. 40%, £19.99   **(GF) (N/S) 28**
This offers the nose and palate no more pleasure than the brand.

(4)   **ASDA** Napoleon French VS Brandy, France, Alc. 36%, £7.74   **(GF) (N/S) (V) 28**
A cheaper alternative, but it does not have the aroma, elegance or taste of the brand.

(4)   **ALDI** Carriere VS Cognac, France, Alc. 40%, £9.99   **(GF) 28**
The pleasure to the nose and palate is a good notch down from the brand.

(4)   **SOMERFIELD** VS Cognac, France, Alc. 40%, £11.99   **(GF) (N/S) (V) 28**
The added caramel and oak are rather too aggressive for this to be a good alternative to the brand.

(3)   **ASDA** French Brandy, France, Alc. 40%, £6.46   **(GF) (N/S) (V) 28**
For cooking – fine. However, this won't cut it alone as an after-dinner drink.

(2)   **COOP** Napoleon Brandy, France, Alc. 36%, £8.99   **(GF) (N/S) (V) 25.2**
This is very poor. Napoleon would be upset to put his name to something of this quality.

Bacardi White Rum

BACARDI WHITE RUM, BAHAMAS, ALC. 37.5%, £11.59   **26.25**

In the UK white rum is popularly drunk with cola, or used as an ingredient in cocktails. However, it's regularly drunk neat in the Caribbean.

(5) **CO-OP** Superior White Rum, Caribbean,   **(GF) (N/S) (V) 26.25**
Alc. 37.5%, £8.99
A cheaper alternative for use in cocktails or with a mixer, but it won't impress the neat Bacardi drinkers.

(5) **CO-OP** Premium Fair Trade White Rum, Paraguay,   **(GF) (N/S) (V) 26.25**
Alc. 37.5%, £9.99
Cheaper, but it's still a notch down in aroma and taste quality compared to the brand.

(4) **ASDA** Carta Blanca Superior White Rum, Caribbean,   **(GF) (N/S) 26.25**
Alc. 37.5%, £7.73
Drunk neat, this is a big step down from the brand in quality. But in a cocktail or with a mixer, it should be fine.

(3) **ASDA** Imported White Rum, Caribbean, Alc. 37.5%, £6.76 **(GF) (N/S) (V) 26.25**
The taste is sufficiently inferior that, even served with a mixer, you would notice the difference.

(3) **KWIK SAVE** White Rum, Caribbean, Alc. 37.5%, £7.99   **(GF) (N/S) (V) 26.25**
Try another shop. Not good value taste-wise and not an alternative to the brand.

(3) **SOMERFIELD** White Rum, Caribbean, Alc. 37.5%, £9.49   **(GF) (N/S) (V) 26.25**
At this price, trade up to the brand, which is at least three times the quality.

(1) **ALDI** Old Hopking White Rum, Caribbean, Alc. 37.5%, £7.49   **(GF) 26.25**
Leave it. The burn tastes are so powerful they would ruin the strongest of cocktails.

Bells Blended Scotch Whisky

Number indicates units of alcohol per bottle

(9) **MORRISONS** Finest Scotch Whisky, Scotland, Alc. 40%, £8.29 **(GF) (N/S) 28**
Grab a bottle! The flavours are different, but as harmonised as the brand, and it's cheaper.

(8) **ALDI** Highland Black 8-Year-Old Scotch Whisky, Scotland, **(GF) (V) 28**
Alc. 40%, £8.99
Pick it from the shelf. It's cheaper and presents a similar taste quality to the brand.

(8) **THRESHERS** Glen Rossie, Scotch Whisky, Scotland, Alc. 40%, £9.49 **(GF) (N/S) 28**
Different, but of comparable quality to the brand. A good buy for the Thresher shopper!

(8) **CO-OP** Finest Blend Scotch Whisky, Scotland, Alc. 40%, £9.59 **(GF) (N/S) (V) 28**
Only a sip away from Co-op's Premium – and it presents comparable quality to the brand.

(7) **ODDBINS** Glen Clova Scotch Whisky, Scotland, Alc. 40%, £10.99 **(GF) (N/S) 28**
Take one home. It costs less than the brand and presents at least the same quality.

(7) **MARKS & SPENCER** Kenmore Scotch Whisky, Scotland, **(GF) (N/S) (V) 28**
Alc. 40%, £11.99
Does not have the peaty smoke of the brand. But it is of similar quality, and cheaper.

(7) **MAJESTIC** Fine Oak Cask Matured Scotch Whisky, Scotland, **(GF) (N/S) 28**
Alc. 40%, £11.99
Many drinkers will prefer this subtler tasting whisky. It's cheaper, too!

BELLS BLENDED SCOTCH WHISKY, SCOTLAND, ALC. 40%, £12.34   28
Scotch Whisky must be produced in Scotland, and is a blend of grain and malt whisky.
Bells offers smooth red fruits and finishes with gentle warmth and a peaty smoky twist.

(5) **SOMERFIELD** Prince Charlie Scotch Whisky, Scotland, **(GF) (N/S) (V) 28**
Alc. 40%, £7.98
A cheaper alternative, but a small step down in quality and flavour.

(4) **SAINSBURY'S** Scotch Whisky, Scotland, Alc. 40%, £7.98 **(GF) (N/S) (V) 28**
Without a mixer the oak dominates too much, so it's not an option for the neat Scotch drinker.

(4) **KWIK SAVE** Special Reserve Scotch Whisky, Scotland, **(GF) (N/S) (V) 28**
Alc. 40%, £7.99
Needs to be drunk with a mixer! Not as elegant, and more aggressive than the brand.

(4) **ASDA** Special Blended Scotch Whisky, Scotland, Alc. 40%, £7.96 **(GF) (N/S) (V) 28**
Better than Asda's regular, but still a big drop down in taste quality from the brand.

The Glenlivet Speyside Whisky

Number indicates units of alcohol per bottle

---

(9) **ASDA** Speyside 12-Year-Old Malt, Scotland, Alc. 40%, £13.78 **(GF) (N/S) (V) 28**
Grab it. Much cheaper and the flavours beat along the same path as the brand.

SAINSBURY'S Single Speyside 12-Year-Old Malt, Scotland, **(GF) (N/S) (V)28**
Alc. 40%, £15.99
Put it in the trolley. Big saving and a comparable taste to the brand.

THE GLENLIVET, 12-YEAR-OLD MALT, SPEYSIDE, SCOTLAND, ALC. 40%, £22.97   28

Taste-wise Speyside malts are generally sweeter and less peaty than ones from the Islands and Islay. However, they are more assertive than malts from the Lowland region.

---

(5) **MORRISONS** Speyside Malt 10-Year-Old Malt, Scotland, **(GF) (N/S) 28**
Alc. 40%, £14.99
Worth a punt for the Morrison shopper, but it's a notch down on smell and taste.

---

(5) **ODDBINS** McClelland's Speyside Single Malt, Scotland, **(GF) (N/S) 28**
Alc. 40%, £15.99
Side by side the Brand wins on all the taste fronts, but at this price it's a good buy.

---

(3) **ASDA** Single Malt Whisky, Speyside, Scotland, Alc. 40%, £9.47 **(GF) (N/S) (V) 28**
Under half price, but its youthful distillate notes will fail to impress the Brand drinker.

Auchentoshan Lowland Malt Whisky

Number indicates units of alcohol per bottle

AUCHENTOSHAN 10-YEAR-OLD LOWLAND SINGLE MALT WHISKY, SCOTLAND, ALC. 40%, £22.99   28

This triple distilled silky Lowland malt is a real palate-pleaser for drinkers who want a Scottish single malt whisky without the peaty, smoky aromas and tastes.

---

(5) **ODDBINS** McClelland's Lowland Single Malt Whisky, Scotland, **(GF) (N/S) 28**
Alc. 40%, £15.99
A cheaper option to the brand, but the aroma and taste are a small step down.

The Macallan Highland Malt Whisky

Number indicates units of alcohol per bottle

(9) **WAITROSE** 12-Year-Old Highland Malt, Scotland, **(GF) (N/S) (V) 28**
Alc. 40%, £16.99
A beat-the-brand buy. Much cheaper, but of comparable quality to the brand.

(8) **MARKS & SPENCER** Inverey 12-Year-Old Malt, Scotland, **(GF) (N/S) (V) 28**
Alc. 40%, £19.99
Different! Lighter colour, and more peaty, but of comparable quality to the brand.

THE MACALLAN 10-YEAR-OLD HIGHLAND SINGLE MALT WHISKY, SCOTLAND, ALC. 40%, £24.99   28
This is malt is matured in sherry casks. It's a smooth, mahogany-coloured dram against which all other Highland whiskies are judged.

(5) **SAINSBURY'S** Highland Malt 12-Year-Old, Scotland, **(GF) (N/S) (V) 28**
Alc. 40%, £15.99
Worth a punt! Smooth and great value, but still a notch down from the brand.

(4) **ALDI** Glen Orrin 6-Year-Old Highland Malt, Scotland, **(GF) (V) 28**
Alc. 40%, £8.99
Well under half the price. Admittedly a big drop down in quality, but still very drinkable.

(4) **ASDA** Highland 12-Year-Old Single Malt, Scotland, **(GF) (N/S) (V) 28**
Alc. 40%, £13.78
Similar colour and nearly half price. But it lacks the seductive charm of the brand.

(4) **MORRISONS** Highland 10-Year-Old Single Malt, Scotland, **(GF) (N/S) 28**
Alc. 40%, £14.99
Comparable colour, but the aroma and flavour are a big step down from the brand.

(4) **ODDBINS** McClelland's Single Malt, Scotland, Alc. 40%, £15.99 **(GF) (N/S) 28**
Much cheaper than the brand. It's a good notch down in quality, but still worth a punt.

(4) **MAJESTIC** Mature Highland 8-Year-Old, Scotland, Alc. 40%, £16.99 **(GF) (N/S) 28**
A big drop down in taste quality from the brand, but still worth the money.

Laphroaig Malt Islay Whisky

Number indicates units of alcohol per bottle

---

(9) **ASDA** 10-Year-Old Islay Pure Malt, Scotland, Alc. 40%, £13.78 **(GF) (N/S) (V) 28**
Great buy! Cheaper, little difference in smell and of comparable taste quality.

---

(9) **MORRISONS** 10-Year-Old Pure Islay Malt, Scotland, Alc.40%, £14.99 **(GF) (N/S) 28**
A beat-the-brand buy from Morrisons. Very much cheaper and of comparable quality.

---

(9) **SAINSBURY'S** 10-Year-Old Pure Islay Malt, Scotland, Alc. 40%, £15.99 **(GF) (N/S) (V) 28**
Grab a bottle from the shelf. It's cheaper and will hit the spot for Islay drinkers.

---

(9) **WAITROSE** 10-Year-Old Single Islay Malt Whisky, Scotland **(GF) (N/S) (V) 28**
Alc. 40%, £16.99
Grab it from the shelf. This tastes as good as the brand and is much cheaper.

LAPHROAIG 10-YEAR-OLD SINGLE MALT WHISKY, ISLAY, SCOTLAND, ALC. 40%, £22.99
28

This is a peaty malt whisky from the Laphroaig distillery that sits on the Island of Islay. A top single malt (from one distillery and from malt rather than a blend of grain and malt).

---

(5) **MAJESTIC** Islay Whisky 8-Year-Old Single Malt, Scotland, Alc. 40%, £16.99 **28**
This is just a whisper away in taste quality from the brand. Well worth a punt!

---

(5) **MARKS & SPENCER** 10-Year-Old Single Islay Malt Whisky, **(GF) (N/S) (V) 28**
Scotland, Alc. 40%, £19.99
Cheaper, and gets very close to the brand in aroma and pungency of flavour.

---

(4) **ODDBINS** McClelland's Single Islay Malt Whisky, Scotland, **(GF) (N/S) 28**
Alc. 40%, £15.99
Does not deliver the peat and smoky notes. A step down in palate pleasure.

Talisker Island Malt Whisky

Number indicates units of alcohol per bottle

TALISKER 10-YEAR-OLD SINGLE MALT, ISLE OF SKYE, SCOTLAND, ALC. 45.8%, £25.99
32.1

Malts from the Islands are generally not as smoky and peaty as the ones from Islay. This presents a palate-warming, harmonious mix of heather, red fruits, smoke and peat.

---

(5) **MAJESTIC** Island 8-Year-Old Single Malt, Scotland, Alc.40%, £16.99 **(GF) (N/S) 28**
This tastes similar to an Oban malt. More sherried and less peaty than the brand.

Jameson Irish Whiskey

Number indicates units of alcohol per bottle

(8) **CO-OP** Delaney's Irish Whiskey, Alc. 40%, £10.99　　　**(N/S) (V) 28**
Buy it. Different distillery from the brand, but it delivers comparable taste pleasure. .

(6) **ODDBINS** Slieve Na gCloc, Irish Whiskey, Alc. 40%, £16.99　　**(GF) (N/S) 28**
If you enjoy the flavour of smoky pea, then this is well worth the extra premium. .

JAMESON TRIPLE DISTILLED IRISH WHISKEY, ALC. 40%, £13.98　　28
This famous blended (malt and grain) Irish whiskey is smoother than most blended whiskies from Scotland. This is mainly because it is triple distilled rather than double distilled.

(5) **ASDA** Irish Whiskey, Alc. 40%, £10.74　　　　**(GF) (N/S) (V) 28**
Veers more towards the taste of Scotch than an Irish whiskey, but it's still worth a punt. . .

(5) **MORRISONS** Clancey's Irish Whiskey, Alc. 40%, £10.99　　**(GF) (N/S) 28**
Drinkable and a cheaper option, but it doesn't have the smoothness of the brand. .

(5) **SOMERFIELD** O'Briens Irish Whiskey, Alc. 40%, £10.99　　**(GF) (N/S) (V) 28**
A cheaper alternative, but the overall palate pleasure is a notch down.

Cinzano Bianco Vermouth

Sugar, Sulphites (E221–E228),　　　　　*Number indicates units of alcohol per bottle*

(9) **ASDA** Vermouth Bianco, Italy, Alc. 14.7%, £2.77　　　**(GF) (N/S) 11.03**
Buy it. A slightly different flavour twist, but it's of comparable quality to the brand.

(9) **TESCO** Vermouth Bianco, Italy, Alc. 14.7%, £2.77　　　　**(GF) 11.03**
Put it in your trolley! Cheaper than the brand and presenting similar flavours and quality.

(9) **CO-OP** Vermouth Bianco, Italy, Alc. 14.8%, £3.29　　　**(GF) (N/S) 11.1**
Grab it. The aroma and flavours are similar to the brand, and it's cheaper.

CINZANO BIANCO VERMOUTH, ITALY, ALC. 15%, £4.84　　11.25
A sweet white vermouth that is produced from a white-wine base, flavoured with herbs and spices. Drunk as a long drink over ice, or as an ingredient in a cocktail.

(5) **SAINSBURY'S** Vermouth Bianco, Italy, Alc. 14.7%, £2.99　　　**11.03**
A cheaper alternative, but it doesn't taste as good as the brand.

Martini Extra Dry Vermouth

Sulphites (E221–E228),   *Number indicates units of alcohol per bottle*

⑨ **ASDA** Extra Dry Vermouth, Italy, Alc. 14.7%, £2.77   **(GF) (N/S) 11.03**
   Buy it. Very much cheaper, similar quality, but a little drier than the brand.

⑨ **TESCO** Extra Dry Vermouth, Italy, Alc. 14.7%, £2.95   **(GF) 11.03**
   A good buy. This tastes better than the brand and is very much cheaper.

MARTINI EXTRA DRY VERMOUTH, ITALY, ALC. 15%, £4.75   11.25
The famous ingredient in 007's cocktail! "Extra dry" suggests that this vermouth will be as dry as a Muscadet or Chablis, but it's not. Drier than Bianco though!

⑤ **SAINSBURY'S** Extra Dry Vermouth, Italy, Alc. 14.7%, £2.99   **11.03**
   A cheaper alternative. But compared to the brand, it's a step down in flavour quality.

Martini Rosso Vermouth

Sulphites (E221–E228), Sugar,   *Number indicates units of alcohol per bottle*

⑨ **ASDA** Rosso Vermouth, Italy, Alc. 14.7%, £2.77   **(GF) (N/S) 11.03**
   Grab it from the shelf. A little more spicy, but it tastes as good as the brand.

⑨ **SAINSBURY'S** Rosso Vermouth, Italy, Alc. 14.7%, £2.99   **11.03**
   Put it in the trolley. A big saving and it delivers similar quality to the brand.

⑧ **CO-OP** Sweet Red Rosso, Vermouth, Italy, Alc. 14.8%, £3.29   **(GF) (N/S) 11.10**
   Certainly medium-sweet, but not red! As good as the brand – and much cheaper.

MARTINI ROSSO VERMOUTH, ITALY, ALC. 15%, £4.75   11.03
A sweet, mahogany-coloured vermouth that looks very similar to a tawny port or an amontillado sherry in the glass. Can be drunk neat or used to make cocktails.

SWC Ruby Port

Sugar, Sulphites (E221–E228),   *Number indicates units of alcohol per bottle*

(8)   **MORRISONS** Ruby Port, Calhem Filho, Alc. 20%, £4.49   **(GF) (N/S)** 15
Pick a bottle from the shelf. It delivers similar sweetness and richness to the brand!

(8)   **ALDI'S** Fletcher's Ruby Port, Alc. 20%, £4.69   **(GF)** 15
This hits the spot, as it's cheaper than the brand and of comparable quality.

(8)   **ASDA** Ruby Port, Smith Woodhouse, Alc. 19%, £4.98   **(GF) (N/S)** 14.25
Put it in the trolley! At this level, it's difficult to separate this "own label" from the brand.

(8)   **SAINSBURY'S** Ruby Port, Taylor & Fladgate, Alc. 20%, £4.99   **(GF) (N/S)** 15
Cheaper than the brand and presents at least the same taste quality.

(8)   **COOP** Ruby Port, Smith Woodhouse, Alc. 19%, £5,49   **(GF) (N/S)** 14.25
Buy it. Bottled by the same producer, it delivers comparable quality to the brand.

SWC RUBY PORT, SMITH WOODHOUSE, PORTUGAL,   14.25
ALC. 19%, £6.99
All port is made in the Douro Valley in Portugal. As the name suggests this is a ruby red
port that has been produced for early consumption. The taste is of velvety rich red fruits,
which makes it a really easy drinker. One bottle contains around 70g of sugar.

Warre's Otima Tawny Port

Sugar, Sulphites (E221–E228)   *Number indicates units of alcohol per bottle*

(6)   **MARKS & SPENCER** 20-Year-Old Aged Tawny Port, Alc. 20%, £21.99 **(GF) (N/S)** 15
If you want assertive tastes of dark chocolate and sultanas, then this is worth every penny.

WARRE'S OTIMA 10-YEAR-OLD TAWNY PORT, PORTUGAL,   15
ALC. 20%, 50CL, £7.99 (£11.98 for 750ml)
Depending on its age, the colour of tawny port varies from red-brown to mahogany. Otima
tastes of sweet red fruits, threaded with
nuts and sultanas. A 750ml bottle contains around 70g of sugar.

(5)   **SAINSBURY'S** Tawny Port, W & J Graham, Alc. 19%, £4.99   **(GF) (N/S)** 14.25
This is a cheaper option. However, it comes second to the brand on all taste fronts.

(5)   **WAITROSE** Tawny Port, Smith Woodhouse, Alc.19%, £6.25   **(GF) (N/S)** 14.25
A cheaper alternative. However, the brand beats it for palate pleasure – as it should.

(5) **CO-OP** Tawny Port, Smith Woodhouse, Alc.19%, £5.99   **(GF) (N/S) 14.25**
Worth a punt! However, it doesn't have the nutty and sultana complexity of the brand.

(4) **ASDA** Tawny Port, Smith Woodhouse, Alc.19%, £4.96   **(GF) (N/S) 14.25**
This is very much cheaper, but the taste is at least two steps below the brand.

(4) **MORRISONS** Tawny Port, Symington Family, Alc. 19%, £4.99 **(GF) (N/S) 14.25**
From the same stable as the brand, but a very big step down taste-wise.

Warre's Late Bottled Vintage (LBV) Port

Sugar, Sulphites (E221–E228)   *Number indicates units of alcohol per bottle*

(9) **ODDBINS** 1998 Noval Late Bottled Vintage, Portugal,   **(GF) (N/S) 14.63**
Alc. 19.5%, £10.99
This smells better, tastes better and is much cheaper than the brand – buy it.

WARRE'S 1994 LATE BOTTLED VINTAGE, PORTUGAL,   15
ALC. 20%, £15.39

A big step up in quality and price from ruby port. LBV spends more time in the barrel than vintage port before it's bottled, but the very best deliver similar quality. One bottle contains around 70g of sugar.

(5) **ASDA** 1998 Late Bottled Vintage Port, Smith Woodhouse,   **(GF) (N/S) 15**
Portugal, Alc. 20%, £6.61
Worth every penny! However, the brand does taste better (though not £8 better).

(5) **ALDI** 1998 Souza Late Bottled Vintage, Alc. 20%, £6.99   **(GF) 15**
Worth a punt. Not as elegant as the brand, but well worth £7.

(5) **MORRISONS** 2000 Late Bottled Vintage Port, Portugal,   **(GF) (N/S) 15**
Alc. 20%, £6.99
A cheaper alternative to brand. Not as soft on the palate, but it hits the spot taste-wise.

(5) **SAINSBURY'S** 1998 Late Bottled Vintage Port, Silva & Cosens, **(GF) (N/S) 15**
Alc. 20%, £6.99
Certainly an option. However, it comes second to the brand on the taste fronts.

(5) **MARKS & SPENCER** 1998, Late Bottled Vintage,   **(GF) (N/S) (V) 15**
Alc. 20%, £9.99
Not as good as the brand, and no better than the other "own labels".

Tio Pepe Dry Sherry

Sulphites (E221–E228)   *Number indicates units of alcohol per bottle*

---

(9) **WAITROSE** Fino del Puerto, Jerez, Spain, Alc. 16.5%, £5.39   **(GF) (N/S) 12.38**
Put it in the trolley. It's cheaper and presents comparable quality to the brand.

TIO PEPE EXTRA DRY FINO SHERRY, JEREZ, SPAIN, 15%, £7.70   11.25
Tio Pepe, like most finos, is slightly fortified with grape spirit to bring it up to 15% ABV.
The same colour as Chablis wine, it's dry with a yeasty and salty bite.

---

(5) **ASDA** Dry Fino Sherry, Jerez, Spain, 15%, £3.74   **(GF) (N/S) 11.25**
Cheaper alternative to the brand! An enjoyable drink, but a small step down in quality.

---

(5) **ASDA** Dry Manzanilla Sherry, Jerez, Spain, 15%, £4.56   **(GF) (N/S) 11.25**
Manzanilla is a fino with a bit more of a salty tang. The brand just edges it here.

---

(5) **CO-OP** Pale Dry Fino Sherry, Jerez, Spain, Alc.16%, £4.59   **(GF) (N/S) 12**
A tad more alcohol, but a cheaper option. However, taste-wise the brand beats it.

---

(5) **MARKS & SPENCER** Dry Fino Sherry, Jerez, Spain,   **(GF) (N/S) 11.25**
Screwcap, Alc. 15%, £5.99
This is cheaper than the brand and gets very close to it on all the taste fronts.

---

(5) **ODDBINS** Fino Valdespino Sherry, Jerez, Spain,   **(GF) (N/S) 12.38**
Alc. 16.5%, £5.99
Just a sip away from the brand in taste quality, but still worth a punt!

---

(4) **MORRISONS** Fino Crisp & Dry Sherry, Jerez, Spain, Alc. 15%, £3.89   **(GF) (N/S)**
Very much cheaper, but there is a big drop in quality compared to the brand.

---

(4) **SAINSBURY'S** Manzanilla Sherry, Jerez, Spain,   **(GF) (N/S) 11.25**
Alc. 15%, £4.69
Drinkable but, next to the brand, it's a big step down in aroma and taste.

Harveys Bristol Cream Sherry

Number indicates units of alcohol per bottle

(10) **ODDBINS** Valdespino Cream Sherry, Jerez, Spain, **(GF) (N/S)** 12.78
Alc. 17.5%, £5.99
Grab it from the shelf. Better quality than the brand and it's very much cheaper.

(10) **WAITROSE** Rich Cream, Jerez, Spain, Alc. 17.5%, £6.55 **(GF) (N/S)** 12.78
A beat-the-brand buy! It's cheaper and offers a taste that lasts well beyond the swallow.

(9) **ALDI** Fletcher's Cream Sherry, Jerez, Spain, Alc. 17%, £3.59 **(GF)** 12.75
Aldi shoppers, this is a beat-the-brand buy! Almost half the price and of comparable quality to the brand.

(9) **ASDA** Rich Cream Sherry, Jerez, Spain, Alc. 17.5%, £3.80 **(GF) (N/S)** 12.78
Put it in the trolley. The taste has a bit more bite, but it's cheaper and of similar quality to the brand.

(5) **MORRISONS** Cream Sherry, Jerez, Spain, Alc. 17.5%, £3.89 **(GF) (N/S)** 12.78
Grab a bottle. A more assertive flavour than the brand, but this offers just as much palate pleasure.

HARVEYS BRISTOL CREAM SHERRY, JEREZ, SPAIN, ALC. 17.5%, £6.99 12.78

A rich and concentrated sherry that hits the spot for flavour satisfaction. But one bottle contains nearly 40g of sugar.

(5) **CO-OP** Classic Cream Sherry, Jerez, Spain, Alc. 17.5%, £4.39 **(GF) (N/S)** 13.13
A cheaper alternative to the brand. But glass for glass this comes second.

The Retailers

ALDI

The latest dietary and food intolerance information on Aldi's drink and food products can be obtained from Customer Service:

Telephone: 08705 134 262

Address: Aldi Stores, PO Box 26, Atherstone, Warwickshire CV9 2SQ

Information-only Website: www.aldi.co.uk

ASDA

The latest dietary and food-intolerance information on Asda's drink and food products can be obtained from Customer Service:

Telephone: 0500 100 055

Address: ASDA House, Southbank, Great Wilson Street, Leeds LS11 5AD

Shopping and Information Website: www.asda.co.uk

CO-OP

The latest dietary and food-intolerance information on the Co-op's drink and food products can be obtained from Customer Service:

Telephone: 01706 202 020

Address: United Co-operatives Ltd, Sandbrook Park, Sandbrook Way, Rochdale OL11 1RY

Information-only Website: www.coop.co.uk

KWIK SAVE

The latest dietary and food-intolerance information on Kwik Save's drink and food products can be obtained from Customer Service:

Telephone: 01706 202 020

Address: United Co-operatives Ltd, Sandbrook Park, Sandbrook Way, Rochdale OL11 1RY

Information-only Website: www.coop.co.uk

MAJESTIC (DRINK ONLY)

The latest dietary information on Majestic's drink products can be obtained from Customer Service

Telephone: 01923 298 200

Address: Majestic House, Otterspool Way, Watford, Herts WD25 8WW

Shopping and Information Website: www.majestic.co.uk

MARKS & SPENCER

The latest dietary and food intolerance information on MArks & Spencer's drink and food products can be obtained from Customer Service:

Telephone: 0845 302 1234

Address: Marks & Spencer, Retail Customer Service, Chester Business Park, Wrexham Road, Chester CH4 9GA

Wine Shopping and Information Website: www.marksandspencer.com

MORRISONS

The latest dietary and food-intolerance information on Morrison's drink and food products can be obtained from Customer Service:

Telephone: 01274 356 000

Address: Customer Service Department, Wm Morrison Supermarkets plc, Parry Lane, Bradford BD4 8TD

Information-only Website: www.morrisons.co.uk

ODDBINS (DRINK ONLY)

The latest dietary information on Oddbins' drink products can be obtained from Customer Service:

Telephone: 0800 328 2323

Address: Oddbins Ltd, 31–33 Weir Road, Wimbledon SW19 8UG

Shopping and Information Website: www.oddbins.com

SAINSBURY'S

The latest dietary and food intolerance information on Sainsbury's drink and food products can be obtained from Customer Service:

Telephone: 0800 636 262

Address: Sainsbury's Supermarkets Ltd, 33 Holborn, London EC1N 2HT

Shopping and Information Website: www.sainsburys.co.uk

SOMERFIELD

The latest dietary and food-intolerance information on Somerfield's drink and food products can be obtained from Customer Service:

Telephone: 0117 935 9359

Address: Somerfield Stores Ltd, Somerfield House, Whitchurch Lane, Whitchurch, Bristol BS14 0TJ

Information-only Website: www.somerfield.co.uk

TESCO

The latest dietary and food-intolerance information on Tesco's drink and food products can be obtained from Customer Service:

Telephone: 0800 505 555

Address: Tesco Customer Service, Tesco Stores Ltd, Tesco House, Delamare Road, Cheshunt, Herts EN8 9SL

Shopping and Information Website: www.tesco.com

THRESHERS (DRINK ONLY)

The latest information on Threshers' drinks products can be obtained from Customer Service:

Telephone: 01707 387 258

Address: Thresher Group, Enjoyment Hall, Bessemer Road, Welwyn Garden City, Herts AL7 1BL

Shopping and Information Website: www.threshergroup.com

WAITROSE

The latest dietary and food intolerance information about Waitrose's drink and food products can be obtained from Customer Service:

Telephone: 0800 188 884

Address: Waitrose Customer Service Department, Waitrose Limited,
Doncastle Road, Bracknell, Berkshire RG12 8YA

Shopping and Information Website: www.waitrose.com